Peter Bayne

The Free church of Scotland

Her origin, founders and testimony

Peter Bayne

The Free church of Scotland
Her origin, founders and testimony

ISBN/EAN: 9783337283209

Printed in Europe, USA, Canada, Australia, Japan

Cover: Foto ©Lupo / pixelio.de

More available books at **www.hansebooks.com**

THE
FREE CHURCH OF SCOTLAND

HER

ORIGIN, FOUNDERS

AND

TESTIMONY

By PETER BAYNE, LL.D.

AUTHOR OF
"THE CHRISTIAN LIFE" "THE LIFE OF HUGH MILLER" ETC. ETC.

SECOND EDITION

EDINBURGH
T. & T. CLARK, 38 GEORGE STREET
1894

PREFACE TO THE SECOND EDITION.

IT has been to me a source of deeper satisfaction than I can express, that surviving friends of the Disruption time, and not a few Free Churchmen of the highest eminence and authority, have assured me that I had in this volume struck a chord to which many hearts in Scotland have vibrated. I rejoice without measure that the emphasis with which I lay the accent on the spiritual independence of the Church, under Christ her Head, as the true doctrine of Christian Catholicity, held by the Churches of the Reformation in protest against the narrower theories of the Roman, Greek, and Erastian Churches, and in antithesis to Catharist pride and Donatist isolation, has met with some enthusiasm of response in England as well as in Scotland. I am very much mistaken indeed if there is not, among the evangelical communities of England, a considerable poignancy of yearning towards that fellowship, that unity, that sense of Christian sympathies and a common Church life, which glows with divine warmth and beauty in Paul's Letter to the Ephesians. What is known as the Ritschlian school of theology, with its fresh insistence on the Protestant doctrine of the Kingdom of Christ, which has come so rapidly to the front of late in Germany, is noteworthy as a sign of the time, in connection with movements in Protestant Britain towards a more distinct realisation, under many forms, and with forest-like freedom, of Catholic concord.

The Free Church, while standing firm to the main body of Catholic doctrine, has reawakened to the idea, not unfamiliar to Knox and Calvin, that theological formularies require perennial revision, and has not scrupled to let a ray of nineteenth century light fall upon the venerable standards of Westminster. In preparing the first edition of the present volume, which was done with great haste, I had no opportunity to touch upon this phase of Free Church history, which, in the course of half a century, has naturally become important. It was, however, my happy fate to be present, something less than twenty years after the Disruption, on one of those occasions when the spirit of the new and the spirit of the old first looked upon each other in the General Assembly of the Free Church.

An alarm had arisen in the West — always distinguished for vivacious unrest, combined with pious aspiration — that heterodoxy, in singular metaphysical forms, had shown itself among the students of the

Free Church College in Glasgow. Professor Gibson was much puzzled and seriously terror-struck, and Dr. Begg, whose ideas of pulpit practicality were strict, and sympathy with metaphysical verdancy limited, brought all the pith and power of his eloquence to heighten the impression which Dr. Gibson had made upon the Assembly. A sense of painfulness and spectrality pervaded the atmosphere. Gloom sat upon all faces, the grave anxiety being particularly marked on that of the Earl of Dalhousie. At this moment a young man, with light golden hair and general aspect of calm brightness, like a figure out of a Daniel vision, appeared in the midst, and drew upon himself all eyes. He spoke with remarkable clearness, but with a *minimum* of noise, and with no more excitement than goes with a gentle wind in spring. As his words flowed on, it was felt that, as in a transformation scene, the whole situation changed. The respected Professor Gibson and the sharply logical Dr. Begg, cased in the panoply of their own mature orthodoxy, had been unable, he gently suggested, to sympathise with the eccentricities of growing minds. A more recent student might recognise in these speculations of the sprouting sages of Glasgow one more illustration of that confident prowess, that genial puissancy, wherewith metaphysicians of a certain age commonly undertake to conquer that unconquerable difficulty, the origin of evil. The speaker was Mr. Rainy, who had suddenly become famous in the Church as the successor of Dr. Gordon.

I have the most vivid recollection of the change, visible as the illumination that follows in the wake of a cloud-shadow moving across a landscape, which accompanied his words. The darkness went. The light came. The gloom rose from every brow. The face of Dalhousie became actually radiant with acquiescence, relief, admiration. The difficulty had vanished; and from that hour the young mind of the Church put its trust in the new leader. The students of Glasgow, whose posturings and puissant strokes and audacious battle-cries in their conflict with the old Dragon of Wantley, the old origin of evil, had shocked Gibson, startled Begg, amazed Dalhousie, and driven many good ladies almost into convulsions, became, in due time, efficient ministers of the Free Church.

In this spirit, and for many a year under the same leadership, may all the difficulties of the Free Church be vanquished!

P. B.

May 1894.

PREFACE TO THE FIRST EDITION.

PROFESSOR GIBB and I have been friends since we were schoolfellows in Aberdeen in 1843, and it is in no small measure owing to his encouragement, and the sympathy and furtherance of Professor Salmond, that this volume sees the light. The authorities on which I rely are sufficiently indicated as I proceed, special acknowledgments being due to the standard work on the Conflict by Dr. Robert Buchanan. I studied theology in the New College in Cunningham's time, but never applied for licence, or was ordained. When Candlish was in summer quarters with his family at Kilcreggan in 1856, I became intimately acquainted with him. The book falls far short of what I hoped it might be, but I offer it to my brothers and sisters of the Free Church of Scotland as an expression, sincere though inadequate, of the interest taken by me in the Jubilee, and of the affection, pride, and gratitude with which I look upon this branch of the Reformed Catholic Church.

Paul thought that he had been specially raised up to do apostolic work in calling the Gentiles. Calvin thought that he and Luther had been specially raised up to do apostolic work in unveiling the Holy Catholic Church, obscured by worldliness and superstition. We Free Churchmen are justified in holding that the group of extraordinary men, who led the Church out of Bondage in 1843, were similarly fitted and appointed to do apostolic work. Let us not imagine that theirs was not a true inspiration, or that we are not under sacred obligation to have regard to it, because it was bounded by the limit of Scripture.

They would have rejoiced exceedingly to see the

Church of Scotland formally reconstructed, but they held, one and all, that the condition on which alone modern States and statesmen contemplate Establishment, namely, the spiritual subordination of the Church to the State, makes the acceptance of Establishment a sin. Prior to 1843, the Church of Scotland was the only State Church in Christendom which Cunningham and Candlish recognised as placed upon a basis which Christians could scripturally defend. By an act of usurpation on the part of the Court of Session, connived at by the British Parliament, the supreme spiritual jurisdiction of the Church of Scotland, bestowed upon her by Christ, and recognised as hers in the Treaty of Union between England and Scotland, was violated. When soft-hearted people pleaded for mild measures with the schismatic Presbyters of Strathbogie, and referred to the oath of allegiance which had preceded their vows of ordination, Cunningham pointed out that their oath of allegiance was to a constitutional sovereign, and could not pledge them to violate the constitution. The oath of allegiance could not pledge any man to pay taxes not granted by Parliament; and Queen Victoria, said Cunningham, had no more constitutional right to exercise ecclesiastical jurisdiction north of the Tweed, than to raise money at her will and pleasure. If Cunningham was wrong, then *cadit questio;* the Free Church is a ludicrous mistake. But it is absolutely indubitable that Cunningham was right. There is at this hour no authority on the other side. The Confession of Faith is embodied in the Treaty of Union; and the O'Connell is not born, and never will be born, who can drive coach or curricle through the memorable and glorious clause in which, mainly through the influence of Scotsmen, the spiritual independence of the Church stands enrolled in the Westminster Confession of Faith. But the Treaty of Union has not been formally repealed. You cannot ask Parliament to re-enact it. You cannot well ask Parliament to pass a law promising not to violate it in future. You want no freedom or jurisdiction beyond those which Christ has bestowed. The only course, therefore, that seems at once rational and Christian for the Presbyterians of Scotland, is to proceed with their movements towards union on grounds pertaining to the Church and the country, leaving the State entirely out of consideration. If any Presbyterians in Scotland or elsewhere hold that it was the State that appointed the Lord Jesus Head of the Church, and that therefore the officers of the Church are at liberty to ordain and depose in the name and by authority of the State, they are in schism,—that is all. Let it be ascertained, then, to begin with, whether Presbyterians of all branches in Scotland agree in holding the doctrine of the Headship.

In 1856, Candlish said that the Established Church of Scotland was thirteen years old, while the Free Church dated from 1560. This was, in an obvious sense, true. But there is a sense in which the Free Church was born in 1843, and it is a sense which ought to be kept in mind at the Jubilee. It is no far-fetched or paradoxical statement that, ere 1843, the Church of Scotland had become *too* Scottish: too much, that is to say, a merely local and national Church. In the sixteenth century, under the influence of the cosmopolitan Knox and of the colossal Calvin, whose word, *teste* Hooker, was law through all the Reformed Churches, she shook off the errors of the old Romish Kirk, and arose refreshed as one of the sisterhood of Reformed Churches. In the seventeenth, eighteenth, and part of the nineteenth centuries, though she never quite forgot her catholicity, she had, without knowing it, dwindled into a narrower Church than that of Knox and Henderson. In 1843 she was called once more to go forward,—to realise that the world was her field,—to take note that the Church of Scotland is not mentioned in the New Testament, nor even the Church of Galilee, but that the Church of Christ has marching orders until the planet be filled with the glory of God, as the waters cover the sea. It is for the Free Church of Scotland, bringing from her treasuries things new as well as old, and old as well as new, to recall the sympathies and sentiments of those days when John Knox and the bishops of the Church of

Edward VI. were engaged in one enterprise of Reform; and when English theologians, essentially Presbyterian, were hewing out the Articles of the Church of England from the Latin of Calvin.

The Evangelicals of the Church of England — and there are millions of them — detest sacerdotalism, believe in the Real Presence only in the sense of Christ in the souls of His people, and are essentially Presbyterian. But they have no voice. They are spirits in prison. They make pitiful appeal to the Civil Law, and receive their reward in decisions like the Lincoln judgment. From time to time some Bible Christian finds that he can bear it no longer, and writes to his bishop, as the Rev. Charles Stirling, of New Malden, wrote to the Bishop of Rochester, last November, that he must resign connection with an Established Church whose "communion tables are turned into 'altars,' her ministers into 'sacrificing priests,' her churches into 'mass-houses,' and with auricular confession inculcated, practised, and where possible enforced." Meanwhile the Free Church of Ireland, Episcopalian but Reformed, finding that in some church a cross had been placed, or was to be placed, immediately behind the communion table, disallowed and prohibited even so much of will-worship. Now I have no manner of doubt that John Knox would have been ardently in sympathy both with Mr. Stirling and the Free Church of Ireland, and that, if sacerdotalism and Erastianism were away, he would have entered cordially into communion with Episcopalian Churches.

In my humble but earnest opinion, the part providentially assigned to the Free Church, in connection with her Jubilee, is chiefly this — to initiate a Reformed Catholic League, putting no questions about ecclesiastical names, or limitary distinctions, open to Presbyterians, Congregationalists, Episcopalians, Methodists, and stipulating only that their law is the Bible, and that their Head is Christ.

P. B.

May 1893.

CONTENTS.

CHAPTER I.
The Challenge, ... 1

CHAPTER II.
Glimpses of Origins, 6

CHAPTER III.
The "Little Kingdom," . . 22

CHAPTER IV.
The Evangelical Revival—"Tamson's Men," 36

CHAPTER V.
Thomson in a Characteristic Attitude, . . 42

CHAPTER VI.
A Sudden Change, ... 48

CHAPTER VII.
Non-Intrusion, ... 53

CHAPTER VIII.
The Veto Act, ... 58

CHAPTER IX.
The Chapel Ministers, ... 66

CHAPTER X.
Chalmers at Work, ... 75

CHAPTER XI.
Chalmers at Play, ... 83

CHAPTER XII.
The Resurgent Church — The Sudden Storm — Auchterarder, ... 92

CHAPTER XIII.
Preparing for the Fray, ... 109

CHAPTER XIV.
Lord Brougham in fine Form, ... 116

CHAPTER XV.
The Church takes up her Position — A New Leader, . 120

CHAPTER XVI.
The Agitation deepening — The "Witness," . . . 133

CHAPTER XVII.
The Rise of Candlish, ... 143

CHAPTER XVIII.
The Dean of Faculty, ... 151

CHAPTER XIX.
The Church or the Court of Session, . . . 158

CHAPTER XX.
LAW AND GOSPEL—THE LETHENDY CASE, ... 162

CHAPTER XXI.
LAW AND GOSPEL—THE REEL OF BOGIE, . . . 169

CHAPTER XXII.
LAW AND GOSPEL—MARNOCH, ... 178

CHAPTER XXIII.
THE ASSEMBLY OF 1841—PATRONAGE, ... 184

CHAPTER XXIV.
THE MODERATES STRIKE THEIR FLAG, ... 188

CHAPTER XXV.
THE SCOTTISH HILDEBRAND, ... 192

CHAPTER XXVI.
GUTHRIE, ... 202

CHAPTER XXVII.
CANDLISH IN SHOALS AND QUICKSANDS, . . . 216

CHAPTER XXVIII.
LORD MELBOURNE AGAIN, . . . 224

CHAPTER XXIX.
THE CLAIM OF RIGHTS, ... 229

CHAPTER XXX.
FORECASTINGS OF THE CONVOCATION, ... 242

CHAPTER XXXI.
THE CONVOCATION, ... 250

CHAPTER XXXII.

The Court of Session's last Triumphs, ... 266

CHAPTER XXXIII.

The Debate in the Commons—An imaginary Speech by Guthrie, ... 273

CHAPTER XXXIV.

Thank God! they come, they come! 297

CHAPTER XXXV.

The Queen's Letter, ... 305

CHAPTER XXXVI.

The Free Church, ... 308

CHAPTER XXXVII.

The Testimony, ... 313

CHAPTER XXXVIII.

The Sustentation Fund, ... 318

CHAPTER XXXIX.

The Missionaries, ... 325

CHAPTER XL.

Royal Chalmers, ... 331

CHAPTER XLI.

Cunningham, Scholar and Controversialist, . . 334

CHAPTER XLII.

Candlish and Union—James Hamilton, . . . 339

THE FREE CHURCH OF SCOTLAND.

CHAPTER I.

The Challenge.

THE greatest of the men who, with more or less of arbitrariness, may be marked off as a group, and named by pre-eminence the Founders of the Free Church of Scotland, was Thomas Chalmers. A shining figure, with a moral radiancy about him that conveyed to noble natures, though not of enthusiastic temperament, as notably to Jeffrey, a suggestion of majesty approaching to inspiration. Strength and tenderness, decision and sympathy, poetry and prose, were in him singularly if not uniquely blended. He was an early lover of Keble's poetry, —a fact which, if we think of it, will in his position mean much. But, indeed, it was a part, *magna pars*, of his originality to combine into living and harmonious unity what one might call polar opposites. Aglow with spiritual ardour, moving always in the light of a heavenly ideal, he was yet passionately practical. He soared in spirit with Keble round the whole circle of the Christian year, and he would have won Bailie Nicol Jarvie's heart by discussing methods and measurements, ways and means. He believed in Churches as incarnations of Christ; he believed in Churches as stone walls and as State Establishments. His name summons up to the imagination all that is best in the dream or in the reality of State Churches: their dignity, their comparative repose of intellect and feeling; their order, their permanence; their division of the vineyard, the world, into separate parochial portions, so that none may escape the labourer's eye, so that to each and all of them may be brought down the sunbeams and the dews of God. But if no man ever appreciated more highly than he the commodiousness, comeliness, and utility of an Established Church, no man ever laid it down as a more imperious necessity that the Church should be free and not in bondage, alive and not dead.

In the spring of 1838 we find Chalmers delivering a series of lectures in defence of State Establishments of religion in the metropolis of England. The great world was moved beyond what it is easy for the present generation to imagine. Hanover Square Rooms were thronged with a glittering crowd,—members of the House of Commons, barons, earls, marquises, dukes, one of these being of the Blood Royal. Chalmers had always been chivalrously courteous in his references to the Church of England, and nine Anglican prelates now hung upon his lips. He counselled them to quit the plea of "exclusive apostolical derivation," and, depending on the realities and practicalities of Christian beneficence, to make themselves standard-bearers in the sacred enterprise of diffusing throughout the families of England "those waters of life which can alone avail for the healing of the nation." The words might have penetrated to John Henry Newman, as he sat bodeful at Oxford, agonised with the suspicion that his adored Church of England, instead of being an integral part of the Holy Catholic Church, would turn out after all to be a mere national and political institution.

But it was not the Church of England, much as he agreed with its Bible party, highly as he honoured its Shaftesburys, dearly as he prized its capabilities of securing for the poor the ministrations of the rich, that Chalmers took as the type and model of those ecclesiastical establishments which he championed and loved. It was a Church that had never sought to bask in the glitter of baronial coronets, but which, whether in friendly alliance with the State or hunted like David as a partridge, had maintained her spiritual independence and asserted her right to govern herself by the law of her heavenly King. He claimed, indeed, on behalf of the Church of Scotland, no exclusive derivation from the apostles, no sacerdotal privilege, no superiority of a clerical caste above the body of Christians; but he treated it as indisputable that, in spiritual matters, she was as autocratic as the State itself.

Chalmers did not seem to have the slightest shyness or dubiety in laying this view of the Established Church of Scotland before his audience. He treated it as something for which an intelligent English audience might be held to be prepared; a matter of acknowledged fact, historically blazoned, and familiar to educated men. "We own," he said, "no Head of the Church but the Lord Jesus." "There is not one thing which the State can do to our independent and indestructible Church but strip her of her temporalities." "She was as much a Church in her days of suffering as in her days of outward security and triumph; when a wandering outcast, with nought but the mountain breezes to play around her, and nought but the caves of the earth to shelter her, as now, when admitted to the bowers of an Establishment. The magistrate might withdraw his protection, and she might cease to be an Establishment any longer; but in all the high matters of sacred and spiritual jurisdiction, she would be the same as before. With or without an Establishment, she, in these, is the unfettered mistress of her doings. The king by himself, or by his representative, might be the spectator of our proceedings; but what Lord Chatham said of the poor man's house is true in all its parts of the Church to which I have the honour to belong—'In England every man's house is his castle: not that it is surrounded with walls and battlements—it may be a straw-built shed; every wind of heaven may whistle round it; every element of heaven may enter it; but the king cannot—the king dare not.'"

At this point Chalmers reached that climax of oratorical vehemence which recalled to learned observers what they had read of Demosthenes, or what Cicero says of the tempest-like, torrent-like power of supreme oratory. Eye-witnesses have spoken of the almost convulsive working of Chalmers's features on such occasions, the eyes gleaming as with liquid fire. His magnificent audience, as if moved by a spell, rose by a common impulse and gazed upon him. Confident as he was of his position and foothold,—ardent as was the assentient sympathy of his aristocratic and hierarchical hearers,— he had practically uttered a challenge to which the answer was given at the Disruption.

CHAPTER II.

Glimpses of Origins.

"WE own no head of the Church but the Lord Jesus." Did Chalmers, when he referred to this as a differentiating mark and chief note of the Church of Scotland, indulge in one of those generalities of Christian sentiment that are too vague to be available for purposes of practical definition? Assuredly not. Those who have known Scotland and the Church of Scotland best have been on this point of the same mind with Chalmers. Knox, Henderson, Melville knew the character of their Church, and Queen Elizabeth and the Stuarts made no mistake about it. When Thomas Carlyle pronounced the white heat of enthusiasm into which his countrymen rose in their fidelity to Christ's Crown and Covenant to have been the main influence in forming the national character of Scotland, he was not misled by a sonorous phrase or a symbolic pageant. It will be indispensable for us to look somewhat closely into this matter.

The Reformation, it is allowed on all hands, was in Scotland a movement among the great body of the people. The Bible in the vernacular tongue entered early from

England, and between all sections of what may be called the Bible party in England and in Scotland there has been, since the middle of the sixteenth century, beneath superficial differences, a profound sympathy. As against the Papacy, the statesmen Reformers who sat about the Council-board of Edward VI., and the preaching Reformers who cradled the Church of Scotland, were cordially at one. Neither in England nor in Scotland was there at that time a passionate preference *for* or a passionate decision *against* Episcopacy. The sentiment was then as good as universal, both in Great Britain and on the Continent, among those on the side of the Reformation, that the sacerdotalism of Rome ought to be abjured, and that Episcopacy, if retained at all in the Reformed Church, should be little or nothing more than a superintendency among equals for purposes of order.

But on one point the Reformers of Scotland set their faces as flint against the statesmen Reformers of England. They had learned, either directly from the New Testament, or from that apostle of the second stage of the Reformation, who was its Augustine and its Cyprian in one, that, in rejecting the Papacy, they did not go beyond the pale of the Holy Catholic Church, or pass out of allegiance to her sole King and Head. More and Fisher could not have written in their blood a darker sentence upon Henry VIII.'s sin of assuming the headship over Christ's Church than Calvin supplied them in the word by which he characterised it, "blasphemy." But for his fear to make himself a partaker in that sin, John Knox might probably have accepted the bishopric which Edward pressed upon him. Placed by the providence of God between the discredited Catholicism of the Papacy on this hand and the Erastianism of the English monarchs on that, the Reformers of Scotland found it assigned to them as a sacred duty to vindicate, exalt, bear witness to, the Crown Rights of the Redeemer, the privileges, powers, duties of the Holy Catholic Church, the visible kingdom of Christ upon earth.

Such was the august part which the Church of Scotland, " the Presbyterian Church, so proud and stubborn," as Hallam calls her, undertook. She undertook it in express remembrance and recognition, amid her own troubles and while the dust of the great Reformation earthquake was in the air, of the share of " all nations " in the Catholic Church. She undertook it—this has been fairly admitted even by her adversaries—in a spirit of antique Christian superiority to the things of this world, uninfluenced by the spectacle of the glittering emoluments that reconciled the Church of England to Erastian bondage. Christ and the Bible,—these were the watchwords of the Church of Scotland. The Church claimed no right to add to Scripture, nor did she profess to transfer from the individual soul, by any infallibility of her own, the responsibility of ascertaining the meaning of Scripture. But in all spiritual matters the Bible was her law, and in framing her own bye-laws in spiritual matters, her appeal was to Scripture alone. " The Lord Jesus Christ, as King and Head of His Church, hath therein appointed a government in the hand of Church officers distinct from the civil magistrate." The Headship of Christ means, in one word, that Christ is to be all in all to His Church, and that she, clad only in spiritual armour, and bearing none but spiritual weapons, is to conquer the planet in His name.

We cannot do anything more practical in regard to this or any other Christian doctrine than ask what countenance does it derive from Christ. And it must be granted that the doctrine of the Headship bears this test well. From first to last, the Divine Personality, whose presence is the greatest of New Testament miracles, identifies His work with the foundation of a kingdom. His gospel, as announced in what is now generally regarded as the earliest of the evangelical records, that of St. Mark, is the gospel of the kingdom. So much was this a matter of course, that even Nathanael understood it: "Thou art the King of Israel." It was the Divine kingship that the Apostle Peter attested, on a cardinal occasion, in response to Christ; and it was upon this truth, to wit, the truth of His kingship, that He promised to plant His Church. In that truth—His kingship—would lie the secret of her strength. While she loved and exalted her King—while His Spirit irradiated her tabernacles—while she continued to advance to ever new conquests in His name—the gates of Hades should not prevail against her.

That the kingdom thus announced was spiritual, and not without mystery, cannot be denied. Peter, overjoyed when he first caught the sunrise gleam of it in the words of Christ, was perplexed and offended to learn that, after all, it was bound up with suffering, with sorrow, with self-sacrificing pain. Officious followers, who would take Christ by force to make Him a king, received no encouragement. An attempt to bring Him in as a decider, in cases of dispute as to property, drew from Him a distinct disclaimer of right or obligation to interfere with the ordinary course of civil and criminal administration: "Who made me a judge or a divider over you?" Physical force was indispensable for that. And when His amazed and no doubt bitterly disappointed adherents found that He did not dispose of the officers who came to arrest Him by calling down fire on them from heaven, He told Peter to put up his sword into its sheath, and calmly surrendered to His captors.

Pilate would have learned, were it but from the clamours of the crowd, that Jesus was accused of blasphemy in claiming to be the Son of God, and of treason in claiming to be the king of Israel. From his first questioning of the accused, he had probably arrived at a confused notion that he had to deal with some singular Jewish fanatic, and it seems impossible to doubt that the personality of Christ had made an impression on him. He therefore tried in an ineffectual way to turn the crowd in His favour. But the renewed cries about the kingship startled him, and returning to Christ's presence, "Art thou then," he asked, "a king?" To this the answer was explicit, "I am a King. To this end was I born, and for this came I into the world." The words immediately following, if we must take them with rigorous literalism as they stand, refer to a general witness-bearing, on Christ's part, to "the truth." But nothing is more distinctive of the manner of Christ than His sound logic, His avoidance of abstractions and generalities, and His specification of concrete particulars. Every rabbi and every philosopher professed to teach truth, but did not claim a kingdom. It appears to be in the highest degree probable, therefore, that His reference was to "this truth," namely, the truth that Pilate had expressed, *i.e.* the truth of the kingship. At all events, we have the declaration before Pilate that the object of His coming into the world was to establish a kingdom.

It certainly need in no case surprise us that the truth connected with Christ's kingship should have perplexed Pilate, for spiritual kingship, resting on no visible power or pageant, might well be a mystery to the servant of Rome. Nineteen centuries, however, of Christian civilisation have taught mankind that spiritual force is no vain imagination, no vapour of a heated brain. Where, to-day, are all the kingdoms of the world, that stood strong on that evening when Pilate broke impatiently away from Jesus Christ, without waiting to hear what kind of truth could be bound up with His crazy kingdom? The spiritual power is the mightiest of powers, whether in the individual breast or in the society of men. And this at least is certain, that in the course of nineteen centuries the spiritual kingship of Christ, though it has turned into new channels the whole current of civilisation, has but given earnest of its potentiality, and promise of its ultimate conquests. Having done *so much*, since He told Pilate He had been born to be a King, the Church and the world may trust Him to do more. And all that is wise and thoughtful in the intelligence of our time, both religious and scientific, agrees on one point with those Reformers and Covenanters who rejoiced in Christ as their King, namely, that He was and is the epitome of Christianity, and that the Church is likely to be of use to the world in proportion to the sincerity, simplicity, and efficiency with which she aims at realising His kingdom upon earth.

Since, then, He by no means left the truth as to His kingdom in the inchoate state which Pilate imagined, it will be well to ask whether anything can be learned from Him with precision upon the subject.

It is impossible to read the Gospels intelligently once without perceiving, and if we read them fifty times we shall be only the more firmly persuaded, that Jesus Christ addressed Himself to man's spirit, working from the spirit outward, and that He dealt with principles, not with forms. Inflexible as adamant in matters of principle,—"make the tree good," "sell all thou hast," "ye cannot serve God and mammon,"—He was flexile as water in relation to methods, forms, non-essentials. His words were spirit and life. "The flesh profiteth nothing." Not institutions, but the spirit and life of institutions, did He aim at renewing. Knowing human nature, apprehending all the essential facts of human society, He foresaw their possible modifications, and provided a moral life, a spiritual truth, that might circulate through them all.

Take this matter of His Church. Though not forgetful of the natural aptitude subsisting between new wine and new bottles, He took, as if it were a matter of course, the Hebrew synagogue as serving all essential purposes required by Him in giving an object lesson on the discipline of the Christian Ecclesia. Nothing could be simpler than the whole matter as we have it traced, with light but unerring touch, in the eighteenth chapter of St. Matthew's Gospel. If Christian is offended with Christian,—if the law of the brotherhood, the law of duty and charity, seems to be broken,—the offended brother is, first of all, to try personal remonstrance, obviously of as quiet a kind as may be, with the offending brother. "If he shall hear thee, thou hast gained thy brother." If he turns a deaf ear, the method of informal remonstrance is still to be persisted in; but now the presence of two or three more is invoked, so that kindly reason may soften the obdurate one. If he still is perverse, then "tell it unto the Church;" and if he flouts the Church, "let him be unto thee as an heathen man and a publican."

This is the utmost stretch of ecclesiastical discipline as warranted by Christ. So long as the Christian brotherhood, the Christian Church, is in this world, it is inevitable that the refusal of Christian fellowship, the treatment of a man as a heathen or publican, will have indirect effects. It is in the nature of the case impossible that his social repute should remain unaffected. But, beyond this necessary implication, the Church is not supplied with an iota of force, whether her own or the State's, wherewith to give effect to her withdrawal of spiritual privileges. A heavenly sanction of the earthly decision is promised,—that is all. Alas, how different would the history of Christendom, Primitive, Popish, or Protestant, have been had Christ's limits of discipline been observed! But though absolute renunciation of physical force took place in the exercise of Christian discipline, it was transacted directly under the Master's eye and with intervention of none between Him and His Church. "Verily I say unto you, Whatsoever ye shall bind on earth shall be bound in heaven: and whatsoever ye shall loose on earth shall be loosed in heaven." To obey Christ is the liberty of Christians.

Perfectly simple as Christ's sketch of discipline is, it comprises by implication all that is essential to the freedom and the autonomy of the Church. Is it not obvious, even on grounds of common sense, that such a society should be governed by a spiritual law of its own, and not as a department of the political administration? The right to include or exclude members may be looked upon as inherent in the very nature of free association. We need not hesitate, then, to say—what has indeed been generally held—that the opinion of Erastus, to the effect that the Christian Church has no power of any kind except what it derives from the State, is a mere extravagance of flighty argumentation. It ought to be distinctly realised that, even in the heyday of Moderate ascendancy, the Church of Scotland always rejected, and completely rejected, the flimsy speciosities of Erastianism. Dr. George Hill, of St. Andrews, one of the most illustrious leaders of the party, and one who, by the candour of his judgment and the comprehensiveness of his intellectual glance, and his admirable lucidity and tolerance, would have shed lustre upon any party, says of the Erastian view, that "it seems impossible for any person whose mind comprehends the whole subject, not to perceive that the opinion is false." This golden candlestick of Moderatism had no difficulty in realising the Church as apart from and independent of the State. "As the

Church did exist before it was united with the State, it may exist without any such union." "It will possess, in this state of separation, when it can derive no aid from civil regulations, all the authority which Christ meant to convey through His apostles to their successors, and of the exercise of which the apostles have left examples." "When the Church receives the protection and countenance of the Civil Power, she does not, by this alliance, lose those rights and powers which are implied in Church government as such." "If the Church, instead of deriving any benefit from the State, were opposed and persecuted by the Civil Magistrate, it would be not only proper, but necessary, to put forth of herself those powers which, in more favourable circumstances, she chooses only to exercise in conjunction with the State." In short, "the power inherent in the nature of the Christian society" is derived "from Divine institution and not from civil regulation." No recognition of the independent spiritual jurisdiction of the Church could be more unequivocal, nor is its validity in any measure impaired by the addition that, when arrangements as to emolument are made between States and Churches, the latter must take into consideration, in the exercise of their jurisdiction, the views and requirements of the former.[1]

Among the principles which Christ enunciated as absolutely binding on His followers—immutable amid the wildest fantasies of superficial change—was that of their equality among themselves. "All ye are brethren." And since men will err in the application of principles,

[1] Hill's *Lectures*, Book vi. chap. iii.

as well as from sheer ignorance of their existence, He explains His meaning still further: "Ye know that they which are accounted to rule over the Gentiles exercise lordship over them; and their great ones exercise authority upon them. But so shall it not be among you; but whosoever will be great among you, shall be your minister: and whosoever of you will be the chiefest, shall be servant of all." The Divine wisdom of this appears first in its clear apprehension of the indispensability of official subordination in all cases of co-operative effort, in all forms of organised activity. The man who cannot defer to, and take directions from, his official superior, is an incurable, infra-human anarch.

But Christ not merely realises this necessity; He realises, in the second place, and provides against, the tendency, which has manifested itself in all ages, of official superintendence to pass into lordship. Hence hereditary aristocracies and superstitiously reverenced castes. It is impossible not to see in Christ's reference to lordship amongst the Gentiles, a conclusive proof that He had His eye upon these things. It is inconceivable that one who was thus on His guard against the petrifaction of officialism into caste and lordship, should stamp Divine precedence upon one class of officials. As the times altered, and the signs of the times, the grades and forms and names of officialism might change, but lordship was never to be allowed to emerge; Christian equality was never, under whatever pretences of sanctity or promises of advantage, to be compromised.

A Divine discernment of principles, a Divine opportunism—regard to circumstances of time, requirement, and capability—in the application of principles; such was the method of Christ. Even upon His own extemporised organisation of the Seventy He did not permit the mark of perpetuity to rest. He dissolved and discarded it when done with. The duty of oversight—call it episcopacy, if any one likes—will remain as long as organised activity remains. The gift of leadership is altogether invaluable in action where large multitudes are engaged in common operations, and the accompaniments of its exercise are quickening and delightful; but if, under stress of circumstance and by lapse of time, the true Christian superintendency or episcopacy had become inextricably involved, say, with the baronial lordship of feudalism, might it not have been in closest accordance with the spirit and method of Christ to divest it of its baronial garnitures, and reduce it to the parity of Christian brotherhood? On this point the Church in which Principal Hill was a leader, and of which Chalmers was a defender, had been sensitively jealous, impressing friends and foes alike with her insistence upon Presbyterian parity.

And now we must touch, if but briefly, upon the delicate and difficult question of the formation of the pastoral tie between ministers and their flocks. Under primitive, and what might be styled normal, conditions, the act of constituting the pastoral relationship involves harmonious co-operation between three parties,— the congregation, the pastor, and the aggregate of congregations. The pastor and the people must have mutual suitability, and the sympathetic co-operation of the aggregate of congregations, guaranteeing in so far as is practicable the quality of the pastor, comes in to heighten the joy and to deepen the consecration. This is simple, natural, and, as we should therefore have expected, correspondent to the pattern shown in the New Testament. The settlement having, on these terms, taken place, the pastor remains to be an "example to the flock," not a priest but a ministering servant, the Christ in him responding to the Christ in them.

But suppose now, that in course of time the beautiful simplicity of the apostolic ideal has been marred, and that the necessity of providing meat and raiment for the pastor has gradually brought parish livings within the circle of those things that rank as property. This will produce modifications. The new elements, hinted at by Principal Hill, introduced into the situation by State connection and the system of patronage, will tend to throw the spiritualities we have been speaking of into the background, and to bring into view sundry other things. Glancing into Lord Macaulay's biography, one comes upon the following jotting from his journal for May 5, 1859: "Glorious weather. A letter from Lord John to say that he has given my brother John the living of Aldingham, worth £1100 a year, in a fine country, and amidst a fine population. Was there ever such prosperity? I wrote a few lines of warm thanks to Lord John." Both Macaulay and Lord John Russell were professedly Christian if not exactly religious men, and this is the approach they make to the New Testament ideal of the settlement of pastors. What a transformation! The Ecclesia, the spiritualities, the souls of the parishioners, seem to have vanished into space, leaving as the sole reality £1100, to live on in a glorious country, which the good Lord John takes out of his waistcoat pocket and hands to his political supporter. Principal Hill was eminently correct in believing that the entrance of the mundane elements, money and patron's property, would greatly complicate the settlement of ministers.

But we, in closing this chapter, shall turn for a few moments to John Knox, or rather to a distinguished personal friend of John Knox's, to wit, John Calvin, who —though, like every other great man of the Christian centuries, he illustrated by his spots the spotlessness of the heavenly Sun, and, while before his time in indubitably remonstrating against the execution of Servetus by fire, was only on a level with his time, far below the level of Christ, in doing, as he did, his very best to bring Servetus to death—possessed a rare gift for wedding apostolic principle and precedent to modern fact. The first and the essential requirement in a pastor, says Calvin, is the call of God. Of this he ought himself to be conscious, but it is beyond the scrutiny of the Church. On this last point, as it is worth while to observe in passing, Calvin's views have been misrepresented. "Calvinists," says Dr. Newman, "make a sharp separation between the elect and the world; there is much in this that is cognate or parallel to the Catholic doctrine; but they go on to say, as I understand them, very different from Catholicism, —that the converted and the unconverted can be discriminated by man." This betrays perfect ignorance of

Calvin and of the Reformed Catholic Church. Calvin says in so many words that God keeps the secret of those who are His to Himself.[1] One of the distinctly blazoned notes of Churches of the Presbyterian order is that they hold conversion to be a sacred mystery, a secret between the individual breast and God, a matter into which no human eye has a right to peer. Accordingly, Calvin pronounces every Christian who has not been proved guilty of open wickedness (*aperta nequitia*) to be eligible for the office of presbyter or bishop.

How, in the next place, was the pastor to be appointed? In rendering an answer, Calvin selects a typical instance from the practice of the apostles. Paul and Barnabas ordained presbyters in the Churches of Lystra, Iconium, and Antioch. The general method they adopted was that followed in the municipal proceedings of cities, Greek and Roman, when officials were elected. They presented the bishop or presbyter to the Church, and the whole congregation testified their acceptance by uplifted hands: *tota multitudo, ut mos Graecorum in electionibus erat, manibus sublatis declarabat, quem habere vellet.* The Apostle Paul associated the people with himself in the appointment of pastors; and if he prescribed this method to himself and Barnabas, we may, thinks Calvin, be sure that he would not concede sole, autocratic, or arbitrary power in the matter to Timothy, Titus, or any one else. It is therefore according to God's will that fit men should be appointed to charges " with consent and approbation of the people," the election being

[1] *Institutio*, Lib. iv. cap. i.

presided over by other pastors, who take care that neither levity nor tumult nor anything unseemly should dishonour the occasion, and who, by laying their hands on the head of the pastor, perform the specific rite of ordination. The imposition of hands is traced by Calvin to the ancient Hebrew form of blessing, and to the gesture of Christ in blessing little children. All reasonable and brotherly, all home-like, heaven-like, and beautiful.[1]

[1] *Institutio,* Lib. iv. cap. iii.

CHAPTER III.

The "Little Kingdom."

"THE little kingdom." This is Macaulay's epithet for Scotland. There is in it perhaps some trace of kindliness, but more of that cynical pungency, not to say disdain, for their mother country, which Scotchmen of the second generation are apt to acquire in England. Magnitude and minitude, however, are not safe criteria of importance to apply to lands or cities. Attica occupied no great portion of the globe, and Judæa was a very little kingdom. Scotland has played a part that wise men will not overlook in the evolution of our most modern civilisation.

But there is one thing above all others that makes it difficult for Englishmen to understand Scotland, and for Scotchmen to understand England. It is hardly too much to say that the term "ecclesiasticism," or rather the thing for which the word stands, is the centre of entirely different associations and suggestions in England from what it stands for in Scotland. From the days of Wycliffe's preachers at the latest,—from the day, we might pretty confidently assert, if not earlier still, when

Chaucer gave his astounding and now unmentionable account of friars,—persons ecclesiastical have been, to use a broad term, unpopular in England. The assertion holds good impressively of the most popular and Radical religionists of England to-day, for one of their foremost representatives, the Rev. Guinness Rogers, prefers to associate "the heroic age" of himself and those for whom he speaks, with the keen, remonstrant oppositionism of the Donatists than with the acquiescence of the Catholic Church. A national, vital, popular ecclesiasticism—an ecclesiasticism affording play to the nation's brain and welling straight from its heart—is an idea that never occurs to an Englishman. But this is what has existed in Scotland, and given significance to the history of Scotland. Buckle was an Englishman, Carlyle was a Scot. Sitting cross-legged in his study, and noting that ecclesiasticism was an extremely powerful thing both in Scotland and in Spain, Buckle concluded without hesitation that Scotchmen were, from cradle to grave, led in the hand by ecclesiastics, and that paramount ecclesiasticism had in Scotland the same intellectually paralysing effects as in Spain. Carlyle knew better. He perceived that the ecclesiasticism of Scotland had been a quickening leaven, a stimulating life, not a paralysing virus. "Scotch literature and thought," said Carlyle, "Scotch industry, James Watt, David Hume, Walter Scott, Robert Burns: I find Knox and the Reformation acting in the heart's core of every one of these persons and phenomena." These words of Carlyle may be said to solve the riddle of Scotch history. "It did not strike Buckle," says another writer, "that mummy-wheat might be very good wheat,—that a nation might develop healthfully and strenuously, although the forms in which it developed were, to a great extent, ecclesiastical." It was in the second half of the sixteenth century, which may in so much be figured to the imagination as the watershed of modern history, that the ecclesiastics of Scotland became somewhat suddenly transformed into tribunes of the people, and contributed a great deal to start that river of political and general progress which has continued to flow in Scotland until this day.

If there is one word which has for Englishmen a sound as consonant to liberty—as suggestive of all that is popular — as ecclesiasticism is the reverse, it is the word "Parliament." In English history Parliament and Church may be looked upon as, on the whole, conflicting powers. And the Parliament has, for the immense majority of Englishmen, been the more trusted of the two. But the old Scottish Parliament was autocratic, and had little connection with the body of the people. And Buckle seems to have had no idea—nor does it appear to have struck Carlyle, whose own idiosyncrasy made him blind to that side of the matter—that one, and a chief reason why the ecclesiasticism of Scotland was popular and vitalising, lay in the fact that the Church furnished Scotland with what was, to all intents and purposes, a Parliament, and practically a most effective Parliament. How true is that remark of Disraeli's, occurring in the bright novel of his early manhood which captivated Goethe, "With *words* we govern men." Call a Parliament a "General Assembly," and the cleverest

Buckle, if a bit of a pedant, fails to detect what it really is.

In the course of that curious and complicated historical drama which worked itself out in Scotland in the latter end of the sixteenth and the early part of the seventeenth century, the General Assembly of the Church gradually arose and grew into strength in Scotland, and became, not in name but in fact, a Parliament of the people. The people loved it for the simple reason that it was their own. Every darling of the nation, be he peer, be he peasant, could find his way into it. It became the representative body of a spiritual democracy, a republic none the less real that it was formally ecclesiastical. The Scottish farmer and cottager might there sit side by side with the foremost divines, and with a sprinkling of the ablest noblemen and the most acute and experienced lawyers of Scotland. From the first it was popular, and at every critical juncture in the subsequent history of the nation the feelings and opinions of the great body of the Scottish people could be better ascertained by consulting the General Assembly than by consulting Parliament. It was, in fact, a Parliament whose edicts had only an indirect political significance, but which sent its roots into every parish in Scotland, and touched all the most personal concerns of the population, moral, social, and domestic. It was by a highly remarkable series of coincidences that the Church of Scotland came into a position to play the memorable part in virtue of which, at one and the same time, she secured her own spiritual independence, and contributed, in a degree which it is hardly possible to over-estimate, to train the people of Scotland in habits of civil and political freedom.

The most cursory glance into the history of Scotland discloses that, though under ordinary circumstances one marked attribute of the people is gravity, yet, at intervals at least, they are capable of intense paroxysms of enthusiasm. Such was that which, on the occasion before us, originated in the preaching of a few earnest men, the deaths of a few martyrs, and most of all the eager drinking of undiluted Christianity from the wells, previously forbidden, of the New Testament. Like the fabric of a vision, the old Roman Catholic Kirk of Scotland vanished, and in its place we behold the Congregation. The clergy and the people outran their rulers, and instead of waiting for a constitution from the Civil Power, framed, in its essentials, the Constitution of the Church, according to the principles of Christ applied to the providential conditions of the time. The ardent "other worldliness"—the pure spiritual passion—of the body of Reformers really facilitated the operations of the aristocracy in robbing the Church. Proudly bold in asserting their sole spiritual allegiance to Christ, the preachers made no desperate clutch at the ample endowments of the old Church, and presented no effectual resistance to the dismantling of those baronial bishoprics, which, whatever pretences and veneers might be made use of, did really introduce an alien influence and element into that equality of the Christian brotherhood which had been laid down as a principle by Christ. Poor as were the preachers in worldly goods, their power began to be felt so soon as they made it practically known how they interpreted the liberty which they claimed for the Church, the visible Congregation, in Christ's name. They demanded freedom for the pulpit, and they exercised that freedom in rebuking King James and his nobles. For words spoken in the pulpit,—spoken in capacity of minister of Christ, whether in pulpit, Presbytery, or General Assembly,—every Scottish pastor refused to give account to king, council, or any court of civil or criminal justice, until he had been first tried by the Church.

Who can fail to understand that, under these circumstances, an immense force of a popular nature— an epoch-making organ of public opinion—would spring into existence? Scotland was then, from circumstances that have been alluded to, drawn more prominently than ever before or since into the evolution of world-history. All the parties that were leading on the stage of Western Europe had their representatives among the Scottish hills. There the Guises held the threads of intrigue in the interests of France. There the dark genius of Spain plotted and devised and laid the train of its conspiracies. A strong and influential party took their clue from England, a party in close connection with Queen Elizabeth. And there was a plurality of Scottish parties, each with a nuance of its own,—the party of the king, the party of the nation, the party of the aristocracy, the party of the Church. All these might be said to be in some sense the party of the General Assembly.

James was no perfect king, though very far indeed from the preposterous caricature of Macaulay. Casaubon, as we may learn from Pattison's masterly biography, passed over from the court of Henry IV., in France, to that of James, in England, to bear witness that he, the finest Greek scholar in Europe, had passed from a monarch who was an illiterate barbarian to one who was a friendly and gentlemanly scholar. But James was none the less likely for his scholarship to be irritated, at the time preceding his accession to the English throne, by the liberty with which, as he said, every Dick, Tom, and Harry criticised his affairs in the pulpit. Ministers of a republican Church, the preachers were likely to be somewhat bold in their strictures upon monarchy, and we need not be much surprised that James should have suspected a flavour of treason in the Rev. Mr. Black's assertion from the pulpit that "kings were devils' bairns." In point of fact, however, these assertors of the liberty of the pulpit in the sixteenth century were the pioneers of Milton in demanding the liberty of the press in the seventeenth, and of the editors and telegraphists of our own time. Neither the liberty of the pulpit nor the liberty of the press has been exercised in all instances without abuse. And it is well to remember that, allowing for occasional extravagances, the pulpit criticism which sometimes charmed and sometimes infuriated James was in the main sound and seasonable. Queen Elizabeth, the best judge then living, was on the side of the preachers, and against the voluble and veering king. Queen Elizabeth knew that it was not possible to be on both sides in the quarrel between papal and Protestant Christendom. The repelling of the Armada was a practical business; the resistance of Spain involved decisive measures against those Popish lords and their followers who might make things inviting for a landing by the Spaniard in Scotland. James, like his son, lacked backbone; and Elizabeth, as well as the Scottish preachers, knew the fact. Literally, however, and to very serious purpose, the Presbyterians and their General Assembly formed, in those days, part of the garrison of the island against the Armada, and furnished for Scotland no ineffective substitutes, both for a free press and a popular Parliament. We may now begin to appreciate the reasons why the Church has been more of a people's institution in Scotland than in England.

Another of those reasons was that the fervour of the Reformation had burnt, one might say, out of the mind and memory of the people of Scotland the old Romish conception of the Church as constituted by the clergy. An Englishman would as soon think of Parliament as superseding or extinguishing the nation,—putting itself for the nation,—as a Scotchman would of the clerical class styling itself a priesthood, and superseding the people. In Scotland, from the days of Knox, a Church, republican in form, combining congregational completeness and parochial autonomy with synodical order, in which all members, lay and clerical, are spiritually equal, and the clergy are but the ministering servants of the flock, has been the object of trust and affection. Secessions have taken place because the Church has not seemed to be true enough to her own original ideal. In proportion to the fervency of faith and of religious enthusiasm among the people of Scotland, has been, at any particular period, the warmth of their devotion to the Church, and their zeal for her spiritual independence.

It has greatly contributed to intensify and idealise the affection of the Scottish people for their Church, that the humiliation of the Church has always gone *pari passu* with the wounding of the national feeling, and that the Presbyterian clergy have always proved themselves true interpreters of the patriotic sentiment of the people. We have seen that the preachers of Scotland, in Elizabeth's time, supported the sturdy Protestantism of that straight-hitting Deborah against their own wavering Solomon. In this the body of the people went heartily along with the preachers. When James mounted the throne of England, he departed more and more widely from the robust and simple policy of Elizabeth, and both he and his son Charles bestirred themselves to break the proud neck of the Scottish Church. But the nation, strange as it may seem, appears to have been actually made more sensitively jealous of its political independence from having furnished England with a sovereign, and to have for this as well as for higher causes, responded with extraordinary enthusiasm to the Church's efforts to maintain her independence in spiritual matters. Cromwell trampled down both Church and State in Scotland, as he had previously done in England, thus inflicting a bitter sense of humiliation upon the Scottish people. He expressed, in the most emphatic manner at his command, the estimate he had formed of the importance of the General Assembly as an organ and focus of the national feeling by forcibly dissolving it. He was careful, however, to avoid touching the spiritual liberties of Presbyteries and congregations, contenting himself, when a pastor proved refractory, with sweeping away the temporalities of the parish. The Governments of Charles II., which restored Episcopacy, and James II., which plotted to restore Popery, were largely obnoxious to the patriotic sentiment as well as to the religious convictions of Scotchmen. The Presbyterian Church and the body of the people had thus been knit together in all changes of government, and the final establishment of Presbyterianism at the revolution of 1688 was a triumph for the nation as well as for the Church. Burns, a good judge, names the Covenanters as serving freedom's cause. He must be deaf indeed to the intimations, blind to the symbolic blazons of history, who does not perceive that the Church of Scotland has been pledged by her whole career to maintain her spiritual independence,—an independence including the right to proclaim Christ's truth to kings, to guard the privileges of the members of the Church in the formation of the pastoral tie, and to exercise discipline within her borders.

At the Union between England and Scotland, special care was taken that the Presbyterian Church of Scotland should retain her spiritual independence, and should not be subjected to the supremacy exercised by the Crown over the Episcopalian Church of England. A few years subsequently, through the machinations of the political party that was bent upon reinstating the Stuarts, an Act was passed in the British Parliament by which it became possible for Presbyteries, if they so desired, to neutralise or evade, in the interest of patrons to livings, the call by which congregations signified their assent to the settlement of ministers among them. It was felt at the time that this Act, commonly known as Queen Anne's, practically establishing patronage, was intensely at variance with that spirit of Christian democracy which had always characterised the Church of Scotland. But the great religious excitement, which for two centuries had been the main factor of history in Western Europe, had now been succeeded by comparative quiescence, nay, even by the beginnings of reaction. The eighteenth century brought with it indifference and scepticism in religious matters. The full-flooded rivers of controversy that, from the days of Luther to the days of Sancroft, had rolled impetuously along, had now dwindled down to laggard streamlets, gradually losing themselves in sand.

It was natural, in these circumstances, that the party of intrepid and uncompromising Presbyters who, from the days of Knox, had taken the lead in the Church of Scotland, should find themselves superseded by a less fervid, more accommodating, less democratic, and less independent set of leaders, whom the fiery progeny of the Covenanters named Moderates. It is unwise to sneer vaguely at the eighteenth century, or at these Moderate divines, who formed one of its most characteristic products. The life of man—the life of the race—cannot be all excitement, all enthusiasm. Periods must intervene when activity is partially suspended; periods when human nature has recourse to the sweet restorer, sleep; autumnal and wintry periods, when the mind lies fallow in preparation for new springs of quickened consciousness and keen spiritual aspiration. The eighteenth century was one of those fallow periods. The Reformation century, the Puritan century, had been times of spiritual revolution. They were followed by a century of rest. Moderatism was one of many symptoms of a spiritually languid age. It was not a dead age. Far from that. It produced Butler and Reid. It produced Hume and Kant. But it was, comparatively speaking, cold, and its coldness was felt mostly in regions where one naturally looks for heat, as in the religious province.

The representative figure of Moderatism, as a party in the Church of Scotland during the eighteenth century, was Robertson. A memorable man; not of the highest order, either intellectually or morally, but of a high order. To him, as to the greater and nobler Scott, Carlyle did injustice; and it is one of the melancholy facts of life, that no lesson is more readily learnt by a new generation from its fashionable teachers than to sneer at the teachers who preceded them. But the Scottish preacher who promptly achieved a European reputation as an historian, whose works were among the treasured literature of Voltaire at Ferney, and were referred to with reverent admiration by Gibbon, was no ordinary man. Robertson's *Charles the Fifth* is a masterpiece of broad historical delineation, showing all the prominent figures as they moved in successive groups in the pageant and procession of the greatest of modern centuries. In breadth, in the arrangement of masses of light and shade, in the discernment of cardinal facts, —qualities which after all may be more informing than the mastery of picturesque detail by more popular historians,—it would be difficult to name a superior to

Robertson. It is time for intelligent Scotchmen of all parties to do justice to this illustrious man, and to acknowledge that his career and reputation go far to prove that moderation, even in the Moderate party, had not quite ceased to be the reconciling, ennobling, refining, and exalting virtue that all philosophic schools, and conspicuously the New Testament, unite in pronouncing it. The serene intellectual poise of Robertson, in the century after that of the Puritan battles, and when toleration was still practically regarded by many devout persons as a sin, can hardly be over-praised. He did justice to Cardinal Ximenes. He did justice to Martin Luther. As a master of grouping and of historical perspective, neither Froude nor Macaulay can stand comparison with him, and beside him Ranke is but a rambling annalist.

But Robertson was an historian first, a Presbyterian Churchman second; and though it were unpardonable to doubt the sincerity of his personal religion, he was courtly, rationalistic, and absolutely out of touch with that fervent enthusiasm and that burning zeal which had always been notes of the religion of his countrymen. His religion was a philosophy, an ethical theory, at best a law, rather than burning enthusiasm of devotion to a Master, and awestruck adoration of a God. And profoundly mysterious, immeasurably suggestive as is the fact, it is indubitable that, when philosophy essays to supersede and to play the part of religion, learning to look down with disdain upon religious persons, upon the common sorts and conditions of men, it fails to touch the hearts of nations, or to realise the effects produced by vital religion. In proportion as the spirit of philosophic moralising, giving a polite go-by to all the mysteries of the inner life and the celestial outlook, gained the ascendant in the Church of Scotland, in like proportion did the people become dissatisfied with her ministrations, congregation after congregation, sometimes in single instances, sometimes in groups of two, or three, or five, receding from her communion, and coming gradually together again, not to set up a new form of creed or constitution, but to realise for themselves a Presbyterian Church more loyal, as they believed, to the original ideal, as portrayed in the New Testament and restored in the sixteenth and seventeenth centuries. With these seceders a party in the Established Church continued to cherish the warmest sympathy; but they considered it their own duty to maintain the conflict with the Moderates within the Church, standing by the fundamental principles of her Constitution, and, like the Republican party of America in its long struggle with the slaveholders antecedent to the great Civil War, looking forward to the day when they, rising into the ascendant, might cause the face of the Church again to shine as in the glories of her dawn. This party was nicknamed by its opponents The Highflyers, and adopted as its own badge the term Evangelical. Mr. Taylor Innes, in his learned work on *Creeds in Scotland*, gives it the appropriate name of the High Presbyterian party.

CHAPTER IV.

The Evangelical Revival—"Samson's Men."

IN the early part of the present century, the Evangelical Revival was still among those things which had on them the dew and the promise of dawn,—the dew to symbolise the tears for the failures of the night and its distresses, the light to symbolise the hope of future achievement and of promised reward. It had begun in England, in the Established Church, in those University rooms and halls where the Wesleys and Whitfield brought with them airs from the heaven of Christian homes. But it quickly caught on among the people, and the Church of the baronial bishops soon proved too narrow to hold it, although it found response in many a simple, childlike, honest soul, many a Grimshaw, Romaine, Toplady, within the Anglican pale. Once more it turned out that the broad stratum of the English population was prone to religion; and once more, as in the days of Wycliffe, and in the days of Cranmer, and in the days of Bunyan, it held good that the religion taken to its heart by the great body of the English people was the religion, not of priests, nor of philosophers, nor of professors, but the religion boldly inscribed, and discernible at the *first* honest glance, upon the Bible.

In our own day we have been impressively told by Matthew Arnold, how much nobler the simple Bible is than the Bible commented on, the Bible touched up, or watered down, by the typical German professor. In "the Protestant faculties of theology" in Germany, "a body of specialists," says Matthew Arnold, "is at work, who take as the business of their lives a class of inquiries like the question about the Canon of the Gospels. They are eternally reading its literature, reading the theories of their colleagues about it; their personal reputation is made by emitting, on the much-canvassed subject, a new theory of their own. The want of variety and of balance in their life and occupations, impairs the balance of their judgment in general." "If you choose to obey your Bibles," says Mr. Ruskin with happy shrewdness, "you will never care who attacks them." Specialism has its uses. "Of Biblical learning," Arnold justly adds, "we have not enough." But it is not criticism that reveals to us the glow and grandeur of the Homeric poems, or opens our ear to the glorious and wonderful hum in them of the glad fightings and busy industries of the early world. It is not criticism that lays bare to us the true mystery and magic of Hamlet. And it is, to quote again from Matthew Arnold, "a truth never to be lost sight of, that in the domain of religion, as in the domain of poetry, the whole apparatus of learning is but secondary, and that we always go wrong with our learning when we suffer ourselves to forget this."

We should convey a misleading impression if we said that Matthew Arnold entertained the same idea of the Bible as has been entertained, first and last, by the great Bible party of England and Scotland. But the Evangelicals, whatever else they held, have seen in the Bible a revelation of the God of righteousness; and Matthew Arnold gives his weighty opinion that, "reading the Bible with this idea to govern us, we have here the elements for a religion more serious, potent, awe-inspiring, and profound, than any which the world has yet seen."[1] The work that has been done by the Evangelical party, both in its beautiful and melodious dawn under the Wesleys and Toplady,—for in both of these, spite of their cobweb differences of dogma, there was the note of a true inspiration of sacred song,—and in its more recent manifestations, attests the truth of these words.

The Evangelical party had never died out in Scotland, and when the wave of the new gospel tide came flowing into the inlets of the Scottish coast, it met with no organised obstruction. The old mills, shall we say,— venturing on an audaciously modern figure,—proved to be workable by the new electricity. Wilberforce, whose slave-trade reputation was preceded by his Evangelical fame, recognised in the minority of the General Assembly his true brethren in religious sentiments, and avowed himself piously scandalised to behold Robertson, a leader in the Church, standing on terms of amicable relation with Gibbon. We shall hope that it is no treason to the later developments of Evangelicalism to

[1] *God and the Bible.*

be less severe upon Robertson for being so audaciously tolerant.

It was, however, in the nineteenth century, in its first quarter, so full of all kinds of thrilling excitement, in war, in politics, in poetry, that the Evangelical party in the Church of Scotland, now thoroughly awake, began to come decisively to the front. In the brilliant Edinburgh of those years, the Edinburgh which still attracted to its University such future statesmen as Palmerston and Lord John Russell, the Edinburgh of Scott, of Wilson, of Jeffrey, of young Carlyle, the Evangelicals of the Church of Scotland began to play a part of more importance, a part more keenly influencing and agitating the Scottish people, than they had enacted for upwards of a hundred years.

They were led by a man whose name represents more perhaps than any other, to all who are really acquainted with the history of Scotland during those years, the beginnings of Evangelical ascendancy in the Church after the long reign of Moderatism. Andrew Thomson's life has not been written, but his name and memory are indelibly inscribed on the mind of his countrymen. He was exactly the man to take away the reproach from what had been called the narrow, the pietistic, the fanatical party. As minister of St. George's, the principal charge in Edinburgh, he preached clear, well-reasoned, tersely-written discourses, strongly Evangelical, which might fail to convince every one, but could be despised by none. In society, assisted by a fine person, a voice remarkable for compass and harmony, a quick and vigorous intellect, a social talent aided by a skill in music, and a manner in which dignity was combined with animation, he carried everything before him. But the sphere in which he shone to most advantage was the General Assembly, where he faced the lordly Moderates, and gathered and formed into an invincible phalanx the scattered remnant of the old Presbyterian following. He was an acknowledged prince among debaters. Brougham, the greatest Parliamentary orator of his time, had said that there lived but one man whom he feared to meet in debate, and he was Andrew Thomson.

He had caught the mantle of the Erskines and Moncreiffs, and recalled the "watchwords of primitive order and popular rights." Wherever a congregation found itself in danger of having a minister forced upon it by a worldly patron and the Moderate majority, Andrew Thomson "lifted up his intrepid voice" and pleaded its cause. Intimately associated, both in personal friendship and ecclesiastical sympathy, with Dr. Thomas M'Crie, the biographer of Knox and Melville, and the greatest living authority upon the Church of Scotland, he took delight in appealing to the heroic age of Presbytery, and. made conscience of keeping always unfurled the banner of the Church's contention for the Crown Rights of her Lord. He was the type of a successful party leader, glowing with an ardour that attracted the young men, ever willing to marshal his squadrons for the charge. Presbyterian Scotland, from hundreds of manses and thousands of cottages, watched the course of Thomson and the progress of the new party with ecstasies of approbation. Sir George Sinclair told the present writer that once, in the south of Scotland, in those times, he entered into conversation with a fellow-traveller in a coach, and got upon the subject of the Church and the Assembly and the prominent ministers. For his companion Andrew Thomson, or, as he called him, "Tamson," was all the law and all the prophets. If Sir George mentioned any minister who was not in Thomson's brigade, he was not thought worth speaking of. But if Sir George was happy enough to know and name one of the other kind, then his companion brightened up in a moment, and he said, with flashing eyes, "Aye, he's ane o' Tamson's men!"

CHAPTER V.

Thomson in a Characteristic Attitude.

BUT we cannot do better, with a view to understanding the situation, than glance into the Assembly of 1820, and observe what was going forward. The old king had died in January of that year, and his son, George the Fourth, had succeeded him. In February an Order was issued by the Privy Council, and was transmitted in due form to the Assembly at its meeting in May, on the subject of prayers for the Royal Family "in that part of Great Britain called Scotland." After citation of one or two Acts of Parliament, "it is ordered," proceeds the document, "by His Majesty in Council, that henceforth every minister and preacher shall, in his respective church, congregation, or Assembly, pray 'For his most sacred Majesty King George, and all the Royal Family;' of which all persons concerned are hereby required to take notice and govern themselves accordingly."

To this Andrew Thomson demurred. The spiritual independence of the Church was imperilled. No power on earth, he affirmed, was entitled to dictate the terms in which she was to pray to God. Thomson moved as follows: "That it be declared by the General Assembly that no civil authority can constitutionally prescribe either forms or heads of prayer to the ministers or preachers of this Church, and that the Orders in Council which have been issued from time to time respecting prayers for the Royal Family are inconsistent with the rights and privileges secured by law to our ecclesiastical Establishment; but that, as these Orders appear to have originated in mistake or inadvertency, and not in any intention to interfere with our modes of worship, the General Assembly do not consider it to be necessary to proceed further in this matter at present." A conventional expression of loyalty followed, and a profession of entire willingness to address supplications to God in behalf of a Royal House by which He had shed blessings on the nation; but the distinct assertion of the spiritual independence of the Church came first.

In his opening speech Thomson laid stress upon the "incontrovertible principle of the Church of Scotland, that it had no spiritual head on earth, and that consequently the King in Council had no right to interfere in its worship." As for the Acts of Parliament on which the Order was rested, he argued either that they were irrelevant, or that they had always been repudiated, in their spirit and purpose, by the truly constitutional party in the Church.

The Moderate leaders opposed the motion; but mark the reason. Not one of them challenged the soundness of Thomson's main contention, that the Church was, by her Constitution, spiritually independent. Dr. Cook, of Laurencekirk,—a name destined to become well known before 1843,—avowed himself prepared to maintain, as well as the Evangelical chief, that no civil authority could constitutionally prescribe heads of prayer to the Church; but he denied that there had been any infringement of her liberties in the present instance. The Lord Justice-Clerk Boyle took the same line, referring to the gracious manner in which the King had recently declared his resolution to support the Constitution of the Church of Scotland, and boasting of his own descent from one who had borne a distinguished part in the ancient struggles of the Church in defence of her independence. He moved, therefore, that "Whereas the independence of the Church of Scotland in all matters of faith, worship, and discipline is fully established by law, the General Assembly finds it unnecessary and inexpedient to adopt any declaration with regard to the late, or any former, Order in Council relative to prayers for His Majesty and the Royal Family."

The original motion was seconded by Mr. James Wellwood Moncreiff; and Andrew Thomson, in concluding a spirited and eloquent debate, reiterated his conviction that the Order was an encroachment on the Church's independence, adding the pathetic and almost prophetic words: "I trust that the breath of official authority will never be allowed to wither one leaf of that Plant of Renown which our fathers watered with their blood, and of which we have been permitted by a kind Providence to eat the pleasant fruits." The motion of the Justice-Clerk was carried by 126 votes against 53.[1]

And did not all this, the reader may ask, arise simply

[1] Sage's *Memorabilia*.

out of an exhibition, on the part of Andrew Thomson, of
the practice, dear to clerical and oratorical vanity, of
making much ado about little or nothing? The true-
blue followers of the old banner throughout the manses
and homes of Scotland did not think so. But be the
question answered, for argument's sake, in the affirm-
ative. Could any illustration bring out more vividly
than is done by this debate, the keen and conscientious
vigilance with which Andrew Thomson and his party
guarded the soleness of that allegiance which the Church
owed to her heavenly King? And could the Moderate
party, Dr. Cook and the Lord of Session, Boyle, and the
rest of them, have more convincingly shown their own
belief in the reality and the justice of the Church's
claim to exercise independence in all spiritual matters
than by the course they took in arguing against
Thomson? Is it not impossible to observe the position assumed by the dominant party, without recognising that it never occurred to them to dispute that the
Scottish Church occupied an entirely different position,
in relation to the State, from that occupied by the
Church of England? True, there might arise difference
of opinion as to whether, in any particular instance, the
State had made some slight encroachment on the sphere
of the Church, or the Church some slight encroachment
on the sphere of the State; but this debate sets it forth,
as with the writing of meridian sunlight, that not a
speaker even on the Moderate side imagined the rights
and powers of the Church to have emanated from the
State, or that the State could, without tyrannical
usurpation, treat her spiritual jurisdiction as non-

existent. It was obviously no secondary matter on which, on such an occasion,— the recent accession of a sovereign,—Andrew Thomson could have ventured to make such a stand. It was because the Church had in her best days guarded her spiritual independence as the apple of her eye that he spoke out; and the strongest of the arguments by which the Moderate party obtained a decisive majority against him was, that the principle which he sought to vindicate had been called in question by no one, and needed no vindication.

In the General Assembly of 1820, Thomson had risen to repel the intrusive foot of Royalty—or what seemed to be such—from the sanctuary of the Church's independence. In the General Assembly of 1825, he proved himself true to her genius and history, by vigilant assertion of the rights of the Christian people. A presentation had been issued by the Crown to the living of Little Dunkeld in favour of an individual who was totally unacquainted with the Gaelic language. The congregation had always enjoyed a Gaelic ministry, and the Presbytery had therefore refused to sustain the presentation. Their decision had been confirmed by the Synod of Perth and Stirling, and was carried for final settlement to the Assembly. Thomson moved that the decision of the Presbytery and Synod should be ratified, and the Crown be respectfully requested to bring forward a presentee who could address the Highlanders in their own tongue. He was supported by another leader of the Evangelicals who had not been a member of the Assembly of 1820, but who, though not so well equipped as Andrew Thomson with the tactical qualifications of a party leader, was still more brilliant in his intellectual attributes than he. Thomson's motion was seconded by Chalmers! The combination was irresistible. The motion was carried by 107 to 89.

CHAPTER VI.

A Sudden Change.

ON the 9th of February 1831, Andrew Thomson, then about fifty years of age, took part in the proceedings of the Presbytery of Edinburgh, displaying the full vigour of his mental and physical energies. He walked home with a friend, engaging, as was his wont, in cordial talk. At his own door, in turning round for a parting word, he fell dead.

Seldom has all that human wisdom could have wished for or prescribed, with reference to a not far distant future, been more mysteriously baffled than by the death, at that moment, of Andrew Thomson. He would have shone so grandly in the Ten Years' Conflict! He was the realised ideal of a party leader,— for the dazzlement of genius, as has been abundantly attested both in the ecclesiastical and the civil history of Britain, has something in it at variance with consummate excellence of party management. Scotchmen were proud of Chalmers, but they placed their more sober trust in Andrew Thomson. Holding, through M'Crie, as has been said, with the past of Scottish

Church history, he was intensely modern in his aggressive assaults upon the slave-trade and the whole system of slavery, in his opposition to the Test and Corporation Acts, in his sympathy with the great liberal current in the movement of his time. Early in the century he had founded *The Christian Instructor*, the pioneer of a thousand such periodicals; had drawn into it, with wise comprehensiveness, the flower of religious literary talent both within and without the pale of the Church; and had made it an instrumentality, prized and treasured in ten thousand Scottish families, for keeping himself in touch with the conscience and heart of Scotland. He flung from him as a foolish prejudice that jealousy of culture in association with devoutness, and of comeliness and joyfulness in the worship of God, which has been vaguely supposed to be an attribute of Presbyterianism. Possessing great taste and capacity in music, himself a musical composer, he led the way in that reform of Church music which has since been so beneficently developed.

Seldom has Carlyle, even in those clouded years when the reader is frequently reminded of the saying, "Son of thunder, but thou hast become marvellously weak in thine old age," missed the mark so completely as in his reference to Andrew Thomson in the *Reminiscences*. "Once," says Carlyle, "I recollect transiently seeing the famed Andrew; and what a lean-minded, iracund, ignorant kind of man Andrew seemed to me." But Carlyle's own statement in connection with the formation of the tie between Chalmers and Irving appears to be inconsistent with the idea that there was anything of the pinched and frigid zealot in Thomson. Irving, Carlyle tells us, gave offence, in the very dawn of his pulpit powers, to a certain "hidebound public" both in Kirkcaldy and in Edinburgh. In the manner and still more in the matter of Irving there was a "novelty" that was "sufficiently surprising," an importunate demand, in particular, that actual practice should be squared with speech and theory—"If this thing is true, why not do it?"—that gave "astonishment and deep offence" to "hidebound mankind." "Both in Fife and over in Edinburgh," says Carlyle, "I have known the offence very rampant." But it was Andrew Thomson who directed the attention of Chalmers to Irving; it was Andrew Thomson who induced Chalmers to come *incognito* and hear Irving in Thomson's own pulpit, and whose word, presumably in opposition to the verdict of the narrowly orthodox, was in favour of Chalmers's choice of Irving as his assistant. If Carlyle's imagination did not, as seems most probable, falsify in this instance the original record of his memory, his impression must have been due to his own jaundiced eyesight, rendered untrustworthy by the setting in of his dyspepsia and by other experiences of what he describes as "four or five most miserable, dark, sick, and heavy-laden years." Carlyle's eye-glimpse of Thomson contradicts all the contemporary accounts we have of the man. These concur in laying stress upon his radiant geniality, his frank and cordial bearing.

Chalmers was overpowered with a passion of tears when he heard of Thomson's death. His hand, he said, had no steadiness to draw the lineaments of one who, though dead, seemed still to look upon him with the vividness of life. In his funeral sermon he brought out forcibly the importance of the fallen leader as a figure in the Edinburgh and in the Scotland of the time. " It is as if death," he said, " had wanted to make the highest demonstration of his sovereignty, and for this purpose had selected as his mark him who stood the foremost and the most conspicuous in the view of his countrymen. I speak not at present of any of the relations in which he stood to the living society immediately around him,—to the thousands in church whom his well-known voice reached upon the Sabbath,—to the tens of thousands in the city whom, through the week, in the varied rounds and meetings of Christian philanthropy, he either guided by his counsel or stimulated by his eloquence. You know, over and above, how far the wide, and the wakeful, and the untired benevolence of his nature carried him; and that, in the labours and the locomotions connected with these, he may be said to have become the personal acquaintance of the people of Scotland, insomuch that there is not a village of the land where the tidings of his death have not conveyed the intimation that a master in Israel has fallen; and I may also add, that such was the charm of his companionship, such the cordiality lighted up by his presence in every household, that, connected with this death, there is, at this moment, an oppressive sadness in the hearts of many thousands, even of our most distant Scottish families." The death of Thomson was a " national loss." He had " but gambolled with the difficulties that would have depressed and overborne other men." Of the blending of softer elements with Thomson's strength Chalmers spoke as lending a peculiar charm to his character, analogous to that of delicate beauty among Alpine crags. From the groundwork of masculine firmness, from " the substratum of moral strength and grandeur," there " effloresced " in tenfold beauty the " gentler charities of the heart." " To myself," said the preacher, " he was at all times a joyous, hearty, gallant, honourable, and out-and-out most trustworthy friend." Such a testimony was at the same time a testimony to the heart that gave it.

CHAPTER VII.

Non-Intrusion.

WE saw that one of the main objects kept in view by Dr. Andrew Thomson in the Assembly leadership of the High Presbyterian party, was the guardianship of the liberties of the Christian people in the settlement of pastors. Not only did he exert himself to the utmost to bring the administrative enginery of the Church to prevent presentees from being forced upon unwilling flocks, but he set on foot a society with a view to buying up patronages, and thus giving free course to the popular choice.

His death took place at that critical moment when the agitation for parliamentary reform was approaching its climax, and the epoch-making Reform Bill of 1832 was beginning to loom in the distance. The public mind throughout Scotland was vehemently excited; the spirit of democratic aspiration, like a quickening, thrilling fire-mist, was in the social atmosphere; and, as had from time immemorial been the case, the democratic aspiration in the State showed itself with conspicuous fervency in the Church. A disposition was manifested in the ranks of the Evangelicals not to wait for the slow operation of a system of purchase, but to assail patronage comprehensively and at once. When the parliamentary Reform Bill was passed, the Anti-Patronage Society declared for the total abolition of patronage.

In the Assembly of 1832, Chalmers occupied the Moderator's chair. It is the place of highest honour attainable by any member, and Chalmers's Moderatorship attests not only his own lofty position in the Church, but the rise in importance and influence of the party of which he was now the acknowledged leader. A little more than fifty summers had passed over him, and years had brought to him not a breath of decay, but only the full maturity and mellow strength of his powers. Few men could enter with more faithful sympathy than his into all that was refined and elevating in Moderatism. But to every argument in its favour he had one unanswerable reply. He had *been* a Moderate! He *knew* that it had lost Christ's miracle-gift, and could cast out no devils. He had tried its sweetest songs, its most eloquent enchantments, on the devils of rustic Kilmany, and not a devil of them would budge. He had paid fine compliments to Christ, and painted up the beauty of virtue, and no one had minded Christ or cared for virtue. He began preaching Christ as Paul, and Luther, and Bunyan, and Erskine had preached Him, and the devils began at once to scamper and the virtue to come in. He had *been* a Moderate; he could *never* be a Moderate again.

The subject of patronage was brought up by applications, technically styled overtures, from eleven Presbyteries and three Synods. These prayed the Assembly to take steps to secure to the call of the congregation its ancient and salutary force, and to prevent its being turned into an empty form by usurpation of all rights by patrons.

Dr. Robert Brown, of Aberdeen, speaking for the Evangelicals, proposed that a committee should be appointed to consider the overtures and report to the next Assembly. Principal Macfarlane, a leading Moderate, moved that the overtures should be dismissed as "unnecessary and inexpedient." He was supported in an elaborate speech by the Right Hon. Justice-Clerk Boyle, the same whom we found so jauntily pooh-poohing Andrew Thomson's protest against State encroachment on the independence of the Church. He spoke with the vehemence natural to a high legal and Conservative functionary, who shuddered at that evil and perilous thing, the will of the people. The question was in his eyes of "gigantic importance." The drift of the overtures, he insisted, was to destroy the rights of patrons, and to introduce popular election with all its flood of evils. Universal confusion would cover the land, and there would be an end of the peace and harmony that had hitherto reigned. If this were indeed desired, the Assembly ought to go manfully to Parliament and ask for an alteration in the law.

To reply to this imposing display of aristocratic and forensic eloquence there arose, amid the questioning amazement of the Assembly, an exceedingly young man, with keen, bright, imperturbably self-confident face, whom the few who knew him named to their whispering neighbours as the Rev. James Begg, of Paisley. That a man of twenty-three, on his first appearance in the

Assembly, should take a prominent part in a leading debate, and should enter the lists against giants like Boyle and Macfarlane, was a thing unheard of. Experienced beholders anticipated doubtless that the bold speaker would blunder into self-effacement. But in this cause James Begg might claim to be a predestined champion. He first drew breath in the parish of New Monkland, on the banks of the Clyde, where the very breezes, as they swept over copse, and corn, and heather, might sing of Covenant wars and Presbyterian contendings. A band from the parish had marched to Bothwell Bridge, and the boy Begg had often looked with reverent admiration on the silken banner, emblazoned with Bible, crown, and thistle in gold, round which his fellow-parishioners had fought and fallen. It was perhaps not so surprising, therefore, that he should have been audaciously eager for the fray when one of the essential principles of his ancestral Presbyterianism was at stake. Nor did he stammer or betray any tendency to nervous discomposure. Logic and lucidity, precision and a trace of sarcastic pungency, characterised his remarks, rather than festoons of flowery eloquence or exuberance of youthful sentiment. The prickly sharpness of some of his observations on the Moderate big-wigs won him the hearts of the students in the gallery, and Moderator Chalmers, who dearly loved a joke, forgot the awful solemnity of his seat, and actually clapped his hands and laughed.

But the most notable thing in James Begg's speech was the nice exactness with which he signalised the object to be aimed at by the Church as essential in the matter of patronage. Total abolition, he admitted, could not be effected by the Church without intervention of Parliament. The indispensable point was that no pastor should be forced into a church against the will of the people. This, he maintained, had, since the Reformation, been a principle of the Church of Scotland, and she possessed power, dormant but sufficient, to give effect to it. What they wanted was Non-intrusion. "I have no fear," he said, "of civil interference. Indeed, if such interference were attempted, it would then become a question for every honest man to determine how long he could consistently remain a member of a Church thus rendered unable to enforce her most salutary laws."

Begg rose unknown, and sat down famous. The fledgling orator who had put the Lord Justice-Clerk Boyle and Dr. Macfarlane to their mettle, whose fine hitting and cheery bumptiousness, and born Scottish sagacity, had made Chalmers forget his dignity in a boyish burst of sympathetic laughter, was henceforward a public man and leader of the people in Scotland. The Moderates carried their point by a majority of forty-two. But from Begg's lip had fallen the word that became a watchword in the ranks of the party, and a chief popular blazon on its banner—NON-INTRUSION!

CHAPTER VIII.

The Veto Act.

IN the Assembly of 1833, Dr. Chalmers was not in the chair, but was all the more able, on that account, to influence the deliberations of the Court. The eleven inferior courts that had overtured the Assembly of 1832 on patronage were now in number forty-two. In the interval he had fully considered the question, and his views on the whole subject were provisionally made up. His preference was decisive for the plan of concurrent legislation on the part of the Church and the State, as compared with that of disposing of the difficulty by legislation on the part of the Church alone. On this point, however, he allowed himself to be overruled by Lord Moncreiff of the Court of Session, whose eminence as a lawyer and devoted loyalty to the Church of Scotland seemed to accredit him as practically infallible in pointing out a way by which the possibility of collision might be avoided. Lord Moncreiff was firmly convinced that the Church was constitutionally possessed of the power to deal conclusively with patronage, and thought she ought to do so at once. He, as well as Dr. Chalmers, was strenuously opposed to the total abolition of patronage, but he had no doubt that the Church possessed jurisdiction sufficient to enable her to frame such a measure as should shred away the evils with which it had become associated.

Chalmers was not, in politics, ardently democratic. The ordinary man, the arithmetical unit of the population, did not impress him as particularly sublime. He had an unaffected horror of the electioneering charlatan, the patriotism made to sell, the village demagogy, the pothouse palaver, the sordid inspirations that with fatal facility transmute the masses into the worst, the most ravenous, the most bloodthirsty of classes. He had been, therefore, upon what good judges now generally esteem the wrong as well as the beaten side in the struggle for parliamentary reform.

But no one had a higher appreciation of man idealised on the model of Christ than he. No one cherished a firmer faith in the power of the most unlettered member of the Christian brotherhood to discern in another the lineaments of the King. He had a tragic feeling of the cruelty of inflicting a godless or uncongenial minister on godly parishioners. He thought with reverent admiration of the zeal of the old Church of Scotland in guarding the Christian people from having such forced upon them. "The great complaint of our more ancient Assemblies," he told the Assembly of 1833, "the great burden of Scottish indignation, the practical grievance which, of all others, has been hitherto felt the most intolerable and galling to the hearts of a free and religious people, is the violent intrusion of ministers upon parishes."

He traced in vivid outline the history of the Church's doings in the matter. First of all, at the very fountainhead of Scottish Presbyterianism, in 1560, the method had been that of election pure and simple. But in 1578, after eighteen years of experience and experiment, a twofold, or perhaps rather a threefold system was matured, and embodied in the Second Book of Discipline. The eldership in the congregation nominated the presentee, with or without conjunction of a patron; and if the people gave their consent, the induction took place. The rule is laid down " that no one be intruded contrary to the will of the congregation or without the voice of the eldership." In 1649, when the Westminster Standards were finally domiciled in Scotland, and in 1690, when the Church arose, at the Revolution Settlement, after the long persecution of the later Stuarts, the same principle of the interdict or veto of the people was recognised and ratified.

The practical operation of the system had been beneficent and pacific. The " popular will," skilfully inserted in its proper place, served as an equipoise rather than as an element of strife. " It was when a high-handed patronage reigned uncontrolled and without a rival, that discord and dissent multiplied in our parishes." The question then arose whether the people, in entering their interdict, in uttering their veto, should or should not specify, explain, and vindicate the reasons why they objected to the presentee. This proved to be a most difficult, delicate, and important question. Chalmers held that the essential thing was the *fact* of non-consent, the *will* of the people, and that exposition or argumentation in support of their decision was unnecessary. The peasant Christian, "while fully competent to discern the truth, may be as incompetent as a child" to show it in argument. "When required to give the reasons of his objection to a minister at the bar of his Presbytery, all the poor man can say for himself might be, that he does not preach the gospel, or that in his sermon there is no food for his soul." "In very proportion to my sympathy and my depth of veneration for the Christian appetency of such cottage patriarchs, would be the painfulness," said Chalmers, "I should feel when the cross-questionings of a court of review were brought to bear upon them." "To overbear such men is the highway to put an extinguisher on the Christianity of our land,—the Christianity of our ploughmen, our artisans, our men of handicraft and of hard labour; yet not the Christianity theirs of deceitful imagination, or of implicit deference to authority, but the Christianity of deep, I will add, of rational belief, firmly and profoundly seated in the principles of our moral nature, and nobly accredited by the virtues of our well-conditioned peasantry. In the older time of Presbytery,—that time of scriptural Christianity in our pulpits and of psalmody in all our cottages, —these men grew and multiplied in the land; and though derided in the heartless literature, and discountenanced or disowned in the heartless politics of other days, it is their remnant which acts as a preserving salt among our people, and which constitutes the real strength and glory of the Scottish nation."

But the Moderates were resolute, and felt it doubtless pleasant to thwart the Evangelical leader who outshone them all. Chalmers's motion, therefore, to give constant and imperative effect to the congregational *veto*, was defeated in the Assembly of 1833 by twelve votes.

Another year went past. Chalmers was no longer a member of the Assembly. But the tide had been flowing vehemently in favour of the popular party. The motion which he had brought forward was, in substantials, re-introduced by Lord Moncreiff, and carried by a majority of forty-six. This was the famed Veto Act of 1834. It decreed that, when a congregation reclaimed against the presentee nominated by a patron, their rejection should take effect.

As it was not a voluminous piece of legislation, and as an accurate acquaintance with it is the simplest and surest guarantee of a just and lucid apprehension of all that followed, the intelligent reader will perhaps like to have before him

The Veto Act.

"The General Assembly declare, that it is a fundamental of their Church, that no pastor shall be intruded on any congregation contrary to the will of the people; and in order that this principle may be carried into full effect, the General Assembly, with the consent of a majority of the Presbyteries of this Church, do declare, enact, and ordain, That it shall be an instruction to Presbyteries, that if, at the moderating in a call to a vacant pastoral charge, the major part of the male heads of families, members of the vacant congregation, and in full communion with the Church, shall disapprove of the person in whose favour the call is proposed to be moderated in,

such disapproval shall be deemed sufficient ground for
the Presbytery rejecting such person, and that he shall
be rejected accordingly, and due notice thereof forthwith
given to all concerned; but that, if the major part of the
said heads of families shall not disapprove of such person
to be their pastor, the Presbytery shall proceed with the
settlement according to the rules of the Church:

"And further declare, That no person shall be held to
be entitled to disapprove as aforesaid, who shall refuse, if
required, solemnly to declare in presence of the Presbytery, that he is actuated by no factious or malicious
motive, but solely by a conscientious regard to the
spiritual interests of himself or the congregation."

Such, in its length and its breadth, is the celebrated
Veto Act, which thousands who never looked at it
denounced as the manifesto of a rebellious Church, but
which has reason and righteousness shining on its face,
and commended itself to what instincts there were of
justice and generous courage even in the prejudiced heart
of Peel, and which was the Pharos light that guided the
true-hearted, patriotic, and indomitable Argylls, the distinguished father and the more distinguished son, in their
long and at last victorious battle with Church patronage in
Scotland. Well considered, and viewed in the light of
the infinite disputation that subsequently arose, it will be
seen to be a masterly bit of legislative work. It would
puzzle an expert to add a bettering touch to the nice
felicity of its defining words. To fling open the door
to free election would have been easy; but it is of the
very essence of Christianity that the one, whether the
individual or the congregation, shall have the benefit

of union and communion with the many, and that the many shall retain vital and vivid connection with the one; therefore it is by the will and consent *both* of the parochial flock and of the aggregate flock and fold, that the settlement shall take place. And how accurately do such words as "consent," "will," "intrusion," "disapproval," steer clear of those absolutely interminable sophistications and debatings that arise when, in such cases, you ask people to state in words the reasons why they disapprove!

On one point these wise and vigilant guardians of the electoral rights of congregations take care that there shall be no mistake. If there is any suspicion of a non-spiritual motive, if there is any reason to fear the direct or indirect action of political boycott, or malice, or bribery, then a solemn inquiry is to be instituted into the matter. The whole affair is to be *bonâ fide* spiritual; and if the State suspects a trick, it will have the best aid of the machinery of the Act in helping to expose it.

Never, surely, did democracy wear a less revolutionary aspect, or come in a less questionable or alarming shape, than when it appeared in the persons of the male heads of families in full communion with the Church earnestly deprecating the appointment of unedifying men to minister to them in sacred things. It was a presumption too potent to be gainsaid,—a presumption warranted by all that has given Scotchmen their good name among the nations of the world,—that these heads of families, communicants, should have in them the living light of Christianity. They might therefore have the clearest conviction that a presentee, even though his doctrine

were orthodox, his learning sufficient, his life moral, was
nevertheless spiritually lifeless, or at all events unedifying
to the congregation. The Veto Act did not lay a finger
on the temporal benefits of the incumbency; and, of
course, the patron, finding one presentee unacceptable,
might present another until a suitable one was found.

CHAPTER IX.

The Chapel Ministers.

BY the Veto Act the great body of the people were restored to their true place in the Church. This was the most conspicuous achievement hitherto realised by the party of Reform. It was marvellously adapted to quicken the interest of the people in the Church, and to warm the attachment with which they regarded their pastors. But another and correspondent change, by which the pastorate itself should be brought into accordance with the original model, from which it had largely fallen, was necessary to the complete restoration aimed at by the movement party.

The pastor, it need hardly be said, is an eminently important figure in the Catholic Church, reformed on the Presbyterian pattern. The real presence of Christ is His presence in the breast of every Christian, and the ideal pastor is the man in a parish who glows most visibly with the presence of Christ, and in whom his flock can see a present Christ. He has a variety of duties, and perhaps it would not be easy to convey a more lucid or more comprehensive idea of these than

Andrew Melville, New Testament in hand, furnishes us with, in a passage that has doubtless been often quoted but will bear quoting again. Melville adopts the view that the variety of names applied in Scripture to pastors is an index to their varieties of duty. "Sometimes," he says, "they are called *pastors*, because they feed the congregation; sometimes *episcopi* or *bishops*, because they watch over their flock; sometimes ministers, by reason of their service and office; and sometimes also *presbyters* or *seniors*, for the gravity in manners which they ought to have in taking care of the spiritual government which ought to be most dear unto them."

This was the ideal of the parish minister, which Andrew Melville believed himself able to draw from Scripture. It speaks well for the practical sense, as well as for the sound Christianity, of Melville, that so little is said in his summary about pulpit fluency and oratorical effulgence. Neither the philosopher explaining abstract truth to an illuminated coterie, nor the pulpit rhetorician moving a polite audience to delicious tears of sentiment, or playing upon them in sunny ripples of hope and joy, seems to have entered largely into Melville's conception of that representative of Christ and of the Church in a parish, who was to share in the whole life of his congregation, to execute discipline as well as preach, to be, in doing as well as in speaking, the brother-servant and leader-friend of his flock. Whatever might be the varieties of the pastoral name, it was in vehement opposition to the genius of Presbyterianism, as found by Melville in the New Testament, that the pastor of one parish should not be in a position of equal and perfect brotherhood with the pastors of other parishes. To deny him his share in any business or concern of Church-session, Presbytery, Synod, or General Assembly, was to outrage the fundamental principles of Christian brotherhood.

During the Moderate ascendancy, however,—in the century of religious indifference and spiritual somnolence,—this life-principle had been violated, and a dangerous and schismatical deviation had taken place from the parity of the pastorate. Circumstances had favoured the rise within the pale of the Establishment of what may be called an alien and accidental congregationalism, retaining the Presbyterian name though really nondescript. It was due mainly to hindrances and complications arising from the State-connection. That connection had in its incipiency been friendly and loyal on both sides. The Church had recognised the authority of the State; the State, often demurring, had on the whole respected the spiritual independence of the Church, co-operating with her in the work of benefiting the nation. A visible Church, exactly as a visible human spirit, must have food and raiment; and the regulating principle of the arrangement between Church and State in Scotland—the regulating principle, observe, which might or might not be adhered to with mathematical accuracy in detail—was that the State should supply the food and raiment, the Church the animating spirit. The alliance between Church and State was based on the mutual recognition of co-ordinate jurisdiction.

The Church was not required to sell her spiritual birthright for a mess of pottage; but it must be admitted that, whatever they did or did not sell for it, the mess of pottage allotted to the pastors of the Reformed Church in Scotland was a pitifully small one. Very different from the butter, in a lordly dish, which the Church of England, less sensitive as to her birthright of spiritual jurisdiction, managed to carry off! The Scottish barons, turbulent and rapacious, had kept their sovereign on starvation wages; and they were the last of men to take due care, when they divided among themselves the splendid properties of the ancient Church, that, in addition to the wretched provision for the then existing clergy of the Reformed Church, there should be adequate or approximately adequate means provided to supply the spiritual wants of the population as it gradually increased.

The matter was not, however, absolutely overlooked. Not to cumber ourselves with detail, we find that, by the arrangement ultimately decided on, when the population of any parish had outgrown the supply of Church ordinances, the Church and the Court of Session, co-operating with each other, were empowered to erect and endow a new charge. But the action, both of the Presbytery and of the Court of Session, was made conditional upon the preliminary consent of landowners "possessing at least three-fourths of the valued rent of the parish." He must take a highly rose-coloured view of the spiritual qualities of landowners, who does not see that this would prove to be a retarding stipulation. Can we fail to realise that, when heritors and clerical gentlemen, lapped in the sweet somnolence of Moderatism, solaced each other over their claret, they might feel it to be in many ways objectionable to multiply charges and to make provision for new ministers? The population increased. The people wanted more means of spiritual instruction than the drowsy lairds and listless parsons supplied. Chapels of ease, as they were called, sprang up. But there were far fewer of them than the increase of the population required, and, such as they were, they by no means reached the standard of normal Presbyterian charges. The Moderate clergy did not like them. As in England, so in Scotland, during the philosophical century, it was Bible religion, that is to say, the religion which your peasant Latimers, your plain Bunyans, Wesleys, and Spurgeons, see flashing on them from the Scripture page, that the people wanted when they asked for more ministers. The people found it also a great advantage that, in the case of the chapels of ease, there were no patrons. But all this was poison to the Moderate clergy and their friends the lairds. The chapel ministers were practically treated as an inferior order, allowed indeed to preach, but excluded from all the courts of the Church.

But the party of the Bible and of the people was now in the ascendant. The Church had shaken off her wintry slumbers, and was putting on her strength. After a spirited debate, the General Assembly of 1834 swept away by a large majority the invidious distinctions which had been permitted to accumulate between the chapel ministers and their more fully-endowed brethren. Fixing her attention upon her own duty, without waiting for the laggard action of the civil power to provide endowments,—placing spiritual things first and material things second, instead of letting the soul wait upon the body,—the Church accepted, as in all senses the equals of their brethren, those ministers who had found themselves charges, often without her help, by the grace of God and the freewill offerings of the people of Scotland. She bestowed upon them all the dignities and powers belonging to the Presbyterian office-bearer.

The most prominent part in this debate was taken by Mr. Murray Dunlop. He was a lawyer of great learning, gifted with the luminous faculty of good lawyers in its noblest form. A man of great general capacity, he was subsequently considered the ablest of the Scottish members of Parliament; but politics were for him the second, not the first. Devoted to his Church with a glowing and beautiful fervency, he entertained for her a sentiment that was religion, heroism, and poetry all in one. The inspiration of a glorious present, the vision of a glorious future, the Church of Scotland arose before him, shaking off the apathy of a hundred years, restoring to the people their liberties and rights, extending to the chapel ministers their privileges, and satisfying all Seceders that the Church of Scotland they had so long loved and waited for, was again willing and worthy to receive them and to gather her whole flock within the ancient fold. "Our anxious people," Mr. Dunlop now said, "from the door of every tent intensely watch the holy banner. Already, blessed be God, they have seen it slightly unfurl in the rising breeze, and lift itself in part from the staff, and the solemn stir of preparation is heard throughout the camp; and at this very hour, with prayer, uplifted hands, and eager eyes, they watch the moment when they shall see it once more broadly unfold itself to the glorious sun, and hail it with one long loud hosannah that shall resound from shore to shore."

Not all, however, in the Assembly were so full of faith and hope as Mr. Dunlop. The prudent, plausible, peace-loving Dr. Cook, always aiming at reasonableness of speech, sincerely averse to quarrelling with the Evangelical reformers, but more averse still to quarrelling with the terrible Court of Session, pointed out that in some instances Presbyteries were actually empowered to deal with questions connected with the temporalities, and expressed a strong apprehension that difficulties might arise with the Civil Power if the chapel ministers were introduced into courts thus constituted. A corresponding fear and reverence in relation to property had been manifested by Dr. Cook in the discussions on the proposal to make good the rights of congregations against patrons. Rights of the Christian people, vindication of Presbyterian parity, Church extension to every corner of Scotland, these were no doubt brave notions, but what might the *other* party to the State and Church alliance say? What if the pace of the Church, in carrying out her own spiritual mission, should prove too rapid for the State?

This constant trepidation as to what the Civil Power might say, called forth a remonstrance from one who had marched with firm step among "Tamson's men," and on whom their leader's eye had often glanced with kindling recognition and exultant sympathy. Very tall, somewhat ungainly, with a huge shock of curling hair and a powerful but not melodious voice, this friend and follower of Andrew Thomson was no courtly orator; but he swayed every audience he addressed, and the more cultivated and capable the audience, the more completely did it own his sway. We shall know him better before we have done,—his name was William Cunningham. Not in the slightest degree disloyal to the connection between Church and State was he. No foreboding of a conflict between the two had distressed him. He was sincerely disposed to defer to and to honour the State in the exercise of all the powers and privileges annexed to the civil jurisdiction. But he was not prepared to admit that the Church should do good only by permission of the State,—that the Church should ask the State, with bated breath and whispered humbleness, to allow her to be true to Scotland and to Christ. This was in his view mere moral cowardice and spiritual paralysis. "The principle," he said, "upon which this House has too often acted seems to have been something like this,—that in consequence of our connection with the State, we have no power to do anything, however closely connected with the interests of religion, which the State has not expressly warranted and authorised; whereas, the true principle by which we ought to be guided—true alike in doctrine and in fact—is this, that notwithstanding our connection with the State, we can and ought to do everything fitted to promote the interests of religion which the State has not expressly prohibited."

This might seem at first glance no great difference, but for Cunningham it meant much. In his view the State was answerable to Christ as well as the Church, and therefore it would be a virtual accusation of unfaithfulness on the part of the State to suppose that it prohibited anything in the spiritual province which Christ's officers in that province found prescribed for them in Christ's law. And Cunningham had deliberately and with all possible publicity committed himself to the statement that, if the Church could not promote the spiritual kingdom of her Lord as well in connection with the State as apart from the State, it was her duty to part. "It is willingly conceded," he had said, "that Christ's Church or kingdom is not of this world, but is purely spiritual, and that, if it can be proved that union or connection between Church and State, of any kind or in any degree, *necessarily* implies the headship over the Church of any other than Jesus Christ Himself,—the subtraction of any of the privileges conferred by Christ on the office-bearers or members of His Church, or the imposition of any restraint upon them in the discharge of any of their duties,—all such union or connection is *unlawful*." Such, to the Voluntaries on this hand, and to Erastians of every tint and of every name on that, was Cunningham's declaration on the eve of the conflict.

CHAPTER X.

Chalmers at Work.

WHO in those days was a more hopeful, happy man than Chalmers? When we think of him, the solemn gladness of those psalms, in which either the Shepherd-minstrel himself, or the nameless Beethovens and Haydns of the old Hebrew Church, expressed the music of their walk with God, recurs to us. He rejoiced like a strong man to run his race, treading like the sun as it mounts the sky, and feeling the pleasure of the Lord prospering in his hand. The Church—the Established Church — had set herself right. The flock was delivered from hireling shepherds, and the true brothers of the Presbyterian pastorate, who had been sent to the tents of Kedar—the ecclesiastical Coventry—of chapel ministration, were raised to the seats of honour,—no mere street preachers, but fully equipped elders to judge the twelve tribes of Israel.

Can we wonder that Chalmers should believe, say in 1835, when the resurgent Church had passed those measures of legislative reform, that he was in a fair way to wipe the last stain of infidel or dissident reproach from the brow of the Scottish Establishment, and that he felt confidence in the willingness of the State to co-operate with the Church in what he viewed as their joint work of benefiting the people of Scotland? It is most instructive, and it is, we must add, profoundly pathetic, to behold this strong Churchman straining his energies to the utmost to demonstrate, by the final testimony of experience, that a rejuvenescent Church could find favour in the eyes of British statesmen. If ever man believed in the theoretic and practical feasibility of the express association of religious institutions and political institutions in promoting the health and wealth of nations, it was he.

The problem he now grappled with was Church Extension. In urging it forward, he appealed not only to Christian principles, but to the evidence of his eyes. His idiosyncrasy, be it remembered, was the combination, perhaps unique, of an impetuosity of spiritual ardour comparable to that of St. Paul, with a utilitarianism as cool, circumspect, and thorough-going as that of Jeremy Bentham. He once expressed to a bosom friend grave and depressing doubts as to the real use and benefit of those splendid exhibitions of pulpit eloquence which were filling the world with his fame; but he exulted in the confidence that he was making a right and fruitful use of his faculties when he trod the slums of Glasgow, the auxiliary of the policeman, bringing celestial fire to irradiate their darkness, and superseding both policeman and relieving officer by the unbought ministrations of Christian charity, quickening into development every germ of self-help, every dormant energy of family affection.

Apply, then, he now in many accents impatiently cried, this experience to the State. Was it not palpable that the people so operated on were like to be better subjects, more law-abiding, less turbulent, less criminal, less pauperised, than if left in heathenish irreligion? Could any man deny that "a depraved commonalty is the teeming source of all moral and political disorder"? This he expected statesmen to admit, when he appealed to them to promote Church extension.

He proposed that over-peopled parishes should be subdivided into manageable districts; that in each of these districts there should be erected "an economical church," so economical that the sittings, if rented at all, might be let cheaply enough to admit attendance by the humblest classes. The Church was ready with "talented and well-disposed licentiates, alive to the great moral necessities of our land, and resolved to enter with the full consecration of their powers and opportunities on that high walk of philanthropy, whose object is to reclaim those degenerate outcasts who have so multiplied in thousands and tens of thousands beyond the means of Christian instruction."

What of endowment? That was a matter that required to be thought of. With characteristic regard to their own interests, the heritors, who by ancient arrangement ought to have borne at least part of the charge, had applied to Parliament for protection to their pockets. Statesmen had been willing enough to listen to *them*. "A recent Act" had screened them from liability in connection with the new territorial churches. There remained "the liberality of the patriotic and the good," in short, the voluntary system without the big V, to fall back upon, and these made generous response to the appeal of Chalmers. But he did not forget that he was working for the poor. They little know this man who imagine that, if he had obtained money enough to decorate the towns and enliven the parishes of Scotland with handsome churches, filled with rich and fashionable congregations, he would have attained his object or reaped his reward. High steeples, advertising crack preachers to attract hearers from miles or leagues around, on the system which has since been so brilliantly developed in London and elsewhere, would have been looked on by him with small enthusiasm. Valuing at all times and in all places the preaching of the gospel, he was not bent only on preaching. "In this way," he wrote, "there would be no increase in the amount of Christian instruction in the country, but only a transference of hearers from one place to another,—a building up of new at the expense of old congregations. It would but make a new distribution of hearers among people who already hear somewhere." It was not as a thing of ornament, but as a thing of use, that this man contemplated the parochial system. "The great thing wanted is, that the thousands now living in practical heathenism, and who at present hear nowhere, shall be reclaimed to the decencies of a Christian land; and this can only be done by planting churches with low seat-rents in the midst of these people, giving them a preference above all others to the sittings in their own local churches, and making it the distinct business of the newly-endowed ministers, each to cultivate, and as much as possible confine himself to, the households of his own assigned locality. In this way altogether new ground will be entered upon; a real movement in advance will be made among a heretofore neglected population. Christian instruction will be let down to the poorest of our families; and our Establishment, if extended in this way, will become, and at a very cheap rate, an effective home-mission in favour of those whose thorough moral and Christian education, both piety and the public good so loudly demand."

The authority of the State in measuring out areas for the territorial churches, and an extremely limited grant of money in each case, say £100, just sufficient to secure that there should be sittings accessible to the poorest self-sustaining parishioners,—such was the modest request of Chalmers and the awakening Church to that State which was supposed to bestow upon her inestimable advantage in their joint labour of promoting Christian instruction in Scotland. What was the reply?

At first there had been some encouraging symptoms on the part of the Government. The Melbourne Cabinet had given a courteous hearing to a deputation from Edinburgh, that came to London to plead for the scheme in 1834. The Whig phalanx, that seemed unassailable after the passing of the great Reform Bill, had even then begun to waver under the skilful attacks of Peel, and was driven from office in that year. But it was against his own judgment as a parliamentary tactician that Sir Robert had pressed his advantage so far, and the consequent rally of his opponents and partial reattainment of popularity placed them more firmly in their seats than before.

Meanwhile Chalmers had been at work. Engaged at one and the same time in fiercest battle with controversial foes, and in pushing on the Church's part of the Extension Scheme, he had issued four pamphlets in one month as successive blows to strike down the hydra-heads of opposition, and had splendidly succeeded in the constructive part of his enterprise. In the General Assembly of 1835 he announced what had been done. Sixty-four new churches had in one year been added to the Establishment, "about as many as the whole preceding century had given birth to," and upwards of sixty-five thousand pounds had been contributed in cash.

The session of Assembly ended, Chalmers himself, heading a deputation, proceeded to London. Whether it was that Lord Melbourne and Lord John Russell were now more stably seated in office, or whether the hydra-heads of opposition, smitten in Edinburgh by four pamphlets in one month, had reappeared and been potently at work in London, a change had come to pass. Lord Melbourne was oppressively apathetic. Lord John Russell was sententious, guarded, prepared to maintain State Establishments of religion, but extremely calm on the subject of Church Extension. The Government, they were told, had resolved to issue a Royal Commission of Inquiry to investigate the subject. That was all. For the fiery champion of State Churches it was a bath of snow-water. Where was that loyalty to the Church's primary duty of bringing Christ's gospel to the poor, which he had looked for from statesmen? In his disenchantment he turned with his deputation, if not for help, at least for solace, to the Tories.

"Gentlemen," said the Duke of Wellington, "you will get nothing. That is my opinion. I am sorry for it, but so you will find it."

The supercilious apathy of Melbourne and the placid languor of Lord John, followed by the issue of a highly-unsatisfactory Commission of Inquiry, stirred the spirit of Chalmers, and drew from him a letter to the Whig Prime Minister, marked by all his ardour in the sacred cause of the poor, and evincing the penetrating power of his logic to pierce through shams into the heart of things. He told Melbourne that the indifference of the Administration to the extension of Christian instruction among unprovided populations betrayed a lurking belief that the instruction, where provided, was not worth much, and that "little or no evil would result on the departure of Christianity and all its services from the land." Such a sentiment, he indignantly exclaims "stamps a nullity on the gospel, and an utter insignificance on the vocation of its ministers." Thus wrote Chalmers more than fifty years ago. As we read the words to-day, is there not something tragic in their sound? How palpably—with ever-accelerating speed—has the current of opinion in Cabinets and Parliaments since then been towards depreciation of the value of "Christianity and all its services"! Herein lies, in fact, the essential difficulty, always making the friction greater, that has emerged in the practical carrying on of the alliance between Church and State. The State of old valued the Church for the sake of the Church's work. The governing classes in Lord Melbourne's days had begun to be profoundly indifferent to the Church's duties as such, and scepticism was stealing upon their minds as to whether even the indirect and educational uses of the Church were worth taking trouble about.

In the constitution of the Royal Commission of Inquiry issued by the Melbourne Government, Chalmers proceeded to point out, there did not appear the smallest consideration of what was due to the Church as an independent spiritual power, co-operating with the State on terms of mutual loyalty for a common object. The names of such men, in the next place, as were familiar with the want of religious teaching in the crowded towns of Scotland, and in whom the Church could trust, Monteith, Spiers, Dunlop, were absent. The selected Commissioners, deficient in all requisite qualifications, had been put in "at the instigation of their patrons or political friends." The Scottish Church was a fellow-worker with the State in the cause of Christ and the people, not on slavish and humiliating, but on honourable and equal conditions; and the terms in which this Commission was drafted evinced ignorance, said Chalmers, "of the fundamental principle of our Presbyterian Establishment," or else a "purpose to offer it violence." Had the Commissioners been of the right kind, the Church might have felt no alarm as to "transgression being made on the line of demarcation between the civil and the ecclesiastical;" but, the Commissioners being hostile, and their instructions "loose and unguarded," the Churchmen of Scotland might well apprehend that their "most sacred principles" would be slighted. And then, for the benefit and illumination of all those Melbournes, Russells, and Peels who might henceforward have any special dealings with the Church, he went into a statement of what had always been, and would always be, an inexorable condition of his championship of State-Churchism. "We do not acknowledge," he exclaimed, "the King to be the head of the Church; and this independence of the ecclesiastical upon the civil was conceded to us at the Revolution, after we had sustained many and grievous persecutions in defence of it, and since guaranteed at the period of the Union between the two kingdoms. We do not admit the subordination of the Church to the State in things which are strictly and properly ecclesiastical; or that we are responsible to any tribunal on earth for the discharge and exercise of our spiritual functions." Spiritual independence he signalised as "the dearest and most hallowed of our principles," and prophesied that, if encroachment were made upon it, many thousands of those Scotchmen who were "still attached to the tabernacles of their fathers" would make known their resentment.

Does the reader now expect to be told that Chalmers flung the Commission of Inquiry in Lord Melbourne's face, and called upon the clergy and people of Scotland to submit to no examination as to the religious state of parishes by emissaries of the Civil Power? There seem to have been not a few in Scotland who were prepared for this course. The agitation was deeply felt throughout the country. A special meeting of the Commission of the General Assembly was called to consider the question of how the privileges of the Church might be guarded.

One particularly excited gentleman deserves special notice. Mr. John Hope, Dean of Faculty, apparently outstripping Dunlop himself in Presbyterian zeal, wrote to Chalmers entreating him to raise his voice, "as our firm and well-tried Presbyterian champion," against "this most flagrant outrage." Mr. Hope pronounced the Government inquiry "destructive of the principle and independence of Presbytery," and described the occasion as "the commencement of the final fight for our Church."

But Chalmers combined the wisdom and self-command of Ulysses with the moral passion and the voice of Achilles. He was to be moved from the stability of his intellectual judgment neither by the whirlblast of popular enthusiasm nor by the seductive flatteries of the Presbyterian lawyer. Calmly studying the terms of the Commission, he perceived that, however "loose" they might be, they did not necessarily carry the tyrannical sense fixed upon them by the Dean. Lord John Russell wrote also a timeous letter to Lord Minto, which served, says Dr. Hanna, "entirely to remove" the misapprehension caused by the language of the Commission. And, let us add,—as perhaps the most important element in the business,—Chalmers's own practical instinct reminded him, on second thoughts, that if two co-ordinate powers, Church and State, were to work harmoniously together, it was, by the nature of the case, requisite and reasonable that they should give full explanation, information, and general furtherance to each other. Having protested, therefore, against both the wording and the manning of the Whig Commission, he nevertheless advised the Church, throughout all her parishes, to welcome the Commissioners, and show them that the poor were hungering for a more liberal supply of the bread of life. " I will submit to any affront," he said, "rather than that the cause should suffer from any want of willing co-operation which I can possibly render to it. I look for many disagreeables in consequence of these appointments; but I will brook anything rather than give up the object of a Christian education for the common people." There is in all this a chivalrous fidelity to honour, an intrepid acceptance of light up to the measure of its dawning, a truth to one's self and one's God, that amounts to a sterling consistency, better than the nicest fitting of cog to tooth and tooth to cog, round the whole commonplace wheel of life.

May we not say that some strange fatality, some singular infatuation, some curious maladjustment of circumstances or malignity of human spite, could alone bring it about that such a man should, within a few years, have come to believe himself absolutely bound by his duty to Christ to bid the Church of Scotland separate from the State?

One thing above all others it is well for us to observe in connection with this letter of Dean of Faculty Hope's to Chalmers, that it was the lawyer, not the divine, who exhibited a sensitive jealousy as to the right of the clergy not to be inspected in the discharge of their teaching and preaching functions. Chalmers had no insuperable qualms about the sacrosanct character of the clergy. He may feel his Presbyterian principles more keenly roused when it is the rights of the people that are menaced!

Meanwhile, be it accurately understood why and for what causes this impassioned advocate valued Church Establishments. It was *not* because he supposed the Almighty to hold Himself more honoured by having His name blazoned on political institutions than on the hearts of nations. The national recognition of God by atheistic Governments he would have pronounced a blasphemous sham. It was *not* because he wished to cripple the operation, in proper circumstances, of Nonconformist preachers, or to bar their attracting audiences from all parts of the compass, or from any extent of area. The more he saw of pulpit power, exerted in the name of Christ, the more cordially was he gratified. The traditions of the Scottish Evangelical party—the Andrew Thomson party—were entirely in favour of generous appreciation of Nonconformist Christianity, and the recognition by the Establishment of the yeoman service rendered by such outfield workers as Wardlaw and M'Crie.

Chalmers valued Establishment because he held that, in order to bring Christian ministrations to the bedside of the poor in congested districts, and to enable the poorest of them to attend the public ordinances of religion, it was necessary to divide large areas into limited districts, to assign a minister to each, and to secure that sittings in territorial churches should be practically free. His own Church Extension Scheme furnished a magnificent attestation of his faith in voluntary effort. It was based mainly upon voluntary effort. Only the stretching out of the little finger of the State did he ask for, to supplement the free-will offerings of the Christian people, and to supplement them in the interest of the poor. And when the people, like all peoples, ancient and modern, really in earnest about religion, made generous response to his appeal, the State treated his adored Church as an Indian village treats the old used-up cow that yields milk no longer, and which, though they do not lay a hand on it, they turn out to die in the meadow, indifferent whether the vultures tear it or no! The day of the vultures is certainly not yet; but can the most imaginative of readers fancy that our lynx-eyed Presbyterian Dean will turn out to be at the head of them?

The Commissioners visited the parishes, pocketed their wages, and went their way. And nothing came of it. The Duke of Wellington was a true prophet: "Gentlemen, you will get nothing."

CHAPTER XI.

Chalmers at Play.

IN the same summer in which he dealt so manfully, so magnanimously, and so hopelessly with Lord Melbourne, Dr. Chalmers visited Oxford. It was a change, for a few halcyon days, from solemn work to not ignoble play. Always ardently scientific, well informed in geology, and intrepid in his conviction that no evil could come to the truth or to the Church from a recognition of facts ascertained by research, he had been elected a Fellow and Vice-President of the Royal Society of Edinburgh, and was also, by election, a Corresponding Member of the Royal Institute of France. He now, in 1835, received an intimation from Oxford, that at the approaching Annual Commemoration the University intended to confer upon him the degree of Doctor of Laws. With the simplicity of a guileless nature, too great to disguise its honest pride, he owned his surprise and delight. "I have long," he wrote in reply, "had the utmost affection and reverence for the University of Oxford, but I never once dreamed of the possibility of in any manner being admitted within its pale." In the presence of a brilliant throng he was invested with the honour conferred upon him, and addressed in sonorous Latin as a paragon of benignity, learning, and eloquence, a strenuous and compassionate advocate of the poor, and *ecclesiæ Scoticæ acerrimus propugnator, ecclesiæ Anglicanæ quoque, idque dubiis et formidolosis temporibus, gravissimus vindex*,—the keenest champion of the Church of Scotland, and also, and that in doubtful and alarming times, a most powerful defender of the Church of England. Three times in the course of the Latin panegyric did the assembled gownsmen of Oxford University make the roof ring with their acclamations.

"The most interesting introduction which I have had in Oxford," wrote Chalmers to his friend, Lady Stuart, "is to Keble the poet, author of the *Christian Year*, a work of exquisite beauty, and most worthy of your personal, nay, of your daily companionship, if you have not yet admitted it into your cabinet." In that year there were not many in England, to say nothing of Presbyterian Scotland, who could speak of daily companionship with Keble's poetry. And it was of this man that Carlyle, in the latest stage of his decadence, spoiling by the ugly sting at the end what would otherwise have been a fine and cordial eulogium on Chalmers, could speak as "ill *read*," and "ignorant of all that lay beyond the horizon in place or in time."

In this Oxford visit there was one cloud that cast momentarily its shadow on Chalmers. "The only expression of regret," wrote a friend who was much with him in Oxford, "which fell from him in my hearing during the course of his visit, had reference to the reserve which characterised, as he thought, the manner of some eminent men connected with a certain theological party to whom he was introduced, and which prevented him from touching, in conversation with them, upon topics of the highest import, with the frank and genial earnestness which was natural to him." The reference obviously is to that famed party whose history, from that year until now, has been the history of High Church life and thought, and, to no inconsiderable extent, of theological and humanitarian literature, in England. Mind and heart linger on the juxtaposition, at Oxford, of Chalmers and Newman. Of how much were they the antithetically contrasted and antagonist types! Simple Chalmers, the kindly, unsophisticated Scot, who saw through a medium of illusion everything called Christian, and sang the praises of the Anglican Establishment as a bulwark of Protestantism. Newman would hardly have granted him the Christian name. But Chalmers was right in thinking that there were mighty elements in the Church of England that sympathised with him,—far mightier than those represented by Newman. Chalmers stood for the religion of men; Newman, for that of priests. The one represented the universal Christian priesthood; the other, a mystically endowed sacerdotal caste. It may seem a startling statement, but the historical evidence of its truth is absolutely overwhelming, that, probably from a time prior to the Reformation, and certainly from the days of Queen Elizabeth until Chalmers and Newman were in Oxford together in 1835, the religion of the great body of Englishmen has been the religion of Chalmers, not of Newman. There is much religion in

Shakespeare; there is no sacerdotalism. Wycliffe, Milton, Bunyan, Whitfield, Wesley, Wilberforce, Shaftesbury, Spurgeon, stand one and all on the religion of Chalmers, as against the religion of Newman. Young men of religious susceptibility, young women of cloistral temperament, adored Newman. But the people of England knew him not. It was very doubtful then, and it is perhaps doubtful now, whether, if we look to essentials and not circumstantials, there is not more of Presbyterianism than of Newmanism in the Church of England. Had Newman been in touch with the Bible Christianity of the English people, as Chalmers was in touch with the Bible religion of the Scottish people, how different the issue might have been! The English people *fear* to see their Church free and self-governing, because they have an invincible suspicion that the Church means the clergy, and that the clergy aspire to be a priestly caste. The Anglican clergy have never been leaders of the people. But Chalmers would have assented, with a fervency that few Anglican clergymen or Anglican laymen can realise, to Newman's solemn conviction, implied in his celebrated utterance as he passed beyond the threshold of the Church of England, that the Church of Christ is no mere national or political institution. The Church of the people in Scotland took over, in the sixteenth century, from the Church of Rome, all the genuine rights, liberties, and powers of the Church of Christ; and since then, in proportion to their zeal for Christ, have the clergy been Scottish patriots and tribunes of the common people.

CHAPTER XII.

The Resurgent Church—The Sudden Storm—Auchterarder.

TIMES were changed in Scotland. The Church had been dead and was alive again. The moral atmosphere was no longer one of slumbrous indifference. That wave of Evangelical religion, sneered at considerably by philosophic personages for other-worldliness, but privileged by virtue of its zeal against slavery, its opposition to the Test and Corporation Acts, its war against the cruelties of the old criminal jurisprudence, its victorious attacks upon tyrannic covetousness in mine and factory, to do a grand spell of God's work for *this* world, had come streaming into the Church of Scotland. The Scottish people, quickly responsive as they had been at all periods of their history to any thrill of new spiritual life, any breath of returning inspiration in their Church, beheld with admiring sympathy the advance of the reforming impulse. They rejoiced to see their Church exercising those rights of expansion, those rights of adjustment to changing circumstances, those rights of bringing into action principles that had fallen into abeyance, which were all included in the right to *life*, received from Christ, and implied, as no one yet appeared to dispute, in the union between Church and State in Scotland. If Whigs were arid to Chalmers, and if Tories gave him cold comfort, the Scottish people backed him bravely in his Church Extension Scheme. We spoke of the first ingathering of the goodwill offerings of the faithful. But contributions to the extent of £305,747, and two hundred and twenty-two churches planted throughout Scotland where need was greatest, gradually proved to this champion of Establishments that something might be done, after all, by the voluntary principle. The just reproach against a Presbyterian Church, that it had let the fundamental principle of parity among the ministerial brotherhood be violated wholesale, was removed by admission of the chapel ministers to complete Presbyterian equality. The right to have no pastor forced upon them against their will, a right inexpressibly dear to the pious farmers and cottagers of Scotland, was secured by the Veto Act. The exclusive spirit of the previous century had decreed, "by an Act of Assembly passed in 1799," that no minister of any other Church should occupy a pulpit of the Establishment. This decree was now swept away. The Presbyterians of England and of Ireland were welcomed to full communion. A body of seceders re-entered the Church.

Vitalised at home, the Church put forth new energy in the task of preaching Christ abroad. Dr. Duff had appeared in the Assembly, and in brilliantly eloquent language, amid the passionate sympathy of his audience, called upon his brethren to aid him in conquering India for Christ. A new scheme was devised for bringing Christ's Hebrew brethren according to the flesh to join the Christian Israel. In one word, the Church—clergy and laity alike—was tingling with the keen activities of rejuvenescence, glowing with the ardours and enthusiasms of reinforced vitality, from shore to shore of Scotland. Taking, in compliment to a mechanical age, the rude standards of coined money and stone walls, we find the progress of the reforming movement, during the few years of Evangelical ascendancy, registered in an increase, *fourteenfold*, of the Church's freewill offerings in the service of her Lord.

Can it, as a matter of common sense, apart from any question of special Divine right, be pretended that this renascence of the Church of Scotland exceeded the natural, normal play of that freedom which, for all organised societies, is a condition of *life?* Might not any professional association—the medical, for example—complain of tyrannical oppression if not allowed to regulate its membership on principles believed by it to be essential to the art of healing? Surely we can return but one answer to these questions; and yet the time was at hand when the impassioned energy of the Church of Scotland, in aiming at the realisation of her heavenly ideal, was to bring upon her rebuke and tribulation, and when the rays of her resurrection glory were to be scornfully disowned and shred away.

Soon after the passing of the Veto Act, the Earl of Kinnoull bestowed the presentation to the vacant parish of Auchterarder in Perthshire upon Mr. Robert Young. When the day came for "moderating in a call," or invitation by the congregation to the man thus designated for their pastor, it appeared that, out of three hundred and thirty male heads of families in full communion, just two signed the call to Mr. Young. Clearly, therefore, the parishioners did not want him for their minister. But they might conceivably be neutral. They might be willing, by silence, to acquiesce in the appointment. An opportunity, therefore, was afforded them of stating whether the appointment was regarded by them with positive disfavour. Nearly three hundred now came forward, and, in exercise of those rights to repel *intrusion* which the Church had conferred upon them, *vetoed* Mr. Young. Doing all things leisurely, the Presbytery gave the parishioners a fortnight to consider their decision. They remained of the same mind. The presentee therefore was rejected. Mr. Young demurred, and the Earl of Kinnoul, though understood to take no serious interest in the matter personally, associated himself with Mr. Young in turning to the Court of Session.

The legal adviser into whose hands Mr. Young put himself, and by whom was determined the manner in which the Court of Session should be asked to coerce the Church into intruding Mr. Young into the parish of Auchterarder, was none other, our readers will be interested to learn, than Mr. Hope, Dean of Faculty, whose flaming zeal impelled him to appeal to Dr. Chalmers when a Whig Commission threatened to do violence to the spiritual independence of the Church.

The Church of Scotland could not have selected a more favourable position in which to fight her battle. Not to vindicate any towering ecclesiastical pretension

—not in defence of any scheme of theological metaphysics — not to extort new power, or privilege, or dignity, or endowment for the clergy — but to secure, for poor country people, for those rustic patriarchs, and simple, prayerful shepherds of whom Burns sang in the *Cottar's Saturday Night*, and whom Scott and Carlyle revered, the right to have no man forced upon them as their minister, was the Church of Scotland now called to contend. Round the sanctuary of the peasant Christian did the Church range her enginery of defence, and bare her bosom to the blow. Wound *him*, she said, and you strike a deadly blow at me; deprive *him* of that right of signifying consent to the appointment of his minister which Paul and Barnabas sanctioned, and which Calvin recognised, and you break the time-honoured league between Church and State in Scotland.

The Court of Session, the supreme tribunal in Scotland in civil affairs, is, of course, guardian of all property, and it was, indirectly, by a question of property that the Court of Session was brought to try conclusions with the resurgent Church. For all true-hearted lawyers, property is a sacred word; and if the dominant lawyers of Scotland were led in this matter into injustice, it is charitable to suppose it was their sensitive regard to property that led them astray. Since the day when a settled ministry first came into existence, long before the time of Constantine, nay, before the rise of the Church of Rome, delicate and difficult problems must have arisen for solution in connection with arrangements arising out of Church property. The lawsuits of a thousand years have been largely occupied with adjudication of property dedicated to spiritual uses. Property originally devised for the benefit of souls has come to be *mis*-applied to countless purposes: the providing of soldiers and revenues for kings, the furnishing of nobles with estates, the enrichment of scoundrel courtiers, the payment of royal mistresses, the procurement of luxuries, race-horses, diamonds, gold plate, for the offscouring of the earth.

As usual, the sure way out of the difficulty, to which recourse has almost *never* been had, is to follow the Divine glance of Christ into the heart of the matter, and to put the spirit and the life in the *first* place, and the meat and the raiment in the *second*. This rule seems really, for a wonder, to have been that which, with creditable and exceptional approximation to exactness, was followed by the Church of Scotland. Nursed among storms, a child of the hill and the moorland, she saw greedy nobles divide among them the splendid possessions of the old Romish Kirk. No magnificence of baronial bishoprics—like the £15,000 a year, £10,000, £5000, which make the Church of England so imposing in the eyes of statesmen — did she set her heart upon. But, in direct allegiance to her Head, she made provision that the spirit and the life, the preaching of the word and the service of the ministry, should be secured in her parishes. She accepted, as mere meat and raiment for these, utterly subordinate to these, the wretched pittance of endowment which was all the niggard State allowed her. The pittance, such as it was, could not, under the circumstances of the time, be dispensed with; nor had any Protestant religionists, at the period when the Scottish Presbyterian Church arose, conceived an objection to friendly union and co-operation between Church and State. The endowment, therefore, as in the theory of all Protestant State Churches, remained, strictly speaking, the State's, or at least under the guardianship of the State, *for the spiritual benefit of the people.* The patron could not touch a penny of the benefice. All he could in any case lose was the satisfaction of seeing some one man of his choice rejected; and he had his remedy by naming another, and, if necessary, another and another, until the right man was found. The rejected presentee, for his part, supposing him to acquiesce in his rejection, could lose no more than his presentation to *this* parish,— all the vacant parishes of the Church remained accessible to him. But if the parishioners were once forced to receive a man who brought no spiritual life and healing to their souls, they might be doomed to suffer as long as their or his mortal life endured. This, beyond all cavil or mystification, was the one poignant and transcendent injustice that could occur in the appointment of ministers; and it was for enacting that this injustice should be made impossible, that the Church of Scotland was called to account by the Court of Session.

It were idle to detail the hitherings and thitherings, the preliminaries, preparations, and manifold circumlocutions, that preceded the opening, on the 21st of November 1837, of this momentous trial. In consideration of its importance, order was made that it should take place before the whole Court. Lord

President Hope and twelve judges, Lords Gillies, Boyle, Meadowbank, Mackenzie, Medwyn, Corehouse, Cunningham, Fullerton, Moncreiff, Glenlee, Jeffrey, and Cockburn, occupied the Bench. The leading counsel for the pursuers or plantiffs was Mr. Hope, Dean of Faculty; the leading counsel for the defence, Mr. Rutherford, Solicitor-General,—men of acknowledged eminence in parts, acquirements, and eloquence. From the 21st of November to the 12th of December the pleadings continued. On the 27th of February the judges began to deliver their opinions. On the 8th of March sentence was pronounced. The report of what was argued by counsel and decided by the judges occupies volumes, but it may prove possible, if only we can direct our glance to essentials, to bring these within a narrow compass.

The Dean of Faculty, whether it was that research had opened his eyes, or whether it was that, being now an advocate, he felt himself permitted, by his professional conscience, to consider solely the interests of his clients, took up a position relatively to the Church of Scotland and the claims of Presbytery wide as the poles asunder from that which he occupied when he called upon Chalmers to show fight against the Whig Commission. He declared, with a sweeping comprehensiveness and a peremptory dogmatism, which could have been surpassed by no parliamentary lawyer of England asserting the axiomatic subordination of Church to State in the land of Henry, Elizabeth, and Oliver Cromwell, that the Church of Scotland owed her very existence to the State. The Establishment, in fact, was the Church. The Government had put down the Romish Church, and "for some time no Establishment whatever existed in its room." But the State could create as well as destroy. "A new and vigorous, a young and untried fabric, full of energy and power, was created by the State in the room of that which the State overturned and abolished. I say *created*, for it was devised, formed, moulded, instituted, and created wholly and of new by the State."

If this is substantially true, if the Dean is practically in the right, then the whole conception formed by historians of the Church of Scotland has been a mistake, and the *differentia*, the contrast, deeply marked in the history of three centuries, between the Church of Scotland and the Church of England has been a dream. That he meant to go the whole length of the Erastian theory, denying all separate jurisdiction in spiritual things, and reducing the Church of Scotland to a department of the State, is proved by his deliberately pronouncing her claims to powers derived from "her great spiritual head" to be "the most pernicious error by which the blessed truths of Christianity can be perverted." The sensitively Presbyterian exhorter of Chalmers can now, by the deft insertion of an adjective, hurl against his Presbyterian mother Church the accusation, dear to confused and weak-headed persons, of being Popish. Hers is the "error which arms fallible man with the belief that he possesses the power and authority of the Divine Teacher whom he worships." Every one who has any real acquaintance with the subject knows that the Presbyterian Church has always jealously abjured pretension to infallibility, and that her claim to legislate or regulate in the name of Christ has meant simply that she is directly responsible to Him. The infallibility claimed by the Church goes as far as the infallibility claimed by conscience,—not a step farther. To sum up spectral possibilities of mischief and of absurdity, as arising out of the claim of the Church to obey God rather than man, and that in no wildly mystical or madly fanatical sense, but as limited by, and in strictest accordance with, Old Testament law and New Testament gospel, which is the whole length and breadth and depth and height of the Presbyterian claim to freedom and self-government, — this constituted surely an extravagant flight of forensic audacity.

It was not difficult for Mr. Rutherford to rebut an argument based upon principles so inconsistent with truth as those of the Dean. Admitting that the Court of Session had full power and jurisdiction in respect of the temporal fruits of the benefice, he had but to refer to explicit statements of the Confession of Faith to make it plain that, in so strictly spiritual a matter as ordination, the Court of Session could possess no jurisdiction over the Church. The sheer intensity of the mistake or misrepresentation contended against forced his argument when at its strongest — historically unanswerable and logically a knitting together of links of iron — to take an exclamatory form. "Enforcing," he cried, "by your Lordships' decrees, the spiritual induction of a pastor! Compelling, under pain of horning and imprisonment, the Church to confer the spiritual gift of the ministry! Have the pursuers reflected for a moment upon the nature of the proposition they maintain? It is simony—a grave ecclesiastical offence, a crime even of deep die, in the eye of the Church, and not considered lightly by the law—to procure presentation for good office and reward; or, in the case of a call, to procure concurrence to the call by similar means. Then what shall it be if the Civil Power compel, by imprisonment, by the dread of punishment,—by brute force, for it comes to that,—the imposition of hands, and that gift of the Spirit which is presumed to pass by the ceremony of ordination?"

As two tea-spoonfuls will tell the taste of two wells, these minute samples reveal the drift and character of the respective pleadings of the Dean of Faculty and the Solicitor-General. We turn, therefore, to the opinions of the judges. The Lord President took the same view of the origin and jurisdiction of the Church as was taken by the Dean. "That our Saviour," he said, with the pungency of scorn, "is the temporal head of the Kirk of Scotland in any temporal, or legislative, or judicial sense, is a position which I can dignify by no other name than absurdity. The Parliament is the temporal head of the Church, from whose acts, and from whose acts alone, it exists as the national Church, and from which alone it derives all its powers." The arrogant sweep of generalisation in this would-be philosophical, but, in fact, merely rhetorical deliverance, blurs and defaces, where it ought to have discriminated and elucidated, the lines of historical testimony and accurate thought. It is safe to conclude that men who characterise all the powers of the Church as temporal, will ignore, with a completeness naturally proceeding from total inability to perceive, the spiritual powers of the Church. The Lord President, therefore, had no difficulty in dismissing, as an illegality, a triviality, not instituted in the sixteenth century, and abolished or turned into an empty form by the Patronage Act of Queen Anne, that call, or expression of consent by the congregation, which the Church now affirmed to be of vital importance.

Lord Gillies followed the President in treating the will of the people, compared with the wish of the patron, as of no consequence. "If the question is put," said Lord Gillies, "whether the call is to be rendered or continued a mockery, or whether patronage is to be rendered a mockery, I have no hesitation in thinking that the call must yield to the presentation." The power, that is to say, of one man, respecting whom there is no guarantee that he is even professedly a religious man, to fix another man, who though externally irreproachable may also be spiritually dead, as the pastor of, say, a thousand devout parishioners for fifty years, is of more importance in the eye of the law than the will of the parishioners to stay his appointment; and if, under those circumstances, the Church comes to the rescue of the parishioners, she must simply be taught by the Court of Session to do her duty of intrusion. Lord Medwyn was an Episcopalian, and could hardly be expected to understand the genius of Presbytery. He also pronounced the right of the patron unassailable. Eight out of the thirteen judges were of this mind.

Law is law, a blind goddess, and no rational enthusiast for law will expect her to execute in all instances the office of the most open-eyed of the Olympian powers, the office of justice. To take care that justice or injustice shall flow in the channel legislatively prescribed for it,—to make sure that injustice, even though raised thereby to its terrible *maximum*, as contemplated in Holy Writ, shall be injustice decreed by law,—this is the ideal of perfection for all Courts constituted like the Court of Session. It would be unreasonable, therefore, to indulge in anything like vituperation of the eight judges who virtually held that the call, drawn by the Church as a rampart round the dearest liberties of congregations, had been but a rope of sand to bind the waves of an advancing tide, and that the boasted jurisdiction of the Church of Scotland in things spiritual was either an absurdity or an attempt to resume the abolished jurisdiction of the Papacy. But it is well to remember that, even on a question of law, a majority of judges of the Court of Session are not infallible, and that the opinion of a minority of the judges, if they are more favourably circumstanced for a consideration of all the evidence, may be of very high importance indeed, if we wish to know, not exclusively the technical and professional value of the decision, but the degree in which it accords with the beneficial working of institutions and the deepest claims of justice.

The minority, to begin with, was formidable in number —five against eight. If we believe—as we certainly may—that an Episcopalian was more or less disqualified to decide upon a thoroughly Presbyterian question, and if we dismiss, as inapplicable to the Church of Scotland, the undisguised Erastianism of another of the judges, we shall reduce the majority to six against five. Of the majority of three, which the Court of Session had found to make its new Thermopylæ against the invasive Church of Scotland, there thus remains but one. To play the part of this Leonidas, we may elect Lord Mackenzie, who held that the Church in her attempts, persisted in for upwards of a century, even under Moderate domination, to maintain the call after the passing of the Queen Anne's Act, had perpetrated "a piece of resistance to the Legislature." Or we may prefer Lord Corehouse, who told the Court that Pope Gelasius, so long ago as A.D. 493, had settled the matter on the side of intrusion, though his Lordship's quotation from Gelasius seems to tell rather the other way, for it recognises the fact of opposition to the settlement of a minister being made by the people, and gives no hint of power on the part of a patron to overrule them, but only of the duty of the clergy to "compel" them "by assiduous admonitions," that is to say, by moral suasion, "to give their consent." Or we can content ourselves with Lord Cunningham, the youngest of the judges, who may be supposed to have been partly influenced by the novelty of his position in concurring with the majority. At all events, if either of these is excluded, we have reduced the majority to a numerical equality with the minority. And this we may expect all candid persons to admit,— that, if the views and sentiments of the three were fairly representative of those of the majority in general, then these judges of the Court of Session, in adjudicating on the Church of Scotland as an Establishment, evinced signal indifference to any aims, objects, ambitions she might entertain, any characteristics she might possess, or any uses she might subserve, as a Christian Church.

The five Lords of Session who repudiated the judgment of the majority were men who knew the history of Scotland, and the part which the Church had played in that history. If the State had created the Church, or even the Establishment, they did not forget that there had been a purpose in the creation, and that this purpose had not been to promote the dignity or influence of patrons, but to bring home the gospel of Christ to parishioners. Had they been deciding a case in connection with the medical profession, they would have considered it germane to the business to keep in view the healing of bodies; and in deciding on a case connected with a Church, they held it right to recollect that a Church is an institute for the healing of souls. Some of these judges of the minority have shed unfading lustre on their country, and are honourably known wherever Scotch common sense and clear-headedness have made themselves a name.

Such were Jeffrey and Cockburn. Until the Biography of Macaulay and the Reminiscences of Carlyle appeared, the world did not know what cordial humour, dramatic versatility, and treasures of true-hearted friendship dwelt in Jeffrey. In his passionate hatred of mawkishness and tea-drinking goody-goody-ism, and of every form of affectation, he was too arid to Wordsworth; but all the world now agrees with him that there is in Wordsworth, with all his merit, a tea-drinking didacticism that "will never do." It was not of the *Prelude*, be it remembered, which has in it the crimsons of Wordsworth's beaming sunrise, but of the *Excursion*, which has in it the pearl-blue and somewhat slumbrous

azure of his afternoon, that Jeffrey uttered those famous
words. If, however, Jeffrey lacked the melodiousness
that goes to the making of a supreme critic, he was
pre-eminently fitted by his combination of practical
sense with intellectual clearness to be a good lawyer
and a sagacious judge. He put aside by a few precise
words, carrying with them their own evidence, the vague
and grandiose pretensions put forward as to the all-
comprehending jurisdiction of the Court of Session.
"It has no proper jurisdiction," he said, "except *in
civilibus*. With a few exceptions, not affecting the
principle, it has no jurisdiction in crimes, and with no
exceptions at all, it has no jurisdiction whatever in
matters properly ecclesiastical ; and especially none as
to the examination, ordination, or admission of ministers,
which are not only in their own proper nature ecclesiastical proceedings, but are expressly declared by the Acts
of 1567 and 1592 to be exclusively for the Church judi-
catures." Too well acquainted with the history of his
Church to be liable to any mystification as to her having
been from the beginning a Church of the people, he
treated the view, that the call had been paralysed by the
touch of law into a hollow form, as absolutely untenable.
Along with Lord Moncreiff and Lord Fullerton, he maintained that even Queen Anne's Act, though it transferred
the presentation from the elders and heritors to the
patron, did not destroy the ancient right of the people
to have no minister settled against their consent.

Lord Cockburn, another man who thoroughly understood the character both of the Church and the people of
Scotland, also exclaimed against the idea that the call had

been legally turned into a mockery. "I could not have been more surprised," he said, "on being told that Presbytery was not the Church of this country, than I have been by learning that calls, except as forms, are no part of our Presbytery; they seem to me to be absolutely imbedded in the constitution and in the practice of the Church."

The Court decided that the Presbytery of Auchterarder, in rejecting Mr. Young because "a majority of the male heads of families, communicants in the said parish, have dissented, without any reason assigned, from his admission as minister," had acted "illegally and in violation of their duty." This judgment was signed on the 10th of March 1838, and the least imaginative reader will feel that this lent a greatly enhanced interest to the proceedings of the General Assembly which met in Edinburgh in the following May. In the bare words of the Court of Session's judgment, viewed negatively, it was possible enough that no fateful import should lie. But if it were taken to imply that the Court required and commanded the Presbytery to ordain a man whom the Church, by her law, pronounced it sinful to ordain, then the inference became irresistible that the spiritual freedom of the Church was called in question. Ordination is a spiritual act, if there is such an act in existence.

CHAPTER XIII.

Preparing for the Fray.

THE General Assembly of May 1838 followed quick upon the signing of the judgment in the Auchterarder case in March. The interest of the occasion, for thinking persons and students of history, is great, for it places before us the two traditional parties taking up their respective positions, in view of the sombre and perilous future. The subject-matter requires nice attention and careful discrimination, but does not lend itself to dramatic effects or yield harvest of sensational incidents.

Chalmers was not a member of this Assembly, although, as it is hardly necessary to say, the action of the Reforming party was exactly conformed to his sentiments. The position taken up by the Evangelicals was defined by Mr. Robert Buchanan in that lucid, expressive, and dignified language which befits so well his own authoritative and noble work on the Conflict. The case tried by the Court of Session had, he explained, risen out of the Veto Act. "The object of that Act was to give full force and effect to the fundamental law of the Church, 'that no pastor be intruded on any congregation contrary to the will of the people.'" He summed up with masterly brevity the evidence that this principle was indeed fundamental in the Church of Scotland. "We meet with it in the very infancy of the Church in her First Book of Discipline; in the Second Book it is pointedly repeated; again at the restoration of Presbytery in 1638; in the directory of the Assembly of 1649; and long after, in 1736, four and twenty years after patronage, in its present form, had been restored, it is declared by the Assembly in the most solemn terms." Such were the lines of circumvallation by which, and now finally and conspicuously by the Veto Act, the Church had guarded the rights of the people. The Court of Session had told the Church that, in erecting those walls of circumvallation, and giving power to the people's will, she had broken the law of the land. Did she then possess spiritual independence, or did her Standards lapse into meaningless platitude, when they spoke of the Church as "hearing the voice of Christ, the only spiritual King, and being ruled by His laws." That was the question the Church was now called to face. Mr. Buchanan concluded by moving that the Church should resolve to maintain at all hazards, as the Presbyterians of Scotland had done, "even to the death," her testimony "for Christ's kingdom and crown."

At this critical moment, when the Court of Session had spoken, and the House of Lords was to be asked to speak with still higher authority, what was the attitude assumed by the party of Robertson and of Hill? Dr. Cook, the vigilant, quick-seeing, active debater and skilful tactician, was the working leader. For one thing,—and the point is of great importance,—he was entirely of opinion that the Court of Session's judgment ought to be carried by appeal to the House of Lords. It had not occurred to him that the Church could be asked to accept the decision of the Court of Session *simpliciter*, and thus to acknowledge that, in keeping up the form of the call for three or four generations, the Moderate party had been merely going through a piece of child's play. But Dr. Cook went farther than was implied in agreement as to this particular case. He accepted with emphasis the general principle of spiritual independence. Alluding to his "reverend and respected friend," Mr. Buchanan, "there is no language," cried the Moderate leader, "which he could use stronger than I would be inclined to adopt to assert the spiritual independence of the Church, and to vindicate the power which we have received from its great Head."

The thorough-paced Erastianism of the majority of the Court of Session—the position that the State had created the Church as it might create a corporation of cordwainers — sent some twinge of honest pain, some touch of true *angina pectoris*, to the Presbyterian heart of Dr. Cook. "I entirely agree with my reverend friend that our Church, the Church of Christ, is not the creature of the State. We had our doctrines, our views and principles, before we were connected with the State; and we would have them to-morrow if we were to sever that connection." Nay, he professed, for himself and his party, a positive enthusiasm for the distinctive principle of Presbyterianism, a readiness to "display the banner of our great King and Head, and if necessary," under it to "perish."

Apart from all that followed,—apart even from the logical consistency of Dr. Cook's present speech and the moral courage or cowardice of him and his party,—these statements ought to be remembered. They link the Presbyterianism of to-day with the Presbyterianism of Andrew Thomson. They prove that, after all the contendings and heart-burnings of the intervening time, the divisions of the Church of Scotland have not theoretically touched any principle accepted by the one party and rejected by the other. The Moderates never in words repudiated the doctrine of the Headship of Christ, never denied that it involved the spiritual independence of the Church, never adopted the creed of Erastian statesmen and perverse or contemptuous lawyers. Throughout their long period of ascendancy, they never abandoned the call, never forgot the watchwords of their Church, never confessed that they were not (at heart) as staunch maintainers of the spiritual independence as Andrew Thomson himself. But it had always been averred by the Evangelicals that the Moderate homage to the principle was homage of the lip. When the question came of sacrificing the rights of the people or of bending to the Civil Power, they had fawned on the power and deserted the people. The Church of Scotland, in her days of martyr heroism, had turned her own cheek to the smiter; the Moderate party turned Christ's cheek, in the person of the poor parishioner, to the blows of Cæsar.

And so, in the Assembly of 1838, while declaring his readiness to perish for the Headship of Christ, Dr. Cook assumed with his party a demeanour of awestruck and overpowered expectancy as to what the authorities might ultimately determine in relation to Auchterarder. If the State should prove to be on the Church's side, then he would shout, and wave the old banner. He did not object—far from it—to appealing from the Court of Session to the House of Lords to have the law ascertained. But if it appeared that the exercise of the spiritual jurisdiction of the Church really affected the property rights of patrons, then the Church, instead of guarding the spiritual will of the people as a sacred thing, should consider herself bound to ask the State to draw anew the line of demarcation between the spiritual jurisdiction belonging to the Church and the civil jurisdiction belonging to the State. The Court of Session declared that, in the present instance, the Church had overstepped the frontiers of her province by barring the way to patrons in intruding ministers upon congregations. If this should indeed be the law, as the House of Lords would determine, then, said Dr. Cook in effect, the Church must conform. When a difference of opinion arises, it is for the State to decide.

In the last resort, and when the question is as to whether the Establishment shall continue to exist or shall not, this is true. The State has the physical force. The Church cannot resist the civil sword. By the unanimous admission of all Presbyterians who know the alphabet of their constitutional principles, the Church not only possesses no vestige of physical force, but claims not an iota of jurisdiction over property. If the State says, therefore, I lay down such and such a condition of

Establishment; and the Church says, I will not or cannot accept it: then the Church cannot be, or continue, Established. This was what eventually happened. This was the consummation devoutly deprecated by the impassioned champions of Establishment who passed the Veto Act. But the fundamental principle on which the Scottish Church had accepted Establishment was that her spiritual freedom should, in the outset, be *conceded*. Until this concession was retracted, she had a right, even as an Establishment, to be governed, under Christ, by her own officers, and to make and apply her own spiritual laws. Since Dr. Cook admitted that, in giving effect to the people's will at Auchterarder, the Church had done no more than exercise her spiritual jurisdiction, he obviously could not, without surrendering that independence, display readiness to accept the State's decision as to whether that independence belonged to her or did not.

In order to understand how it was that the knife of the Court of Session struck the Church in this matter of spiritual jurisdiction under the fifth rib, we ought to conceive distinctly that it was the rite of ordination that the Court interfered with. In effect, the Court of Session said to the Church, Thou shalt ordain this man pastor of the parish. Let an Englishman image to himself how an exclusive club would feel if a Court of law said, Thou shalt admit this man to membership; or how the medical profession would feel if a Court of law said, Thou shalt inscribe this man on the Medical Register. These are, *mutatis mutandis*, nearly analogous cases to that of the Church of Scotland being ordered by the Court of Session to ordain ministers against reclaiming congregations. But the case of the Church, since conscience was obviously and inevitably engaged, was more manifestly unjust and cruel than would be the supposed case of a club or a profession.

The simple and intrepid course of standing to what the Church, in solemn performance of her religious duty, had done, was proposed by Mr. Buchanan. A more equivocal course, asserting the possession of spiritual independence in the abstract, but virtually asking the State to say what spiritual independence meant, was proposed by Dr. Cook. The Assembly decided by 183 voices to 142 in favour of the former.

CHAPTER XIV.

Lord Brougham in fine Form.

THERE was no difference of view between the Reforming and the Moderate parties in the General Assembly of 1838 as to whether the judgment of the Court of Session in the Auchterarder case should be carried by appeal to the House of Lords. It came up for final decision on the 2nd of May 1839, and on that day Lord Cottenham and Lord Brougham delivered their judicial opinions upon the subject.

It was perhaps a matter of course that Lord Cottenham, an Englishman, should take it for granted that, in a case of discrepancy between lawyers and parsons in Scotland, the parsons should be wrong and the lawyers right. But it sent a shock of surprise, as well as of pain, to many in Scotland, to find that Henry Brougham had so little heart-knowledge of his native land. It is curiously suggestive that one who played a part so memorable, so brilliant, so illustrious, as that of Lord Brougham, in the arena of Parliamentary Reform, should, in adjudicating upon the Constitution of the Church of Scotland, have put scornfully aside, as not worth serious consideration, the popular call of congregations to their ministers. With the vehemence characteristic of fiery temperaments when they are particularly in the wrong, he emphasised the point that the call could not possibly entitle the people to more than to have the presentee tested by the Presbytery as to his possession of certain specified qualifications. Fancy this as a method for securing that parliamentary constituencies should not have members intruded upon them! Fancy the look of the free and independent, if they were required to accept Mr. So-and-so, the nominee of Lord This-or-that, to represent them, unless they could prove him exceptionable in a few particular respects! And is it easier for a constituency to discern who are the men fitted to rule the Empire, than for parishioners to discern who is the man that will visit them in their cottages with glimpses of heavenly consolation, and edify them from the pulpit in the name of Christ?

Macaulay says that Hume so strongly disliked the religion of the Puritans, that he was incapable of doing justice to their services to liberty. Men of affairs are apt to treat religion as if it were really and truly nothing at all. So dark was Brougham on the religious side, that it seems to have never flashed upon him that there could be any analogy between the election of a member by a parliamentary constituency, and the choice of a minister by a congregation. Sympathetic in the highest degree with the aspirations of freemen to send representatives to Parliament, he had no intelligent sympathy whatever with the wish of devout parishioners to have a voice in the election of their ministers. "Surely," said Hugh

Miller, in a Letter to Lord Brougham to which we shall have further occasion to refer, "the people of Scotland are not so changed but that they know at least as much of the doctrines of the New Testament as of the principles of civil government, and of the requisites of a gospel minister as of the qualifications of a member of Parliament." He reminds Lord Brougham of a fact which his Lordship might have learned from Burns, or Carlyle, or Scott, that freedom's sword and religion's Bible have been associate powers in the history of Scotland, the religion having generally been in the van of the freedom. "Is it at all possible that you, my Lord, a native of Scotland, and possessed of more general information than perhaps any other man living, can have yet to learn that we have thought long and deeply of our religion, whereas our political speculations began but yesterday, — that our popular struggles have been struggles for the right of worshipping God according to the dictates of our conscience, and under the guidance of ministers of our own choice,—and that, when anxiously employed in finding arguments by which rights so dear to us might be rationally defended, our discovery of the principles of civil liberty was merely a sort of chance-consequence of the search?"

Hugh Miller's Letter was suggested by Lord Brougham's opinion on the Court of Session's judgment; but had it preceded that opinion, it would most probably have had no influence upon his Lordship. Was not property involved? Was not the shadow of property more important than the substance of religion? Brougham talked grandiosely about the patrimonial property of the patron, and took it for granted, as a thing beyond all question, that property, called into existence wholly and solely for the spiritual nourishment of the parishioners, was of more moment than what it subserved. The call, said this great orator, — who loved a joke, — was as mere a ceremony as the wagging of the tail of the people's champion's horse in a coronation pageant. Property, property, property,—the patron's property,—if the rights of the people interfered with that, let the people hold their tongues. This peremptory conclusion of Lord Brougham's forms surely the finest historical exemplification discoverable of the verdict returned in that delectable *cause célèbre*, versified by Cowper, between Nose and Eyes. To which of these litigants did the spectacles belong? Clearly to the nose. The spectacles sat upon the nose. The spectacles dignified the nose. The eyes were merely a part of the pageant. The Court decided therefore in favour of the nose, and decreed that, whenever the nose put his spectacles on, by daylight or candlelight, eyes should be shut. Exactly. The only thing required for the perfect legal vindication of the property of the patron in the settlement of ministers, was the formal abolition of the call, the shutting of the parishioners' eyes.

The House of Lords dismissed the appeal of the Church, and confirmed the judgment of the Court of Session.

CHAPTER XV.

The Church takes up her Position—
A New Leader.

IT was the 2nd of May 1839 when the Lords gave their decision. Within the month the General Assembly was to meet. In the interval, the groundswell of a profound and solemn agitation passed throughout the parishes of Scotland. Not the noisy excitement of politics, not the feverish eagerness of some great expansion in trade, not the angry hum of a nation gathering to defend its frontiers with the sword. It was the fervid exaltation, the solemn interest, with which a grave and earnest people, such as Macaulay, no flattering witness, declares the Scotch to be, regarded the peril of that ancient Church which, more than any other of their institutions, had made them what they were. "A people"—the words are Macaulay's—"whose education and habits are such that, in every quarter of the world, they rise above the mass of those with whom they mix, as surely as oil rises to the top of water,—a people of such temper and self-government that the wildest popular excesses recorded in their history partake of the gravity of judicial proceedings, and of the solemnity of religious rites,—a people whose national pride and mutual attachment have passed into a proverb,—a people whose high and fierce spirit, so forcibly described in the haughty motto which encircles their thistle, preserved their independence, during a struggle of centuries, from the encroachments of wealthier and more powerful neighbours"—was moved by a greater wave of feeling than had rolled over it since the last long billow of the Covenanting enthusiasm ebbed away. In city streets, men who had known each other from childhood paused to speak, with eager sympathy, upon the subject. In remote country manses, by the farmer's ingle, round the peasant's fireside, Scotland's great concern was the theme of conversation; and above all, when men presented themselves before their Creator for social prayer, it lay upon their spirits and rose to their lips.

The Assembly met on the 16th of May 1839. Chalmers, who in his heart of hearts detested strife, and loved to work in the shade, had been recently much engaged in pushing on his Church Extension enterprises and his mission to the poor. Pledged to the theory of ecclesiastical Establishments, he refused to be persuaded that the State could be so infatuated as to strangle the Church for showing herself alive, and putting forth the energies of growth. We saw how, only in the spring of 1838, he had boasted of the inviolable freedom of his Church, and her pre-eminence as the pattern State Church in Christendom, before nine prelates of the Church of England and a Prince of the Blood. And already, as with the sudden blackness of eclipse, her glory of peace and prosperity seemed to be exchanged for that of tragedy and storm. He felt that the things at stake were essential to the very life of the Church, and again he descended into the arena.

Three motions were made in the Assembly: that of the Moderates, promptly put forward by Dr. Cook; that of the Evangelicals, proposed by Chalmers; and that of the trimmers and compromisers, by Dr. Muir.

Dr. Cook was frankly for surrender. The Veto Act had been pronounced by the civil tribunal to "infringe on civil and patrimonial rights." It was therefore to be deemed non-existent. Presbyteries should be instructed by the Assembly to ignore it, and "proceed henceforth in the settlement of parishes according to the practice which prevailed previously to the passing of that Act." Such was the Moderate attitude. Twelve months previously, Dr. Cook had cautiously seen to it that the Moderates should present an unbroken line with the Evangelicals in addressing the Civil Power. But now that Lord Gillies had coldly remarked, "The call must yield to the presentation," and that Lord Brougham had declared the will of the congregation to have no more legal force than the wagging of the champion's horse's tail at a coronation, the Church must be left by the Moderates to do her fighting alone. Not even in *asking* that the Legislature, supreme over both the Court of Session and the House of Lords, should interfere on behalf of the Church, and encourage instead of obstructing her in the performance of her duty to the flock, would Dr. Cook dare to associate himself and his section with the majority. And this craven and crouching demeanour was to be that of the Church of Knox, the boldest, beyond all debate, of the Churches of Reformed Christendom.

Dr. Chalmers did not lose his perfect self-possession at this critical moment. He refused to hurry to the conclusion that the State-Church experiment had broken down. Lawyers might be hampered by the letter of statutes, but he could not yet accept it as a possibility that the State really meant one inexorable condition of Establishment to be paralysis of the Church in her distinctive and essential powers. He would first, therefore, make it unmistakably clear what it was that the Church could and would at once give up to the State as non-essential; secondly, explain what it was that she could not under any conceivable compulsion yield; and thirdly, propose that the State should be asked, in terms of loyal respectfulness, to declare by a distinct parliamentary utterance that the Civil Power was of one mind with the Church as to the line of demarcation between them. The Court of Session said that the Church's procedure in the Auchterarder settlement made inroad upon temporalities. Let the temporalities of the parish, then, remain where the Court placed them, in Lord Kinnoull's hands, or Mr. Robert Young's, or where their Lordships chose. This disposed of his first point. The Church, in the second place, had from time immemorial affirmed that the intrusion of ministers upon unwilling congregations was at variance with her fundamental principles. If the State insisted upon it that she should violate this fundamental principle, then the State would be requiring her to admit sin, and, of course, break up the Establishment. But, since the possibility of this could not be taken for granted, let, in the third place, a Committee be appointed from all sections of the Assembly, to remove, by friendly conference, any misunderstanding between the Church and the State. Such was Chalmers's motion.

Could any statesman, or any Cabinet or conclave of statesmen, have framed a more luminously reasonable, a more courteously deferential, a more manifestly just proposal than this?

All the genius and all the heart of Chalmers glowed and throbbed in his speech on the occasion. It occupied three and a half hours,—we need not take from it more than a few sentences. He laid down what he held to be "the true theory of the connection between the Church and the State." The Church "may have subsisted for many ages as a Christian Church, with all its tenets and its usages, not as prescribed by human authority, but as founded either on the word of God or on their own independent views of Christian expediency,—meaning by this their own views of what is best for the good of imperishable souls. None of these things were given up to the State at the time when the Church entered into an alliance with it; but one and all of them remained as intact and inviolable after this alliance as before it. I hold it to be quite an axiom, a first and elementary truth, that we are never in any instance to depart from the obligations which lie upon us as a Christian Church, for the sake either of obtaining or perpetuating the privileges which belong to us as an Established Church.

"But though, on the one hand, we cannot either

rescind or refrain from enacting what we hold to be vital, ere we make a voluntary withdrawment of ourselves from the State, we should make every attempt to obtain its concurrence, and that in order to avert the calamity of a disruption betwixt us; and this, too, in the face of every ungenerous misinterpretation, to which our desire of preserving the connection between the parties with all its advantages is liable. There is nothing of the sycophantish, nothing of the sordid, in the most strenuous attempts which principle will suffer us to make, to maintain unbroken the alliance between Church and State. But let me give some idea to the Assembly of the extent of that degradation and helplessness, which, if we do submit to this decision of the House of Lords, have been actually and already inflicted upon us,—a degradation to which the Church of England, professing the King to be their Head, never would submit; and to which the Church of Scotland, professing the Lord Jesus to be their Head, never can. Ask any English ecclesiastic whether the bishop would receive an order from any Civil Court whatever on the matter of ordination, and the instant, the universal reply is, that he would not."

The speaker here quoted a letter sent by Lord Melbourne to one who had appealed to the King to command the Archbishop of Canterbury to give him ordination. The letter announced that Lord Melbourne "cannot advise the King to give any command for controlling the judgment of a bishop on the subject of ordination to holy orders."

"To what position, then," Chalmers went on, "are we brought if we give in to the opposite motion, and proceed in consequence to the ordination of Mr. Young? To such a position as the bishops of England, with all the Erastianism which has been charged, and to a great degree I think falsely charged, upon that Establishment, never, never would consent to occupy. Many of them would go to the prison and the death rather than submit to such an invasion on the functions of the sacred office. Should the emancipation of our Church require it, there is the same strength of high and holy determination in this our land."

Chalmers's motion was the modestly but manfully resolute intimation by the Church to the State that, if established it all, she must be established as a Church, having for primary, professional, inexorable duty, obedience to Christ. Dr. Cook's motion was the frankly submissive, undisguisedly craven, confession that the Church was not competent to draw the line marking off her own professional province of soul-healing, and that the measures which had embodied her reforming ardour must be ignored as nonentities.

Between Dr. Cook and Dr. Chalmers, tenderly treading as one who balanced himself on a ridge between two precipices, came Dr. Muir. The State speaks, and the State cannot be in the wrong; but the Church also may be considerably in the right: and if we are justly compliant in the performance of our own duties, and truly obsequious with reference to the duties of the State, then all may be well. One could not exactly disagree with Dr. Muir's motion,—it was too innocently platitudinarian for that; but one instinctively felt that it would be no brave man's part to take refuge in its evasive phrases.

In this gathering of impassioned champions of Establishment, however, there were not a few who would have dearly prized any presentable excuse by which they might escape giving a decisive verdict on either side. Accordingly the battle of debate protracted itself on Dr. Muir's motion, and, as the hours of evening rolled on into the night, the Assembly began to grow weary and call for the vote. It was then that, in a part of the Assembly far from the Moderator's chair, dimly seen below the gallery, a member was observed to rise and claim audience. There was considerable reluctance to hear him; calls for the division were audible; and it was only when several, who seemed to know him and expect something from him, "shouted to give him a hearing," that the opposition became silent.

He came forward in the direction of the Moderator's chair, "passing his hand through his hair, as was his wont when he became excited," and showing a phenomenally large development of brain. Who was this? Few could tell. Whispers went round that he was the preacher appointed not long since to what Andrew Thomson had made the first of Edinburgh pulpits, St. George's. A superlative preacher,—that was notorious, and his friends said he was intellectually a giant, but he was absolutely untried in the Courts of the Church,— Candlish they called him. So ran the whispers, but they would sink into breathless expectation when the new speaker looked the Assembly in the face.

A very short man, but with a frame suggestive of great strength, arms long as Rob Roy's, hair shaggy and unkempt The facial expression sad and lowering, the features almost ugly, the mouth large with sensitive lips, something in them of the sensitive child or the pouting woman. The whole face redeemed into nobleness by the towering forehead and the dominant expressions of elevation and intellectuality. Not a good-looking man by any means, but as if bathed in a light of spiritual beauty. He is in the very prime of physical and mental strength, thirty-three years of age; having taken long to ripen, more ambitious to excel than to shine; an observer, a thinker, a student, a superlative preacher, he now comes to the front because his Church and his country call him, and because the few who have the secret of his Herculean powers tell him that his hour has come. This is Robert Smith Candlish, the Newman of the Scottish Church movement; the man who, more expressly than any other, took the torch from the hand of Chalmers when the old leader fell; the most sincerely loved, the most intensely hated, the most conspicuous, and the most representative of the Founders of the Free Church.

He began by putting aside, by mere lucidity of word and accuracy of description, some of the less important mystifications and confusions of Dr. Muir's illusive motion. But presently he moved into the heart of the question, bringing into glare of foreground light some essential matters which had been cautiously stowed away by Dr. Muir among masses of woolly phrase. "I have a still graver objection to the motion of my respected Father. I have looked, and I do not find, from the beginning to the end of his resolutions, one single word recognising the privileges of the Christian people. The reverend Doctor has pleaded for the power of the Church, —in its Courts, composed of its rulers and office-bearers,

—but without securing and carrying out, along with that power, the rights of the Christian people. And this, to my mind, is substantial Popery. It is a position which must go far to establish a system of spiritual despotism. In truth, it is only when the rights of the people in the Church of Christ are secured that the power of the ruling Courts can be safely pleaded; and it is then, also, that that power can be pleaded to its highest point. . . . For it is undoubtedly the right and duty of the rulers in the Church to moderate and control, with a high scriptural authority, the movements of all the other parties who act together in this matter."

Here is the case of Presbyterianism in a nutshell, as against the Roman and Anglican system on the one hand, and the systems which deny all jurisdiction to the aggregate of congregations on the other. To separate the people from the Church, or the Church from the people, is to misconceive the very nature of the Church. "Inasmuch as ye did it not unto the least of these, ye did it not unto Me." In every Christian there is a living Christ. *This*, we must always repeat, is the real presence. It was his realisation of this that made Luther's religion at once so Divine and so human. Hence, though opposing the insurgent peasants, he acknowledged the soundness of their claim, that the congregation (*Gemeinde*) should choose its own minister. The instincts of the spiritual life—the cravings of the indwelling Christ—cannot be scheduled in any documentary form for general inspection. If the flock declares the ministrations of the patron's nominee to be unedifying, that is enough. He shall not be intruded on them. On the other hand, according to the Presbyterian theory, the flock is to have all the advantage which the wisdom and experience of the Church as a whole can afford them. As a free State is not a State without order, without law, without discipline, so a free Church is not an anarchic multitude of congregations, but an aggregate of congregations in fellowship with each other, under a common jurisdiction, benefited by the Christian wisdom of the whole. The Church can have no interest apart from the spiritual interests of the people. Presbyteries, Synods, Assembly, exercise their office for the people.

"We have simply," said Candlish, drawing his speech to a conclusion, "to submit to our people this plain and palpable alternative: Will you have us submit without a struggle and without an effort to a system of patronage the most arbitrary and unrestricted,—to a system of patronage which, but for the milder temper of the days in which we live, might bring back those melancholy times when, not ministers in their robes, but bands of armed men, introduced the pastor to his people? Will *you* submit, or will you have *us* to submit, to that iron yoke which your fathers were unable to bear,—or will you give us your sympathies and your prayers while we stand up for the rightful power of the Church of Christ, and assert at once and together *our* prerogatives as the rulers, and *your* liberties as the people; while we go respectfully but manfully to the other party in the contract by which we are established, to the State,—to the authorities of the nation,—testifying to them what is their duty, and soliciting them to the performance of it? I have no doubt whatever that, when the question is thus put, it will be fully and cordially and unanimously answered throughout all our parishes. But if the trumpet give an uncertain sound,—if we merely assert the rights of the rulers in the Church, while we sacrifice or hold in abeyance the people's liberties,—it will be no wonder if we have not—we shall not deserve to have— with us the heart or the prayers of one single man who is worthy of the name of Scotsman. I rejoice, then, Moderator, amid all our difficulties, in the prominency which must now be given to this great element in our question, the standing which the Christian people have in the settlement of their pastors. We shall rally our countrymen once more, now that the old banner is again broadly displayed—the banner which we find fully and clearly inscribed—Cæsar's crown indeed, but along with it and not less clearly or less fully, underneath Christ's crown, and shielded by it—the purchased liberties of His redeemed people."

It was a solemn hour when the speech of which these few sentences may convey some idea rang out in its clearness, its earnestness, its threefold elevation of thought, feeling, and language, upon the Assembly. This was no mere ambitious young cleric, like our bluff friend Begg at twenty-three, giving a taste of his quality to the men of established reputation. The ablest men in the Assembly, Cunningham, Guthrie, Begg himself, as they looked with admiration on this new speaker, felt that he was of the transcendent sort, a leader among leaders. As the tones of Candlish penetrated, with metallic clang, to the remotest corners of the Assembly, it was felt that a new act was opening in the drama, that a new and mighty actor had stepped upon the stage. But Candlish was as modest as he was great, and sought no higher honour than to be the loyal lieutenant of Chalmers.

The motions of Dr. Cook and of Dr. Muir were swept away. That of Dr. Chalmers was carried. The Church had taken up her position, and with studious respectfulness to the State, had defined it. The endowments might be confiscated, and yet the Establishment might stand. But the Church could not be false to her Divine ideal. She could not fail in duty to Christ her King. She could not cease to guard the liberties of Christ's people. Would the State, by trying to force her to do these, compel her to leave the Establishment?

CHAPTER XVI.

The Agitation deepening—The "Witness."

THE heroic age is always with us if we only have the glow of heroes; and in 1839, both before and still more after that midnight meeting of Assembly at which Candlish, like a new star, suddenly cleft the gloom, the old heroic fire was making its presence felt in Scotland. Not once or twice in her eventful history has "glory" lit her path. Her struggle for independence against overwhelming odds in the beginning of the fourteenth century drew on her the eyes of Europe, and the spearmen of Bannockburn were enrolled with the men of Marathon and the men of Morgarten among those in whose praise mothers sing ditties to their boys. Again, in the sixteenth century, she had the rare honour bestowed upon her by God of standing out before the nations, and solemnly uprearing the standard of the Holy Catholic Church, as distinguished from that of the Roman Catholic, then terrible with the strength of youthful Jesuitism, and that of the Tudor-Catholic raised by Henry, and resolutely held by Elizabeth. A revolution, occupying two centuries, was then being unrolled, and there were confusions and minglings and tumults innumerable. It could not fail that the work most appropriate to statesmen should sometimes be effected by Churchmen, and that the work strictly belonging to the State should sometimes, in practice if not in theory, be done by the Church. But the main fact stands out impregnable, that it was at the call of her local Church, speaking as part of the Church of all nations, that Scotland rose into heroic mood, and that the watchwords of her witnessing to Christ's crown mingled with the march-music of mankind, the hum and movement of the great westward-going procession of civilisation.

He who was a Scottish boy in that summer of 1839 and the summers immediately succeeding, will remember how the old inspiration thrilled the land. No agitation so intense in its serenity, so noble in its elevation, so devout in its spirit, has since occurred. The spectacle of the old Church, making herself visible through the resplendency of the indwelling Christ, smitten sorely by the archers only *because* of the burning of the spirit and the life within her, set the chords of sympathy vibrating in ten thousand bosoms.

In remote Cromarty, Hugh Miller found sleep fly his pillow, while his thoughts, wildly at work, traced as in zigzags of lightning the outlines of that memorable Letter which he addressed to Lord Brougham. In " broad Scotland" there was no man who knew his country better, no man more patriotically and intelligently proud of Scotland, or of whom Scotland had juster cause to be proud, than the Cromarty stone-cutter. Unique among self-educated workmen in the breadth, the calmness, the moral purity, and the philosophical balance of his ideas, was Hugh Miller; one of the few Scotchmen who have written an English style that Addison himself might have pronounced classical; a masterly observer in science, and a scientific describer whose powers were looked upon by Sir Roderick Murchison with admiring despair.

He was the man of all others to appreciate at its true worth and importance the stress laid by Candlish on the right of congregations to have no pastor forced upon them. "There does not exist"—the words are Hugh Miller's—"a tenderer or more enduring tie among all the various relationships which knit together the human family, than that which binds the gospel minister to his people." From his sleepless couch he rose to fling upon paper, in passionate splendour of language, his Letter to Lord Brougham, finishing it in one week. He told his Lordship how he felt on the subject of his Church. "To no man do I yield in the love and respect which I bear to the Church of Scotland. I never signed the Confession of her Faith, but I do more,—I believe it; and I deem her scheme of government at once the simplest and most practically beneficial that has been established since the time of the apostles. But it is the vital spirit, not the dead body, to which I am attached; it is to the free popular Church, established by our Reformers, not to an unsubstantial form or an empty name,—a mere creature of expediency and the State; and had she so far fallen below my feeling of her dignity and excellence as to have acquiesced in your Lordship's decision, the leaf holds not more loosely by the tree when the October wind blows highest, than I would have held by a Church so sunk and degraded."

The Letter containing these words, and others of a like purport, was forwarded in manuscript by Miller to Mr. Robert Paul, an Edinburgh banker, who happened also to be a friend and a sympathetic fellow-Churchman of our new lieutenant of Chalmers who electrified the Assembly at midnight. It had occurred to Candlish and other discerning persons, that the Church, amid her tribulation from Erastian lawyers and godless journalists, might derive advantage from a reasonable, judiciously-conducted, well-written newspaper, which should state her case fairly and fully. The difficulty was to find an editor. Mr. Paul, meeting Candlish on the street, asked him to read the manuscript which Miller had sent him. In his study, in a fagged and listless hour, Candlish began to glance over it. "I began to read it"—the story comes best from his own pen—"in a thoroughly indifferent mood. I never can forget the rapture—for it was nothing short of that—into which the first pages threw me. I finished the reading in a state of great excitement; so much so, that, though it was late, I could not rest till I had hastened with the manuscript to Mr. Dunlop, beseeching him to read it that very night. The following day Mr. Dunlop and I met with Mr. Paul and a few friends, and either then, or within a day or two thereafter, it was agreed to ask Mr. Miller to become editor of the *Witness* newspaper, then about to be started."

Within a few weeks, accordingly, of this meeting, the first number of the newspaper appeared. The

Witness at once assumed a place of influence and distinction among the organs of public opinion in Scotland. Hugh Miller's powers had ripened late, but they were now in perfect maturity as well as perfectly fresh and unexhausted. No man loved Scotland more fervently than he, no man knew her history with more intelligent and sympathetic apprehension, no mind was so opulently stored as his with the imagery of her shores and hill-ranges, or with the noblest traditions of her people. But if we will realise the full and peculiar greatness of Hugh Miller, we must understand that, while one of the shrewdest and most circumspect of practical thinkers, he saw, in the characteristic claim of the Church of Scotland to exercise self-government in the name of Christ, no vague theological dogma, no visionary fancy subversive of civil government, no Popery, no sacerdotalism, but the simple and sole method of applying Christ's New Testament law to the management, in spiritual concerns, of Christ's Church. He was the man to laugh to scorn the stupid charges of usurpation and tyranny, which flippant and superficial persons always bring against an energetic, living, growing, self-reforming Church. He was the man to make the people willing in the day of the Church's power. His name soon rang through the households of Scotland; and his paper carried enthusiasm for the struggling Church to the ends of the earth.

It was among the chief advantages for Hugh Miller, in beginning to edit the *Witness*, that he was thoroughly acquainted with the character of the leading minds among the clergy of Scotland, and perfectly knew and could sympathetically respond to the thoughts and feelings of the best religious society. The two men of whom he spoke as having done most to form his own character were Chalmers and Stewart of Cromarty. The latter was an exception to Scottish preachers in general, from the quietness of his manner, and had something in him of the nature of a recluse, not without indolence and almost averse to fame. But in religion he was utterly in earnest; and, being in earnest, and possessed of a subtly inventive intellect and vivid imagination, he could not possibly handle Bible themes without betraying his originality. Put the Bible into a man's hand, and bid him preach you a sermon, and you will find him out. If he is a Bunyan, or a Spurgeon, or a Stewart, he cannot preach from the Bible and continue unknown. From remote Cromarty, Stewart's fame pervaded Scotland. Next to Chalmers and Candlish, he was known to be the most remarkable preacher in the Church. Miller knew him in close colloquy, and thus had the full advantage of his influence. But his shy and retiring nature kept Stewart, so long as his sense of duty was at rest, in the secluded freedom of Cromarty, out of the afflictive dazzlements of a city pulpit. Years hence, when many changes had taken place, and Candlish was wanted for other than pulpit work, and Scotland was searched for one to take his place, all eyes gradually turned to Cromarty. Stewart was called to become pastor of what, under Andrew Thomson and Candlish, had become one of the noblest congregations in Christendom. Such a call seemed providential, and the tenderly conscientious Stewart feared to disobey it. But he said that the thought of

Edinburgh pressed on him like a gravestone, and, shortly before he was to have left Cromarty, he was found dead in his bed.

We may look upon it as one of the most splendid services of Candlish to the cause, that he so promptly enlisted Miller into the vanguard of the Church's host. It was the first proof—or at least the first that made itself conspicuous to all the world—rendered by Candlish of his superb quality as a party leader. Chalmers was by genius and character the kind of man who does not succeed in generalship, and, in the present instance, he was not without a certain feeling of distrust in relation to the popular aspects of the conflict. He held, and held justly, that mere election by the people, without patron or Presbytery, was no ideal method of settling ministers. He had no tincture in his composition of enthusiasm for the natural man, though profoundly reverent of Christian democracy. "I am sickened to despair," was his cry, when he feared that the Church was to bring out the big drum to call the rabble to her aid.

While, therefore, there was no one who could appreciate Hugh Miller better than Chalmers, no one who could do him more ample justice, whether as a literary artist or as a man of massive sense and of sincere religion, no one who could value the *Witness* more when he saw it at work, yet there was a *nuance* of difference, in respect of liberalism, between Chalmers and the two extraordinary men who now joined hands to assist him in the fray. The emergence of Candlish into a commanding position in the Assembly, the advent of Miller as an influential journalist in Edinburgh, signalised the accession of powerful elements of a popular nature to the moving forces on the side of the Church. It was almost with bated breath that Dr. Chalmers, the world-renowned champion of Church Establishments, had referred to patronage. The stone-mason, in his Letter to Lord Brougham, spoke plainly enough on this point. "With many thousands of my countrymen, I have been accustomed to ask, Where is the place which patronage occupies in this Church of the people and of Christ? I read in the First Book of Discipline (as drawn up by Knox and his brethren), that 'no man should enter the ministry without a lawful vocation; and that a lawful vocation standeth in the *election of the people*, examination of the ministry, and admission of them both.'" Our readers, if they recall the glimpse we took into the *Institutio* of Calvin, will not be at a loss to perceive where Calvin's esteemed friend and fellow-worker Knox found the suggestion of this arrangement.

Miller is careful to make it clear that what the people demand is no mere right to schedule objections, and to have their relevancy or irrelevancy adjudicated on by lawyers or ministers, but to express, in so far as rejection goes, their will. On this point he shuts out by italics the possibility of mistake. "We challenge, as our right, *liberty of rejection without statement of reasons.*" A minister is loved and trusted for positive qualities, and if these are not present, though no shadow of accusation may attach to their absence, the congregation reject him. "We look in him for qualities which we can love, powers which we can respect, graces which we can revere. It matters not that we should have no grounds on which to condemn: we are justified in our rejection if we cannot approve."

The Letter, whether it influenced or failed to influence Lord Brougham, was read not only by thousands in Scotland, but by not a few open-minded, forward-looking persons in England, one of these being Mr. Gladstone. It is known that he was profoundly impressed by the men who were then conspicuous as defenders of the Church of Scotland. But he lay under the spell of Newman, and he had a long way to traverse—may it be hoped that he has traversed it now?—before attaining to the point in Christian evolution which had been reached, in 1839, by Miller and by Candlish.

At the time when the publication of the *Witness* began, there were sixty-three newspapers issued in Scotland, and all except eight were hostile to the Reforming party in the Church. Miller had done a good deal previously in pamphleteering, and his letters on the Herring Fishery had enabled Carruthers, the biographer of Pope and felicitous editor of the *Inverness Courier*, to perceive that a prose writer of great power had arisen. His literary skill charmed the Edinburgh people, and won golden plaudits from Jeffrey, while his hard hits and knack of getting "the laughers" on his side recalled his triumphs as a pamphleteer. "Rival editors," says one who worked with him in those days, "he tomahawked and scalped." He carried the fastidiousness of the stylist into newspaper composition, making laborious corrections, "speaking out to himself as he wrote, and trying every sentence upon his ear, as a money-changer weighs a piece of gold on his practised finger-tip." So severe was his labour,—so passionate was his absorption in his great enterprise,—that "I can never," he used to say, "remember the names of my fossils on publication days till about tea-time, when they begin to come back to me, reappearing to memory like letters written in invisible ink when you hold the paper to the fire."

Among the laymen of Scotland, no one contributed so much to the advocacy of the Church's cause as Hugh Miller. Words from his pen, telling epithets, expressive similitudes, forceful and lucid arguments, would obviously, as has been well remarked, be caught up by speakers at public meetings, and echo from platform to platform throughout Scotland. The paper, says Mr. Landreth, was "a peacock's tail, for supplying party-plumes and ornaments." Never, probably, in the history of journalism, has a party been better served by an organ of public opinion than was that which took the lead in the Church of Scotland during her conflict with the State by the *Witness* under the editorship of Hugh Miller.

CHAPTER XVII.

The Rise of Candlish.

WE return to Candlish. That speech in the Assembly of 1839 was a revelation to many; but there were a few who had marked him from afar as one who was sure, when his time came, to be the observed of all observers. An Edinburgh man by birth, he had an intellectual affinity for that Athenian place, and during his whole career shone as a distinctively Edinburghian celebrity. All the same, he was bred and educated in Glasgow, and his blood allied him to Galloway and Ayrshire.

His father, James Candlish, between whom and himself there were points of peculiar physiological resemblance, was a man of great brain power, ardent in his patriotic sentiments, and devoted to the minstrelsy of Scotland. Burns addressed him as "my ever dear old acquaintance." Too speculative theologically for the Church, he chose another vocation, and became a consummate teacher of medicine. One day, when forty-six years of age, he was making a speech to the Royal Medical Society, and felt a queer sensation "as if his head would have burst," or

as if the brain had been "too big for the skull." He
went home, and before midnight was dead. Five weeks
afterwards his son Robert Smith Candlish was born. The
"Smith" came from the mother's side, who belonged
to Ayrshire. Among the immortal belles of Mauchline
she is distinguished as the Miss Smith who had "wit;"
and one who knew her informs us that the first glance
at her "firm mouth, and eyes which seemed to see one
through and through," proved convincingly that the
characterisation in this instance carried with it the
accuracy and suggestiveness common to those of Burns.
With the gentleness and loving-kindness of a devoted
mother, she combined the qualities which are of most
price in fathers, an admirably methodic habit, and "an
authority which, in the quietest conceivable way, was
absolute, decisive, and indisputable." She was the object
of her son's most tender affection and loyal and reveren-
tial trust. If his father gave him his towering brain, it
may have been still more to his mother that he owed his
diamond-like lucency of expression, and that incomparable
faculty for business, which seems to have amazed some
good judges even more than his gifts of speech.

Mrs. Candlish, greatly straitened in circumstances after
her husband's death, opened a school for girls in Glasgow,
and a lady who was one of her pupils has put on record
her memories of our Candlish when a boy of eight. He
was a peculiar, not to say queer-looking child, with large
forehead and small body, delicate fair complexion, and
very long eyelashes. Interesting, doubtless, but evidently
impressing some people with a sense of oddness, for un-
complimentary remarks were made, and one day a lady

rather wounded the little man's pride by giving him a penny,—as if he had been a poor little hydrocephalous object, or, as he himself inquiringly suggested to his mother, a beggar. His mother and a brother and sister were his educators, until he went, at thirteen, to Glasgow University.

Despite his boyish years, he distinguished himself greatly, taking an ample share of honours during five successive sessions. He was high in favour with his professors, and ardently admired and looked upon as a leader by his fellow-students, as well as almost reverenced for "purity of thought and unconscious sanctity of character." His reading ranged beyond his College course, and he delighted in Shakespeare. "In disposition he was impatient, yet persevering; versatile, yet persistent; sensitive, and sometimes irritable; but always kind, manly, generous." No period can be fixed upon to date the beginning of his religious life; but one who may be trusted expresses the belief that it commenced in "very early years," and says that during his undergraduate career he was characterised by a "spirituality" so "dominant and habitual," as to suggest its having grown up with him and become to him "as the breath of life." So early in the century as 1826, when in his twentieth year, we find him, from sheer force of mother wit, anticipating what, after infinite disputation, has now become the judgment of all sensible men on Mosaic geology. The very words, "Mosaic geology," he disallows. "Is there," he asks, "any geology at all in Moses? or are his works intended to teach us matters of science? Nothing seems to me more absurd and dangerous than to implicate revelation at all in disputes on subjects not in the least connected with religion, and on subjects, moreover, when speaking on which the Scriptures must have accommodated themselves to the opinions and language of the day, and on which, in fact, they can scarcely with any propriety be said to have advocated any theory at all."

In this same year, a request being addressed to some of the Glasgow professors for "the most able young man they could recommend," to act as tutor at Eton to Sir Hugh Hume Campbell of Marchmont, the offer was made to Candlish and accepted. In his twenty-first year accordingly he is installed at Eton, and makes his observations upon the new world thus opened to him. He is one of about thirty tutors, "some Fellows of Cambridge, and many of them clergymen." He thinks them "in general, very pleasant men," but feels the want of a "*friend*," accentuating that lack of sympathy which a kindly Scot is likely to experience amid the cold courtesies of English acquaintance. He pronounces in favour of the Scottish system of blending, in education, the home influence and the school influence, as against the English system of herding men with men—through preparatory school, public school, College, Parliament, and club—from cradle to grave. "Upon the whole, I cannot avoid preferring that mixture of public instruction and domestic superintendence which forms the system of our Universities. A boy is much more likely to do good when he spends his evenings with his friends, or with those whom his friends have appointed, than when he is exposed to the temptations of idle companions." He has an eye for the sweet spring scenery of southern England, but never lapses into the view-hunting flowery vein. "If I had room I would expatiate upon the beauties of the country here. The hawthorn is just budding."

He takes a keen interest in public matters, and his voice is clear for freedom, sympathy, and toleration. Hopes the Church of Scotland, in petitioning against the Test Act, will demand relief not merely for "Presbyterian Dissenters," but for all. Wishes the Church would petition also for Catholic Emancipation. "Why will Churchmen always be behind their fellow-citizens in learning to advocate the cause of religious freedom?" A true note of Scottish as distinguished from English ecclesiasticism! Once the question of Church patronage turns up. "The law, as it is now (1827) administered, undoubtedly requires revision." He hesitates as to the total abolition of patronage, but would render the sale of livings illegal, fixing the charge upon the land. "If possible,"—he says, with pathetic interest for us who read his history by the light of the intervening years,— "I should like to see some *more effectual check* than there is at present *on the part of the people* upon its abuse." *He* did not know where to insert the italics in this sentence; *we* do.

There was little in the outset of his ministerial life to forecast his future. Of the commonplace badges of evangelical sanctity he had absolutely none, and his fine culture and generous tolerance, aided, perhaps, by his fondness for the works of Barrow and appreciation of the Anglican Service, and coinciding with his early connection as assistant with one or two Moderates, contributed to put about a whisper, entirely fallacious, that he was himself inclined to that side in the Church. At one moment it seemed that he might take flight for Canada, and he made a narrow miss of Regent's Square Church in London. At first the huge-headed, short-bodied, broad-shouldered young preacher, who, child and man, had always something about him to suggest that nature had struck him off in a humorous mood as a magnificent grotesque, did not appear to be at home in the pulpit. "He had an awkward way of habitually shrugging up one shoulder, which gave him almost a deformed look." His voice was not yet tuned to public speaking, and in his bursts of passionate climax it would become a "scream or even screech." Then his "gesticulation" was inchoate. There were what a lady suggestively called "such nervous varieties." Twitchings of face, to wit, clutchings and pullings about of pulpit habiliments. "If I were his wife," adds the aforesaid lady, "I would make his waistcoat and his gown fit better; they were never doing their duty to his satisfaction." Was it a pulpit Apollo that the audience saw before them, or was it a Dominie Samson?

Never fear, said the knowing ones, he will come right. Gradually the harshness left the voice, the jerkiness of its transitions gave way to a noble modulation, and ere long it rang forth with the clearness of a clarion peal, or rolled like the thunder of the breakers on a storm-beat shore. The twitchings of feature subsided. And as for the matter of the preaching, you found, when you listened well, that there had been nothing like it in Scotland since Chalmers was young. It was Puritan, yet Puritanism spiritualised, transformed, transfigured. "Very soon," says one who listened to Candlish in those years,—" very soon I felt with everybody else that a great preacher had appeared, and that a new era was coming in for the Scottish pulpit."

Accordingly, in that time of distress and dismay, when every face you met on Edinburgh streets looked sad, and Chalmers, coming into his class-room as usual, " broke down in the first sentence of his lecture, and rushed out bathed in tears," because Andrew Thomson had fallen, it was none other than Candlish who, after the too short ministry of Mr. Martin, was chosen for his successor in the pulpit of St. George's. The parish was very large, but under Andrew Thomson it had been energetically managed, and under Candlish, helped by one or two ministerial assistants, and by a rare company of volunteers of the angelic order, male and female, from the congregation itself, it became—we need not scruple to say so—a model for Christendom; exemplary in all respects in which a parish can be exemplary, in education of the young, in consideration for the poor, in the preaching of salvation through Christ. And one of its specialties was that the high intellectual character of its preaching drew to it the flower of the intellectuality of the modern Athens. Of barristers and law lords, of University professors and promising students, of eminent doctors and surgeons, and authors and scientific celebrities, of thinkers who were Christian and of Christians who could think, no pulpit in Edinburgh attracted so great a concurrence as that of Candlish. Had it been Herod whose nod commanded Andrew

Thomson to death, he would have said that Andrew had risen from the dead. That reconciliation between intellect and evangelism, between culture of the modern Athens and theology of the Wisharts and Knoxes, the Gillespies and Hendersons and Rutherfords, the covenanted, sword-girt saints of Airsmoss and Drumclog, which had been effected by Andrew Thomson, was represented in finer, more intellectual, more spiritual manifestation by Candlish.

And now, in the evolution of this great providential drama, Chalmers who had so illustriously co-operated with Thomson, and Candlish who had succeeded Thomson as the first of Edinburgh preachers, stood side by side, in unity of purpose but individuality of character, to do battle on behalf of the Church and people of Scotland. In majesty Chalmers was unapproached. In impetuosity, in forward-looking glance and moving impulse, in eager acceptance of the spirit and ideas of a new time, Candlish was potently felt and conspicuously seen. He had always chafed against a calculating, guarded, prudential virtue. "Men's minds," he had written to a confidential friend, "are not open to large and liberal views,—a certain low and feeble and miserably short-sighted policy rather suits them. Everything like high principle and honest zeal seems out of place. All is cold and calculating prudence." He had now found a field in which the instincts and cravings of a puissant heroism were likely to have satisfaction.

CHAPTER XVIII.

The Dean of Faculty.

THE position of the Church at that moment, when, putting aside the surrender motion of Dr. Cook and the evasive motion of Dr. Muir, she adopted the motion made by Chalmers and spoken to by Candlish, looked simple and imposing, but it involved complications. It was simple from the point of view of a Presbyterian Churchman. It became complicated when the Presbyterian Church was viewed as established and endowed by the State.

Dual government is always difficult. Is it denied that the Church of Scotland, as conceived by Chalmers and those for whom he spoke, was indeed a dual government? As an abstract question the point may be open to debate, but practically it was impossible that the association of the two powers, spiritual and secular, in her constitution, should not involve some of the natural consequences of dual government. Regarding the jurisdiction of the Church as independent, and the jurisdiction of the State as independent, each co-ordinate to each, we must still admit the necessity of an

understanding between the two. Loyal in his heart of
hearts both to Church and to State,—believing both to
be divinely ordained,—Chalmers had taken it for granted,
his whole life long, that there was no cause for apprehension that the jurisdictions would clash. Recurring
to the old Platonic similitude, we may say that Church
and State, as viewed by him, were immortal steeds, one
white as snow, one raven-black, driven in the same
chariot by one invisible Christ. It had been the supporting faith, the exultant assertion, of Chalmers, in his
championship of Church Establishments, that there is no
insuperable, no depressingly formidable difficulty in the
way of friendly, efficient, reciprocally loyal co-operation
between these powers, each exercising an independent
jurisdiction, both possessing a right Divine. He had
proceeded on the conviction that, if the Church held
strictly to her spiritual province, the State could not
and would not prove hostile to her. He would not now
bate one jot or one tittle of the Church's claim to that
liberty, that autonomy, that expansive power, which the
State had not given and which the State could not take
away. But with religious earnestness and sincerity he
recognised also the State's right to decide every question
arising within the secular province, or *around* the spiritual
province (*circa sacra*); and he respectfully asked the
supreme civil authority, the Queen's Government, to
remove what he deemed the misunderstanding that had
obscured the line of demarcation between the provinces.

It is a sound rule, eminently promotive of completeness in the statement of facts and of equity in judging
them, and pleasant both in the conduct of controversies

and their historical recital, to take it for granted that people are honest all round, and that changes, inconsistencies, nay even contradictions, do not necessarily convict men of conscious falsehood. In the heat of debate, in the warmth of sympathetic narrative, sharp words will be spoken, that seem utterly to violate this rule, but an effort ought to be made to repress such aberrations. In the conflict of which we treat, motives were frankly imputed, and it is, in sooth, difficult for one to whom it seems sun-clear that Chalmers, Candlish, and Cunningham were in the right, to resist the suspicion that some element of perversity, some ethically, not to say Christianly objectionable motive, influenced one at least of the legal opponents of the Church.

All would have gone differently—this is beyond dispute—had it not been for the part played, against the Reforming party, by John Hope, Dean of Faculty, the same man whom we found schooling Chalmers in the principles of Presbyterianism, and appealing to him to resent and resist the least encroachment upon the liberties of the Church. Let us try to suppose that he believed himself to have been visited by new light, and that he was equally sincere in rebuking the Whigs when they proposed to institute a religious inspection of parishes, and in weaving schemes with the Tories for laying the spiritual jurisdiction of the Church at the feet of the Court of Session. Dr. Buchanan, who entered into the fray against him, cannot be expected to detect much of moral splendour in his motives, but no evidence could be more cogent than Dr. Buchanan's as to the immense effect of his hostility. As an elder counselling the Moderate leaders in the General Assembly, as a pamphleteer riding full tilt against the Evangelical controversialists, and—deadliest of all—as confidential friend and adviser, earwigging statesmen, whom he could approach in their hours of retirement or prepossess by his private and confidential letters, he was the soul of the party whose object was to shackle the aspiring Church, and to force her to take orders, in her most sacred operations, from the Court of Session.

The Dean, consistent or inconsistent, malignant or high-principled, was, without question, a man who could think for himself. He had from the first been an unswerving opponent of the Veto Law. But though he thus made it plain that he called in question the right of the Church, even when acting with the sanction of Her Majesty's Law Officers for Scotland, and at the instance of a distinguished member of the Court of Session, Lord Moncreiff, to make a law regulating the exercise of patronage without consulting Parliament, he did not at that time proceed to the inference that, until she retraced this step, her jurisdiction was suspended, her independence forfeited. It was after the passing of the Veto Law that he adjured Chalmers to bristle up at an alleged violation of the spiritual independence of the Church.

Plainly, also, at the time when he first took in hand the case of Mr. Young and the Earl of Kinnoull, presentee and patron of the parish of Auchterarder, he had not made up his mind to touch the spiritual jurisdiction. The action was laid by him in a shape which admitted of its consequences being confined to the temporalities of the parish. This was in 1835. But in 1837 he changed his plan of campaign, and made it his request, on the part of Mr. Young to the Court of Session, that the Church should be required, by *ordaining him to the cure of souls,* to open his way to the temporal goods of the parish.

This was a change indeed. The Church had no conscientious difficulty in dealing with temporalities. She did, no doubt, say that she had a duty in relation to these. She did not deny that there was a sense, and an important sense, in which it was her part to defend them against aggression. She was bound to tell the Court of Session that they had been set apart for a particular purpose,—the maintenance of a gospel ministry in the parishes of Scotland. Pittance as they were, compared with the glittering heaps that had sunk into the capacious maw of the Scottish aristocracy, they were something,— and the Church's duty was to shield them and make the best use of them, in the interest of the parishioners. But the Church, as she had only a spiritual jurisdiction, had only spiritual arms, and could be under no conscientious call to resist the State, if it, by physical force, applied the property of the people in a way she disapproved. All the Church could do was to wash her hands of the temporalities, by bearing the most effective testimony in her power as to how they ought to be bestowed.

But the face of the matter was changed when the Court of Session, in response to the application of Mr. Young and the pleading of the Dean, required the Church to proceed with Mr. Young's ordination. The face of the matter was changed when the Presbytery of

Lethendy, having obeyed the Church as to ordination rather than the Court of Session, was summoned by the Court to its bar, and publicly reprimanded. It was a very different matter when the Presbytery of Strathbogie, choosing to obey the Court of Session instead of the Church, ordained the patron's presentee in despite of the all but unanimous remonstrance of the parishioners of Marnoch. No one had ever disputed that, if there exists such a thing as spiritual jurisdiction, ordination falls within its province. The Dean, who had shouted to Chalmers to guard the independence of the Church, now called upon the Court of Session to command her to perform, or not to perform, the right of ordination.

Our readers have probably ceased to have much difficulty in understanding how a position so simple as that taken up by the Church of Scotland in the memorable Assembly of 1839 should involve complications. The dual government of the Church of Scotland, if problematical in theory, became a grimly-featured fact under the conjuring of the Dean. The Church had been as careful as was consistent with fortitude. The Assembly had resolved, in so far as was practicable, to stay proceedings in disputed settlements until progress once more became safe and easy. Chalmers, who had fondly dreamed of the seventh decade of his life as to be spent in Sabbatic rest, happy in the contemplation of past labours and the prospect of a heavenly reward, could not in his heart of hearts believe that, now his sixtieth year was past, the crowning glory of his endeavours, the paragon of religious Establishments, the resurgent and grandly efficient Church of Scotland was to be humiliated, disowned, dismantled by lawyers and statesmen for the crime of wakening up to her duty. But he was an honest man, and death itself would have been better for him than to feel that his championship of Church Establishments had been based on false pretences. Was the Headship of Christ after all a mere flag, a rhetorical flourish, a thing for histrionic strutting and bombastic effusion, or was it a sacred reality? Chalmers had again and again, with all the vividness and vehemence of which he was capable, affirmed that a negative answer to this last question would, if unmistakably given, amount to a dissolution of the league between Church and State in Scotland.

CHAPTER XIX.

The Church or the Court of Session.

IF the reader wishes to keep the essentials of this quarrel distinctly before his mind's eye, he is counselled to retain a vivid recollection of the Veto Act and the Chapel Act. All the assumption of the Church lay there. She considered it within her province to decree that the rights of patrons should be so exercised as not to force ministers on congregations, and that her clergy should form one equal brotherhood, not a superior and inferior caste. If any leading statesman had been able to discern that no possible calamity could ensue although Chalmers and his party were treated in a spirit of generous trust, and such adjustments made in the letter of the law as were requisite to prevent friction between the Church and the Court of Session, all might have been well.

But promptitude would have been indispensable; for, although the Church might be most anxious to make no encroachment whatever on the province of the State, she could not allow her own ministers to cast to the winds her ordinances of government, and laugh her discipline to scorn. The Church could not allow ministers to violate their ordination vows, and they had certainly promised, at ordination, to obey her in spiritual things. If her ministers, when commanded by the Church not to ordain a particular man, and ordered by the Court of Session to ordain him, did perform the rite by order of the Court, then, if the Church inflicted no censure on them, the very "weans" and herd laddies on the Scottish braes would have treated her jurisdiction with the laughing unconcern with which, as Death complained to Burns, Dr. Hornbook had taught them to regard his awful dart. And just this question of obeying the Church, or obeying the Court of Session, was that with which the terrible Dean confronted the ministers of Scotland. Hence a complication, a tragic and lamentable complication.

A certain number of the clergy, finding that they could not possibly obey both the Church and the Court of Session,—that there was no third course between exposing themselves to the risk of spiritual punishment from the Church, involving no necessary risk to glebe or stipend, and exposing themselves to temporal punishment, in shape of fine or imprisonment, from the Court of Session,—elected to disobey the Church and to obey the Civil Magistrate. They were ecclesiastical rebels, and sober-minded persons do not sympathise with rebellion for the sole cause that it is ecclesiastical. But these rebels were ministers of that composite thing, a State Church. Hence they had, it must be admitted, something plausible—not more—to say for themselves, something which heroic men, or clear-headed men, might not have said, but which average men would be likely in most places and times to say. They had been taught to reverence Establishments. They had been taught that the elementary logic of Presbyterianism, as contrasted with Popery on this hand and Erastianism on that, pronounced the jurisdiction of the State to be co-ordinate with the jurisdiction of the Church. Was it a sin to obey one rather than the other of two co-ordinate powers, both sacred? They had seen Chalmers, and one who, in the fierceness of his opposition to patronage far outdid Chalmers, namely, Cunningham, smiting the Voluntaries hip and thigh, and seeming, at moments, to fall into the habit, all but universal south of Tweed, of referring to free Churches as sects, and to Established Churches as if they were alone entitled to the name of Church. Cunningham, no doubt, had thundered in the Assembly against the notion that the Church could do no particular act in her own spiritual sphere without going cap in hand to the State to ask permission; but he had admitted there and then that she could not do what the State expressly prohibited. A country minister might have some shadow of excuse for mistaking the Court of Session, when it talked very big, for the State. The Dean had pointedly affirmed at the time of the passing of the Veto Act, and the Court of Session now backed him up in his assertion, that the State had prohibited the Church from restoring to the parishioners rights which had been transferred to the patron. The statute on which the Court of Session relied might be an abominable statute. The Court only asked whether it was law. It might be a violation of the Treaty of Union between England and Scotland. The Court of Session did not mind that. It

might be unchristian, inhuman, in its dealing with
parishioners,—no matter; the only question the Court of
Session could entertain was whether it was law. If it was,
the Court would interpret it, issue decrees in accordance
with it, severely punish for disobeying it, and place all
the power of the State at command of the proper officers
to give it effect.

We may under these circumstances despise and condemn the ministers who, defying the Church and trampling on the people, consented to do the bidding of the Court of Session, but we cannot be blind to the mystifications of their position. They could not be electrified, on a sudden, into the spiritual heroism which made a Chalmers, a Candlish, a M'Cheyne ready to sacrifice all things rather than ordain ministers over parishioners who solemnly declared that they could derive no edification from them. They had vowed to obey the Church, and they knew that the Bible was the Church's law, and, under it, the Confession of Faith. But they might vaguely imagine, or may at least be charitably supposed to have imagined, that all these were included for them, as State-Churchmen, in the law of the land. Let us not be surprised if thousands, and among them influential statesmen, thought that the discipline under which the Church placed these rebels was severe.

CHAPTER XX.

Law and Gospel—The Lethendy Case.

THE Dean was a man of resolute purpose, not to be frightened by complications, not to be turned by any difficulty from the even tenor of his way. He had made up his mind that the Court of Session should in all causes have the last word in Scotland. He played the part, *mutatis mutandis*, of Henry VIII., and made every man tremble who dared to obey the Church and to disobey the Civil Power. We shall take two illustrative samples of his administration.

The Presbytery of Dunkeld had been instructed by the Commission of Assembly in 1838 to induct Mr. Kessen into the pastoral charge of the parish of Lethendy, with special injunction to refrain from any interference with the temporalities of the parish. The motion to this effect had been made in the Commission of Assembly by Mr. Dunlop, and it was carried by an almost unanimous vote,—fifty-two against six,—the Evangelicals being joined on the occasion by leading Moderates. Dr. Brunton, a prominent Moderate, had described the act of the Presbytery "as purely spiritual," adding that "he knew his own province, and on that province he would stand or fall." The Presbytery met, with a view to obeying the Church.

The Dean, armed with an interdict of the Court of Session, forbade the Presbytery to proceed with the settlement. The Rev. Michael Stirling, of Cargill, the senior member, pointed out to his brethren the alternatives between which they had to choose. If they obeyed the Court of Session, they would be secured in their manses and stipends; if they obeyed the Church, they would be guilty of contempt of the Civil Court, a grave offence, punishable with fine and imprisonment. To do the bidding of the Lords of Session would be, in effect, to force into the parish of Lethendy a man whom the people refused to receive as their pastor, and to keep out a man whom the people accepted and the Church approved. Delay was not to be thought of, for the parish had for nearly two years been deprived of pastoral superintendence. Mr. Stirling was a country minister, of unobtrusive character, who had taken little part in public discussions, but he had not a shadow of doubt that, in proceeding with his fellow-Presbyters to ordain Mr. Kessen, he and they were true to the fundamental principles of the Church of Scotland. The ordination, therefore, took place, in defiance of the Civil Magistrate.

The Presbyters were cited to the bar of the Court of Session to answer for their conduct. The judges, twelve in number, wearing their robes of office, occupied the bench. At the bar stood the Presbytery, eight parish ministers, to answer for contempt. As they stood, one or two of the ministers of Edinburgh entered the court and placed themselves at their side. At last the universally honoured Dr. Gordon entered and quietly took his station with them at the bar. This brought a scowl across the brows of their Lordships. "No sooner was the noble and venerable head seen emerging from the crowd at the end of the bar, than a proposal burst from the Bench to turn out those clergymen from the bar; but an indignant and solemn remonstrance from Lord Moncreiff checked this attempt."

The ministers were asked what they had to say for themselves. Mr. Stirling made a brief and dignified statement, professing for himself and his brethren the intention to treat the judges with all the reverence that was their due, but making no apology for what had been done. "In ordaining to the office of the holy ministry, and in admitting to the pastoral charge, to which in the proceedings complained of we strictly limited ourselves, we acted in obedience to the superior Church judicatories,—to which, in matters spiritual, we are subordinate,—and to which, at ordination, we vowed obedience."

They were dismissed for the time, and the Court took four days to consider how they should be punished. "It is commonly understood," says Dr. Buchanan, "that five of the judges voted in favour of a sentence of imprisonment, and six for the more lenient measure of a rebuke; and that the Lord President did not vote at all." On the day fixed they were publicly reprimanded, and warned that, in case of a similar offence, they should be imprisoned.

It will be difficult for any man born and bred in

England to enter sympathetically into the feelings of the Scottish people in contemplating this exhibition. If it requires a surgical operation to get a joke into the heads of the countrymen of Scott, Burns, Professor Wilson, and Carlyle, it requires an operation of tenfold difficulty to cut a way into the skull of an ordinary Englishman for the conception of a clergyman of an Established Church who is *not* a priest, and who *is* a cordial friend of the people. But every intelligent man and woman in Scotland was capable of seeing in those clergymen, who were called from their parishes and reprimanded by the Court of Session, sufferers in the cause of the people, representatives of that ancient league in which the Church and people of Scotland had stood side by side in defence of religion and of liberty. That those clergymen, in obeying conscience and Christ, had disobeyed the law as interpreted by the Court of Session, admits of no dispute. But if modern Englishmen could find leisure to cast back a glance upon their own history three hundred years ago, they would see that law has been gloriously defied in England in the name of justice, freedom, and God.

It is, as we remarked before, only by having recourse to analogy that one has a chance of getting an honest, average John Bull, who, idolising law, hates injustice, to see how, by the action of the Court of Session, wrong was done in the Lethendy case. Suppose the Court of Queen's Bench were to forbid the College of Physicians to appoint to a district a medical practitioner whom they believed to be capable, from his being acceptable to the inhabitants, of doing them a *maximum* of good, and to command them to appoint instead a practitioner who, from the aversion to him of the inhabitants, could do them only a *minimum* of good, and might do them positive harm; and suppose the College of Physicians, proving refractory, were fined, reprimanded, and threatened with imprisonment for their conduct,—then the situation would closely correspond to that presented in Scotland by the Lethendy case. In England, under these circumstances, there would be an outburst of public surprise, a storm in the newspapers; a conspicuous disregard, it might be, of theories upon the subject, but a unanimous cry of amazement and protest at the pedantic spectacle of lawyers ordering and instructing physicians to do their professional duty. The peculiar element that intensified to painfulness the interest with which onlookers in Scotland contemplated the treatment of Mr. Stirling and his brethren, lay in the fact that they were wounded, not merely in their professional point of honour, but in conscience, for they had vowed to obey, in all spiritual concerns, not the Court of Session, but the Church.

It was one of the minor complications of this Lethendy case, that the Crown, as represented by the Government of the day, actually stood on the same side with the Church and the people against the Court of Session armed with the omnipotent letter of a statute. Mr. Clark, the presentee whom the people had rejected, and whom therefore the Church put aside, owed his presentation to the Crown. But the Government had made it a point, in the exercise of the Crown patronage, to defer to the Church, and to proceed upon the assumption that the Veto Act was legal. Accordingly, Mr. Clark, the presentee in question, found himself dropped by the Government. Crown, Church, and people united in support of Mr. Kessen. This was the position of affairs, until the Dean of Faculty may be presumed to have favoured Mr. Clark with a hint that the legality of the Veto Act had been denied, and that therefore all the proceedings by which his presentation had been cancelled were null and void. At all events, it was under the auspices of the Dean that Mr. Clark brought his action, and to the Dean that he owed his victory. By the incantations of this wizard such curious confusion was wrought, that the Crown appeared in the case on *both* sides, as patron of Mr. Clark by grace of the Dean, as patron of Mr. Kessen by grace of the Church and the people. Unquestionably supreme in the civil province, the Crown was in effect reprimanded by its own Court of Session for being an accomplice with the Established Church in the ordination of a pastor in the parish of Lethendy.

One word more, and we need linger no longer on the illustrative aspects of the Lethendy case. Mr. Stirling and his brethren were cast in expenses to the amount of £346,—a virtual fine. But this was not enough for Mr. Clark and his counsel. The former brought a new action, on the ground of the pecuniary loss occasioned to him by the obstruction placed in the way to his entering upon the living, and "obtained a decree for damages to the extent of several thousand pounds." And when at last obstruction vanished from the path of the man whom the people had rejected and the Dean had backed up,—when the obsequious Establishment had hurried the Veto Act into oblivion—when the triumphant Dean had thrust Chalmers, Cunningham, and Candlish into the wilderness, and he and Mr. Clark could congratulate each other on the Disruption,—what then was the result as affecting the personal merits and character of the Court of Session's minister? Alas! that his Presbytery were compelled to libel him for drunkenness, and, in legal phrase, strike his name from the roll! The instinct of the people had been right. He was not the man to be the shepherd and bishop of their souls. And it was for barring his intrusion upon them that a company of quiet country pastors, not rich in worldly goods, but exemplary in simple graces and virtues, and having it as their life-work to make the light of Christ shine in their parishes, " were threatened with the terrors of imprisonment, and harassed with fines heavy enough, had not the burden been borne by the Church at large, to have consigned some at least of its members, and their families along with them, to beggary and ruin."

Such were the results of the attempt of the Dean to absorb the jurisdiction of the Church into that of the Court of Session, in an instance in which the clergy elected to obey the Church rather than the Court. But, as we have seen, it was a possible, nay a probable event that some of the clergy, having been taught to plume themselves on their State connection, having thought it a kind of duty to fling scorn into the eyes of unattached Presbyterians, and being possessed with a vague sense of the awfulness of resisting the law of the land, should prefer to obey the Court of Session rather than the Church.

CHAPTER XXI.

Law and Gospel—The Reel of Bogie.

THE probability became a fact when Mr. Edwards, presented in 1837 by the patron to the pastoral charge of Marnoch, was vetoed by an overwhelming majority of the congregation. The Church ordered the local Presbytery, to wit, Strathbogie, to reject him. The majority of the Presbyters are understood to have done so with the utmost reluctance, but they obeyed. Things then took their usual course. Mr. Edwards applied to the Court of Session, and the Court of Session granted him a virtual command to the Presbytery of Strathbogie to ordain him pastor of Marnoch. The Court of Session said, Ordain. The Church by its Commission of Assembly said, Reject. Which was to be obeyed?

The Presbytery of Strathbogie consisted of twelve ministers. Seven were Moderates, five were Evangelicals. But one of these last, an able man, zealous on the side of Church and people, happened to be Moderator of the Presbytery. The seven Moderates had hitherto obeyed the Church in so far as they could do so without offending the Civil Court, and when they found that Mr.

Edwards returned upon them armed with an injunction from the Court of Session, they exerted themselves to the utmost to yield obedience to the Court without technically disobeying the Church. No more than a few weeks had elapsed since the Commission had forbidden them to proceed with the ordination of Mr. Edwards. It was only at their regular meeting of Presbytery, some considerable time ahead, that they would be officially informed of this prohibition. They did their best, therefore, to get up in hot haste a meeting of Presbytery, with a view to ordaining Mr. Edwards out of hand, and thus obeying the Court of Session in substance without disobeying the Church in form.

One cannot help feeling something like a touch of pity for these sorely bested Presbyters in their artless doubling between Church and State. How happy could they have been with either! They were not a bad kind of men, those Strathbogie Moderates, but they were not of heroic temper, nor in the least ambitious to play a morally heroic part. The Aberdeenshire doctors had not shone in the Covenanting annals of Scotland. From the time when Huntly and the other Popish lords had troubled King James, and cast glances of dubious sympathy towards Spain, there had been a decided absence of Presbyterian enthusiasm in those districts where Bogie runs seaward, through its strath on the bordering shires of Banff and Aberdeen. Associations with the reel of Bogie, and all that it typifies of dancing, mirth, and wild lyric sportfulness in the character of Scots, were more characteristic of Strathbogie than the austere piety of the Covenanters.

The Presbytery of Strathbogie were now perfectly determined to obey the Court of Session, but they did their best to avoid formal disobedience of their ecclesiastical superiors, and attempted a smart trot to the avenue for that purpose. Their Evangelical Moderator, however, showed himself their match in foresight and promptitude, and completely baffled their project of ordaining Mr. Edwards at an extraordinary meeting of Presbytery. The result was, that at the meeting of the Commission of Assembly in June 1839, the Commission had no graver business before it than to decide upon the measures to be taken in the case of a Presbytery of the Church which had given unmistakable evidence of its determination to ordain a minister in direct defiance of the Church, and in express obedience to the Court of Session.

The Church chose its best men to be its mouthpieces on this occasion. Candlish made the motion in which the seven were rebuked, and placed, in so far as at the present stage of the business seemed practicable, in a position in which further offence might be avoided. Had the Presbytery of Strathbogie manifested contrition, or displayed any disposition to return to their allegiance, the past would have been too gladly forgiven; but, since they notoriously persisted in their determination to proceed to the ordination of Mr. Edwards, it seemed to be kindness, on the part of the Church, to prevent them, by suspending their powers as ministers, from committing an offence so grave as to entail a sentence of deposition.

Candlish having stated wherein the Presbytery had offended, dwelt earnestly on the desire of the Church to proceed with gentleness and forbearance. If the brethren, he said, would give the Commission then and there a pledge of loyalty, "an assurance that till the meeting of the Assembly they will take no further steps in the matter," he would joyfully refer the whole question to the next Assembly. It was only when the Church had been "bearded and defied" by her own licentiates, it was only when her ordained ministers had committed "intolerable offence against her authority," that she had been "driven to the wall" and forced to have recourse to penal measures. In vain she had studiously refrained from avoidable collision with the Court of Session; in vain she had endeavoured, pending any appeal to the Legislature, to place the relation between herself and her adversaries on the footing of an armistice. The refractory Presbytery now declined to give any sign of relenting.

He moved, therefore, that the majority should be suspended from the office of the ministry. But the sharpness of the sentence was qualified in two ways. In the first place, it was put within the option of the suspended ministers to be replaced in their office on merely subscribing an assurance of willingness to obey the Church. In the second place, a committee was named to deal with them in the way of friendly conference, with a view to their restoration to the office of Presbyters. The object was to deter them from consummating their rebellion by proceeding to the ordination of Mr. Edwards,—" to prevent them from doing what, if left alone, they might feel themselves bound to do; but what surely, if they are prevented by the interposition of our authority, they cannot reasonably take blame to themselves for leaving undone."

Dr. Chalmers, supporting Candlish, laid stress upon the imperious necessity under which the Church lay, if anarchy was not to prevail, to require obedience from her clergy. "The Presbytery had committed," he said, "an open breach on that authority, under which all statutory enactments, and all judicial sentences, were carried into execution. It was disobedience, not against a rule, but against the power which originated and enforced all rules and ordinances. If it were allowed, there would be an end to all law and all government." He had at first felt that there was no course but to proceed at once to the supreme penalty of deposition; but he rejoiced that a milder expedient had been devised. He avowed his suspicion that the ministers had been the prey of malevolent influences beyond control by the Church. He appealed to his brethren, "in the name of all that is dear in principle, and all that is dear in patriotism," to defend their beloved Church from anarchy within and tyranny without. "Heaven forbid," he cried, "that in the wild delirium of conflict we should forget principles which are equally dear to both parties, or suffer the Church of Scotland to fall by the hands of her own children!"

The decision arrived at by the Commission was practically unanimous. Not only was Candlish's motion carried by 121 votes against 14, but Dr. Bryce, one of the most prominent representatives of Moderatism, "withdrew from his motion the clause which contained an approval of the Presbytery's conduct." It was not with the principles of the Chalmers party that the Moderates had any quarrel, it was with the life-or-death earnestness with which the Evangelicals maintained them. The freedom of the Church, the Headship of Christ, the rights of the people, — these were fine phrases; but reprimands by the Court of Session, menaces of imprisonment, heavy costs, prospective possibilities in the shape of loss of manse and stipend, were deplorable drawbacks to the sentimental romance of Churchmanship.

The Presbytery of Strathbogie, having made up its mind, showed no disposition to flinch. The seven refused even to meet a deputation of the Conciliatory Committee appointed by the Church. As the Commission of Assembly had taken steps for the maintenance of public worship and pastoral ministration in the parishes during their suspension, they had recourse to the Court of Session for additional protection. They asked, in effect, that the Court should empower them to treat the decree of suspension as a nullity, and to continue in the exercise of their presbyterial and pastoral functions as before, and should forbid ministers, who might be enjoined by the Church to perform their office for them during suspension, to execute the Church's commands. The Court of Session met them, to begin with, half-way, giving them a decree excluding all ministers unsanctioned by them from the parochial churches, churchyards, and school-houses. The Church had, of course, no conscientious objection to submit to this exclusion. Church buildings are property, and so are school-houses, and even the grass over the bones of the dead may be relinquished to the secular jurisdiction.

The Church might most sincerely thank the Court of Session for launching at her this decree. The worldling and the atheist seldom scruple to violate all courtesy in applying the terms "false" and "hypocritical" to religious men and to ecclesiastical bodies, and mean persons were sure to suspect that the Church, with all her spiritual professions, was really aiming at the temporalities. The Court of Session now enabled her to shut the mouth of every scoffer by leaving the churches of the rebel seven unentered, and sending men to preach on hillsides and highways, and in barns and upper rooms. It was over the souls of the parishioners of Strathbogie that the Church claimed to exercise jurisdiction. Men appointed by her to minister to the edification of "the body of Christ," the Church made visible in the persons of the parishioners, poured into Strathbogie. Any meadow, any open space by the highway, afforded such scope for preaching as had never been complained of as incommodious by Christ Himself. Every wimpling burn could serve for baptism.

The Church, we may be sure, would send efficient men to represent her in Strathbogie, men of contagious faith and burning word, whom the people would be glad to listen to, and who, by the mere echo of their voices in exhortation and in prayer, would make the cliffs and stony dells of Bogie cry out against the hireling pastors that were bent on forcing an alien shepherd on the flock. For the farmers and peasants of the district, who entered with the keenest interest into the dispute, and were probably more capable of appreciating such an intellectual entertainment than any peasantry in Europe, the excitement must have been pungently delightful.

But this was obviously not what the seven meant when they asked the Court of Session to save them from molestation. Once more, therefore, they applied to the law Lords who had assumed the government of the Church of Scotland, to serve interdicts upon those ministers whom she had sent to preach and dispense the sacraments in the parishes of the suspended Presbytery. The undaunted Dean was ready. The petition was granted. Interdicts were served upon the preachers, forbidding them to preach in Strathbogie.

The Church now deliberately defied the Court. No power on earth had a right to forbid her to guard the spiritual interests of the flocks committed to her care. Nor were her loyal sons afraid to do her bidding and to encounter the foe. "Ministers hastened to Strathbogie at the call of the Church." They were duly served with interdicts. But the Dean, or some other power not unveiled, considered it discreet to shrink from enforcing the interdicts by actual arrests. It would indeed have been a piquant complication of the business if ministers of the Established Church had been imprisoned for preaching in Strathbogie, while all other sorts and conditions of preaching men and women, including infidels and followers of Joanna Southcote, might on mere principles of toleration hold forth in it to their hearts' content. Arrests did not take place, but the risk was boldly encountered. All the leaders were ready to go, and many of the foremost men did go. Candlish went, and Begg went, and Guthrie went, and the haughs and holms of Bogie rang with such eloquence as they had never heard since they emerged from the primeval sea. Reminiscences or imaginations linger probably in not a few heads of secularist caricatures of the period, in which the intruding Non-intrusionists, short Candlish and long shaggy-headed Cunningham, brisk Begg and apostolic Gordon, were seen kicking up their heels, and flourishing their interdicts and snapping their fingers at the Court of Session, in this newest variation of the Reel of Bogie.

CHAPTER XXII.

Law and Gospel—Marnoch.

THE end, however, had not yet come. Mr. Edwards was not installed in the manse of Marnoch, and his object was to be so without delay. The seven Presbyters who had stood by him hitherto were not disposed to desert him now, but they were anxious to proceed as little as possible on their own initiative, or without feeling themselves safeguarded by the law of the land. Turning to the Court of Session, Mr. Edwards obtained what was in effect a positive injunction to the Presbytery to proceed with his settlement.

The suspended seven obeyed. In the dead of winter, —January 1841,—when the land lay shrouded in snow, the parishioners of Marnoch, and with them a multitude of neighbours from all parts of the district, assembled round their parish church to witness the attempt to thrust Mr. Edwards into the charge. When the doors were opened, the whole of the body of the church was occupied by the parishioners, the galleries being filled to overflowing by strangers. The meeting having been constituted, a parishioner of the name of Murray rose up, and, describing himself as a member of the Church of

Scotland, and an elder of the parish of Marnoch, asked the Moderator, the suspended minister of Keith, whether he came there by authority of the General Assembly. Answer was declined, except on condition that Mr. Murray and his fellow-parishioners should recognise the suspended ministers as a Presbytery, which they peremptorily refused to do. Mr. Duncan, agent for the elders and communicants, pressed the claim of Mr. Murray to an answer. "As an elder of the parish, Mr. Murray asks a question. He believes that *you* have no right here at all." Thus pressed, the Moderator said, "We are here as the Presbytery of Strathbogie,— a part of the National Church assembled in the name of our Lord Jesus Christ." At this there was a great manifestation of feeling in the audience, for these Scottish peasants do not identify the Court of Session with the Church of their fathers. In two successive attempts, Mr. Duncan tried to bring the Moderator to an explicit repudiation of the authority of the General Assembly, but in vain. "We are here met," said the Moderator, "as the Presbytery of Strathbogie, and under the protection of the law of the land."

In the name of the congregation, Mr. Duncan now read a protest against the induction, bearing the signatures of the elders and 450 communicants. It expressed the "extreme pain and disappointment" with which the parishioners looked upon the so-called Presbyters "as suspended ministers of the Church of Scotland." Before a competent Church Court, they were fully prepared to substantiate their objections to Mr. Edwards, which, they said, were not frivolous, but grave enough to warrant deposition. They earnestly begged the suspended ministers "to avoid the desecration of the ordinance of ordination," and "solemnly, and as in the presence of the great and only Head of the Church," averred that, should the desecration be accomplished, they would repudiate and disown it, and refuse to regard Mr. Edwards as minister of Marnoch. The proceedings of the pretended Presbytery involved, in their view, "the most heinous guilt and fearful responsibility," dishonour to religion and "cruel injury to the spiritual interests of a united Christian congregation." So said the spokesman of the parishioners.

On finishing this document, Mr. Duncan announced that the parishioners of Marnoch could take no further part in these unconstitutional proceedings, or remain to witness the forcing of a minister on the people. Without tumult or outcry, in silent strength of resolution, the tension of their lips and the hot tears oozing from their eyes alone indicating the depth of their feelings, the people gathered up their Bibles and moved out of the church. Does it not again remind us of Macaulay's words about that people whose "wildest popular excesses" bear trace of "the gravity of judicial proceedings and of the solemnity of religious rites"? Thoughtful onlookers felt that they had never seen before and would never see again a spectacle so full of moral beauty. "No word of disrespect or reproach escaped them." "There were grey-headed men among them," wrote Hugh Miller, "who had worshipped" within these walls "for more than half a century,—men, too, in the vigorous prime of manhood,—others just entering on the stage of active life. All rose and all went away,—many of them in tears. It was the church in which, Sabbath after Sabbath, their fathers had met to worship; it had formed the centre of many a solemn association, many a sacred attraction; and they were now quitting it for ever."

The whole area of the church became vacant. The people passed out into the cold wintry air, and, proceeding to a snow-clad hollow below the knoll on which the church was built, grouped themselves together for a few minutes, and resolved to retire straightway to their homes. Dignity, solemnity, loyalty to all that is morally beautiful in human nature, characterised their conduct from first to last.

Sad as it was for these parishioners to quit the walls in which they had worshipped since childhood, they well knew that the Church of Scotland did not forsake them. The husk of endowment had been snatched away, the kernel of spiritual Christianity was well cared for by the Church. When the people vetoed Mr. Edwards, the patron, as was in a great majority of instances the case, had shown no objection to co-operate with the Church and the congregation in settling another man, and had issued a second presentation in favour of Mr. D. Henry. It is a significant fact that, both in relation to Crown patronage and private patronage, the Church might never have got into difficulty had it not been for the officiousness of lawyers. Mr. Henry, acceptable to the people, was in due course ordained minister of the parish. He had as yet no church, no stipend. But the heart of Scotland had been touched by the spectacle of the Court of Session settlement in Marnoch, and there was no insuperable difficulty either in building him a church or in providing him with a living. A large church, with a church-tower and "a handsome and commodious parsonage" immediately adjoining, arose in the outskirts of the village of Marnoch. "The parish church still stands on the hill, but the parish families have ceased to go up to it ever since that wintry day when it ceased to be occupied by a minister of the Church of Scotland, and passed into the hands of a ministry provided for it by the Court of Session. The National Church, whose principles and whose honour they so nobly upheld in 1841, was in 1843 disestablished like themselves,— and they and their minister have, since the Disruption, formed part and parcel of the Free Church of Scotland."

It is necessary to take a glance—a brief and cursory glance will be enough—within the walls from which the flock had retired, in order to see how the work of ordination was proceeded with by that Presbytery which, submitting to act as part of the official machinery whereby the Court of Session had superseded the Courts of the Church, still affirmed itself to be part of the National Church and obedient to the law of the land.

No sooner was the area laid bare by the departure of the parishioners, than the mixed multitude that filled the galleries rushed, with tumult and flinging of snowballs, into the vacant space. "The unhappy intrusionist ministers were pelted with snowballs and other disagreeable though not very deadly missiles, while shouts and groans and hisses assailed them." There were menacing symptoms of a riot; but a magistrate, of firm nerve and known to be in sympathy with the cause of Church and people, having been promptly sent for, had little difficulty in restoring tranquillity. The ordination then took place with the usual formalities, one of these being that the Dean's minister professed his belief in "the whole doctrine contained in the Confession of Faith." One part of that doctrine is, that the government of the Church is divinely placed in the hands of Church officers, "distinct from the Civil Magistrate.

CHAPTER XXIII.

The Assembly of 1841—Patronage.

IT was out of patronage that all the troubles of the Church had arisen. From the sixteenth century she had been engaged intermittently in conflict with the system, never quite conquering it, always feeling it to be at variance with Christian freedom. Even the Moderates had never adopted it so openly as to try to abolish the congregational call; and the High Presbyterian party, looking upon its reintroduction by the Act of Queen Anne, after temporary expulsion, as a violation of the Union, had constantly and keenly made war upon it.

Andrew Thomson had organised an association for gradually buying up patrons' rights, and giving full effect to the call. One of Thomson's most ardent coadjutors in this movement had been Cunningham; but in Thomson's lifetime Cunningham had not proposed that the Church should, either by legislation of her own or by appeal to Parliament, make a complete end of patronage. Acquainted as he was with every nook and by-way of Scottish Church history, he was aware that, in 1642, when the Church was in great power, she had not considered it her duty to sweep patronage wholly away, but had arranged a method by which its bad effects were minimised. He would have been content to see patronage and parochial liberty reconciled, as they were by the Veto Act, that felicitous measure which, when patrons were devout and noble-minded, and, like the Crown, magnanimously fair both to the Church and to the people, worked with smoothness and beneficence. But when the Church was pertinaciously attacked for having attempted to combine the exercise of patronage with the edification of parishioners, and when great legal authorities attempted to make her jurisdiction in things spiritual a mere ceremonial accompaniment of the Court of Session's jurisdiction in things temporal, then Cunningham looked with fiercer glance upon patronage than he had ever done before, and threw his heart into an agitation for the extirpation of the system, root and branch. His plan was to go frankly to Parliament, and, representing that patronage brought the Church and the Court of Session into strangling complications, to petition for its abolition.

In the Assembly of 1841 he advocated this course, branding patronage as a plant which God had not planted, and showing that it neither received countenance from Scripture nor had ever been heartily concurred in by the Church.

Chalmers had never been an impetuous opponent of patronage. He had clung to the idea that, as one element in settlements, it might have no malignant effect. But he was beginning to feel it to be, in its results, intolerable. Candlish kept pace with Cunningham. A close friendship sprang up between these two. Among the laymen, perhaps the most vehement opponent of patronage was Mr. Maitland Macgill Crichton. Guthrie beat down the plausibilities of its defenders with his great flail of common sense.

The very name of Macgill Crichton seems to sound familiar to those versed in Presbyterian history, and Hugh Miller has remarked how naturally one would have looked for him among the vanquishers of Claverhouse at Drumclog. He was of Herculean build, and had outstripped a mail-coach in a twenty mile race. From spinal cord to finger tips he thrilled with the devout patriotism of old Scotland. His qualities as a platform speaker were excellent, his thinking forcible, his words brief and strong, winged with enthusiasm for his principles and his friends, and prickly with sarcasm for his adversaries. Crichton saw the extreme folly of elaborately setting up an Establishment, and then binding it to conditions that defeated its primary purpose. "While liberty of conscience," he said, "should be preserved inviolate, and all left free to conform or to dissent as they thought fit, the National Church ought to be restricted and crippled by no conditions calculated to repel the people from her communion." "Is it," he asked, "consistent with the purity of the Church, or with the spiritual liberty of Christ's people, that the sacred trust of electing pastors should not only be taken from the members of the Church, but so disposed as common worldly property, that all its holders may be—and, in fact, the great majority are—either alien or hostile to her communion?" With a warmth recalling that of Hugh Miller on the same subject, he denounced the calumny that Scottish congregations were less capable than patrons of electing their ministers. "Can it for an instant be admitted that the voice of the congregation, speaking by the majority of its communicants, in a matter of such dear and sacred interest to themselves and to their children, is entitled to no more weight than the voice of my lord or squire, himself an alien to our Church, who may dictate to the people their future pastor? I proclaim such a statement to be a libel upon my countrymen, the Christian people of Scotland."

But the body of the Evangelicals were not yet able to keep up with Cunningham, Candlish, and Macgill Crichton. It was almost a drawn battle between these and the phalanx of the Moderates, reinforced by not a few of the weaker-kneed members of the opposite party. Dr. Cook had 138 votes, Cunningham 135, in the all but drawn battle, in the Assembly of 1841, on the Abolition of Patronage.

CHAPTER XXIV.

The Moderates Strike their Flag.

BY no means so nearly balanced were the parties on the crucial question, also discussed in the Assembly of 1841, of the attitude which the Church ought now to assume toward the Legislature. The Earl of Aberdeen had already made his well-meant but feeble and ill-starred attempt to pass such a measure as might restore peace between the Church and the Court of Session. His proposal was to give the people power to reject for specified reasons. It bred an infinitude of wrangling and heartburning,—nothing else. The Duke of Argyll had now prepared a Bill which, being substantially at one with the Veto Act, would have removed the cause of contention. The Evangelicals most earnestly desired, therefore, that the Moderate party should combine with them in presenting a united front to the Legislature in support of the Duke's measure. Dubious as it might be whether the House of Lords would in any case lend a favourable consideration to the Bill, they were certainly more likely to do so if it came with the unanimous approval of the

Assembly than if it were opposed by the Moderate party.

A resolution, therefore, was moved by Candlish, pledging the Assembly to offer no opposition to "a measure fitted to put an end to the collision." He appealed to the minority, in a speech of which the feeble echo that remains is evidently inadequate to convey to us any just idea of its pathos or its power; but to judge from what has been said of it, and by its effect at the time, it must have been a rare masterpiece. Its main leverage as an appeal to the Moderates was derived from the terrible position of the majority as shut up by conscience to rend the Establishment in twain if the Bill were rejected, whereas the minority could not allege that they were bound in principle to obstruct it. They had no conscientious objection to Non-intrusion. They had never ceased to affirm that they held the Church to have no King but Christ. Would they not, for their brethren's sakes, for the sake of the Church in whose courts the two parties had so long dwelt together, make a public statement to this effect? More was not asked of them. "By such a statement," cried Candlish, "they will prove themselves the most generous, the most disinterested, the most seasonable benefactors the Church ever saw." So deeply did the Assembly seem to be moved, that he believed himself to have prevailed. "I rejoice," he said, "that I have been the humble instrument under God of bringing the House to its present state of mind." "I am speaking under a weight of responsibility deeper than I ever felt before, I am speaking under an apprehension of the impending calamities with which our beloved Church is threatened."

But he was mistaken. The tokens of emotion had been superficial and misleading. The Moderates praised the speaker, were liberal of polite expressions, but were at heart unmoved. They would not expose themselves to the slightest risk of offending the civil authorities, and held doggedly to the policy of accepting, with bated breath and whispering humbleness, whatever course the legal tribunals chose to mark out. They struck their flag. The State was for them henceforward the Church. They had not the courage even of Oliver Twist, and did not dare to *ask* the Government to pass a healing measure, without first going through the humiliation of hauling down the Veto Act, and thus acknowledging that the independence of the Church, of which they had so often talked, did not enable her to decline to be made an instrument in forcing pastors upon parishioners. The body of the Moderates voted against Candlish's resolution. The Duke of Argyll could tell the House of Lords that his measure was supported by 230 against 125,—a majority of nearly two to one,—but he could not say that the Church was unanimous in desiring its enactment.

One would like to be able to yield something more than a cold theoretic assent—to yield an assent implying some slight sympathetic warmth—to the sincere conscientiousness of the noblest of the Moderates, to Robertson, of Ellon, for example, on this occasion. But it is really difficult to get footing on so thin a razor-edge of conscientious principle as Robertson defined for himself and his brethren. What he objected to was the prevalence allowed to Christian will, apart from specified reasons. "I am not," said Robertson, "without a groundwork of principle for what I state in this House. The Scriptures of truth assert that Christian men, in dealing with one another, when they have a charge to make, should have reasons for the charge; and surely, when Christian men have a charge against the person appointed to be their pastor, they should have reasons to give for it, openly and fairly, that all the world may judge of it."[1]

It is not easy to understand how, except in the heat of debate, Robertson could have imagined that there was any analogy between bringing a charge against a man and declining to have him as a pastor. Does one make a charge against a parliamentary candidate when he refuses him as his representative? Does a woman make a charge against a man when she declines him as a husband? A minister might be a perfect crampfish in all spiritual respects, and yet challenge accusation in any Court in the world. It was a curiously constituted conscience that could resist Candlish's appeal rather than allow Scottish communicants to escape heckling as to their spiritual reasons for disapproving of a presentee. And, alas! the fact remains—closing on Moderate brotherliness and intrepidity like a coffin-lid—that, until the Court of Session cast menacing glances at glebe and stipend, the Moderates, now so jealous of disapproval without reasons, had acquiesced smilingly in the Veto Act!

[1] *Life of Robertson*, by Charteris.

CHAPTER XXV.

The Scottish Hildebrand.

THE work of this memorable Assembly of 1841 was not yet done. The seven ministers forming the majority of the Presbytery of Strathbogie had flagrantly broken the law of the Church. The principal business before the Assembly was to put discipline in force against the rebels. They had disregarded the sentence of suspension. They had profaned the rites of ordination. Would the Church proceed to their deposition? In the sixteenth century, in breaking from the Papacy, she had professed to carry over with her every power and privilege rightly claimed by the Universal Church. Would she now dare, in the blaze of nineteenth century enlightenment, to apply to the Strathbogie ministers and their district the same discipline, in all spiritual respects, under which, in the Middle Ages, pastors and districts had been laid by the Church of Rome?

She did not hesitate. Chalmers himself made the motion that the seven ministers of Strathbogie, who had disobeyed the Church and broken their ordination vows, should be deposed from their office, and forbidden to preach or administer the sacraments. Never had he occupied so agitating a position. Never had there been more painful conflict in his breast between the claims of the Establishment and the claims of the Church. But the victory had been complete; and now, though earnest and sad, he was collected, firm, and calm. The Church, if established at all, must be established as a living organism, not as a dead machine. Acknowledging that the Church was not infallible, declining to conjecture the pleas to which the Strathbogie ministers might have recourse in the inner court of conscience, he took his stand on the palpable fact that, if their rebellion was passed over, the whole fabric of discipline would come to the ground. "The Church would be left without a government." If the Legislature, on being finally appealed to, should lay this down as the condition of Establishment, then the Church must be prepared "to abjure her connection with the State."

In terms of touching pathos, he expressed his amazement at the spectacle of the rude interference of the Courts of law with the Church, exactly at the time when she was doing with conspicuous success what, by the nature of the case, the State must be supposed to wish her to do. "This is a truly mysterious visitation which has come on the Church of Scotland." Her area had been enlarging, her usefulness had been increasing, her beneficent influence had crossed the threshold of families, and, going out into the streets and alleys, had penetrated "to the lowest depths of the people, giving thereby solidity and strength to the basis of the commonwealth." She had been achieving not only "the primary end of Christianity—the salvation of souls," but " the secondary blessings of education, and regularity, and improved habits, both economical and moral." And just then it was, " when so much could have been done by a conjunction between the piety of the Church and the patriotism of the State," that the Civil Court strikes in, and " a cruel arrest is laid on all this prosperity, and the vision of our fondest hopes is scattered into fragments." The Church could not, for the bribe of peace, make a sacrifice of principle, and therefore he moved that the rebel Presbyters of Strathbogie should be deposed from the office of the holy ministry.

The Moderates now gave fresh proof that they had deserted the cause of the Church. Dr. Cook had made up his mind to run no risks, and adopted the position which every State-Churchman, who feels that the State element and not the Church element is the essential matter in the connection, will naturally adopt. He held by the State. The Church, he averred, had exceeded her powers in the Veto Act. The Court of Session, supported by the House of Lords, authoritatively declared this to be a fact. " Consequently, the determination of the seven Strathbogie ministers not to be guided by that Act, but by the injunctions of the supreme civil tribunals of the country, was in perfect conformity with their duty, and ought not to have subjected them to censure, far less should have occasioned their being served with a libel, for the purpose of their being deposed should the libel be proved, or the charges which it contains be admitted." He moved that the ministers should be let alone, remaining in all respects as if no proceedings had been taken against them. A nobleman of no personal weight having seconded Dr. Cook's motion, there rose to reply the Rev. William Cunningham.

It was evident that he was in his most earnest mood, his whole intellectual nature, his whole moral nature, stirred to their depths. Having put aside certain irrelevancies and generalities with which the case had been cumbered, " he would first," he said, " venture to assert, on the facts judicially admitted by these men, that there was abundant ground for maintaining that they had broken the laws of the Church ; secondly, that they had violated their ordination vows ; and thirdly, that they had been guilty of a sin against the Lord Jesus Christ." A buzz of startled and angry remonstrance ran through the Moderate ranks at the word " sin." That kind of alarmed surprise among his hearers at the sweep of his logic, or the audacity of his statement, or the impetuous vehemence of his manner, always acted finely upon Cunningham, making him as calmly self-possessed and proudly defiant as the thunder of artillery and the smoke of battle have made some great generals. He paused ; gave every one time to reflect ; and then went on. " He never, so long as he was a member of a Christian Church, would give his consent to the deposition of any man from the holy ministry, unless he could conclusively prove that the man had been guilty of a sin against the Lord Jesus Christ." " But if they were prepared both to aver and conclusively to prove it, then he believed that the sentence of deposition they were called this evening to pronounce, was a sentence that would be ratified in heaven."

As he proceeded with his argument, it could not but be felt that its links were of hammered iron. In no age of the Church of Scotland had her ministers been permitted to disown her jurisdiction and defy her commands without incurring the supreme penalty. In 1648, when the Westminster Standards had been accepted, and the Church had not yet been subjected to Cromwell's physical force, she had expressly decreed, "if any suspended minister, during suspension, shall exercise any part of the ministerial calling, he shall be deposed." Glancing back to the early Christian centuries, Cunningham showed that the Church of the West had always inflicted supreme punishment upon pastors who defied the restraints of discipline. The ordination vows of the libelled ministers were, in the next place, explicit. "They solemnly promised to be subject to the judicatories of this Church, to maintain the unity of this Church against error and schism, notwithstanding of whatever trouble or persecution may arise." And yet, by their own admission, they had applied to the Court of Session to overrule and cancel the discipline of the Church.

Viewing the matter for a moment in the light of common sense and the general usage of civilised life, he argued that such conduct as that of the libelled ministers was at variance with justice. In entering the ministry, they had accepted the spiritual government of the Church, and practically divested themselves of the right to apply to the Civil Power against the Church. They had "applied for admission into a certain society, which imposed certain restrictions upon that admission. Such is the case even in many corporations, which, with perfect justice and equity, bind their members not to use any privileges they may receive by becoming members, as against the society into which they had been admitted." If there was any one restriction to which a man entering voluntarily upon the ministry of the Church of Scotland might be supposed to subject himself, with clear consciousness that he was doing so, it was the restriction of his right or power to bring the Church as a culprit to the bar of the Court of Session.

Reference had been made to the oath of allegiance taken by the Strathbogie ministers. Cunningham declared that the oath of allegiance bound all subjects to loyalty to Queen Victoria, but "by the Constitution of Great Britain" she had no spiritual jurisdiction in Scotland. "As an ecclesiastical Court, they were perfectly independent of all interference in ecclesiastical matters, even under the oath of the sovereign, who has no more authority (in Scotland) to regulate these matters than to levy taxes without the consent of Parliament." Since the Revolution Settlement, in 1688, "down to the age in which we live, no such claim as this had ever been put forth, nor any such power or prerogative been enjoyed, with respect to Scotland, by sovereigns of Great Britain, or any officer holding his powers from the sovereign."

There remained the sin, in its strictest sense, against Christ, which the speaker had imputed to the ministers. By their own statement they had applied to the Court of Session to suspend the sentence of the Church. "Now this latter step," said Cunningham, "was plainly a renunciation of the allegiance they owed to the Lord Jesus

Christ as the only King and Head of His Church; it was plainly a denial of His sole Headship and supremacy, and of the truth contained in the Confession of Faith, and ratified by the law of the land, that Jesus Christ is King and Head of His Church. It plainly involved a denial of the position that to His office-bearers, and to them alone, is committed the power of the keys. Would any one venture to deny that the Court of Session had assumed the power of the keys, and had thereby broken both the law of God and the law of the land, and been guilty of great sin? And of all this sin these men were the authors and originators." The offence, therefore, of the ministers was "neither more nor less than high treason against Jesus Christ, since it was a blow aimed at the very existence of the Church as a distinct society, exercising functions and enjoying privileges derived from Him, and to be regulated by His word."

Thus did the Hildebrand of the Reformed Catholic Church in Scotland assert the inalienable right and duty of the Church to give effect to the law of Christ in His visible kingdom upon earth. It was not permitted to the Church to transfer to the State that guardianship of the liberties and rights of the visible body of Christ which He had committed to herself. Cunningham did not condescend even to argue with those who traced the spiritual independence of the Church to the concession of the State. The State could not confer what it was a sin on the part of the State to usurp. It was an aggravation of the sin of the ministers that they had consented to act as accomplices and tools of the Civil Power in its encroachments on the spiritual jurisdiction of the Church.

In the impetuosity of his assault upon the Church's foes, Cunningham seemed, in fact, to proceed on the principle of cutting the Church clear of the State and its temporalities together, leaving it to dispose of the wreck of Establishment as it thought fit, and looking only heavenward for guidance and support.

If the Presbyterian doctrine of the Headship is unreservedly accepted,—if the Church cannot, without disloyalty to Christ, abdicate self-government in matters spiritual,—the main contention of Cunningham's speech on the deposition of the Strathbogie ministers is unanswerable. The Moderate party, determined to maintain at all hazards the connection with the State, put forward its ablest man to endeavour to show that the violation of principle was not so clear, the crisis not so grave, as Cunningham averred. Mr. Robertson, of Ellon, respected by both sections of the Assembly, a man of devout character and solid though not shining parts, argued with dexterity on the difficulties involved in the position of the Strathbogie ministers, urging that, as a matter of fact, they had been perplexed between the Courts of the Church and the Courts of the State, and that it was hard to inflict on them the tremendous punishment of deposition for getting mystified between the two. "It was true that these gentlemen had come under the ordination vows; and he had no doubt that they took these vows honestly, and firmly determined to adhere to them in the spirit in which they were taken. But he must also advert to the fact that these gentlemen had previously taken the oath of allegiance to the Constitution of the country, and were bound to adhere to that Constitution as explained by the Civil Courts of the country."

He tried also, with ingenious amiability, to have it taken for granted that they had really, in the silence of their consciences, appealed to the Head of the Church against the sentence of suspension before disregarding it. But the keen eye of Mr. Dunlop discovered in their own statement an awkward comment on this view of their position. "After being suspended," they had themselves avowed, "they discharged no duties till after the decision of the Civil Court" cancelling the sentence of their ecclesiastical superiors. Fear of the Civil Power, and not a conviction that the Church was breaking Christ's law, had been their motive. In short, they had obeyed the State, in direct contravention of the commands of the Church; that was a palpable fact; and if the Crown Rights of the Redeemer had any meaning in the creed of the Church of Scotland, this was to set those Crown Rights at nought. The Assembly voted with Chalmers and Cunningham, against Cook and Robertson, by 222 against 125. That same night the sentence of deposition upon the seven Strathbogie ministers was solemnly pronounced by Dr. Chalmers.

"Ratified in heaven" was most assuredly the comment upon all this, which, if not by word of lip, then by swelling of breast and tears of solemn joy, passed from group to group of patriot Presbyterians throughout Scotland. But the austerity of the Church added immensely to her difficulties. Easy-going, good-natured statesmen were offended and vaguely alarmed. Soft-hearted people wavered. There is a logic of the feelings as well as of the intellect that influences events. The Strathbogie seven might be utterly indefensible, but they had been weak rather than wicked. They would have acted as heroes if they could, and to many it seemed hard to depose them from the ministry and put the brand of sin upon them for not deciding heroically between Church and State.

Dr. Buchanan mentions, somewhat curtly, that the Rev. Mr. Clark, of Inverness, supported by Mr. Brodie, of Monimail, came forward at the last moment, before the motion for deposition was made by Chalmers, and urged that the sentence should be suspension for an indefinite time. Mr. Clark had been an Evangelical of unsullied record, and was distinguished in private life by sympathy, gentleness, and kindness. No one could better represent than he the logic of the heart. By adopting his suggestion, which was not listened to, a golden bridge might have been left for the return of the banished, and the Moderates and their allies in Parliament might have felt that the Church was in a placable mood. But who could now wish that half-measures had been adopted?

CHAPTER XXVI.

Guthrie.

AMONG the supporters of Cunningham in his direct assault upon patronage, and in his terrible argument against the mutineers of Strathbogie, was Thomas Guthrie. A very noticeable figure, he, among the fathers and founders of the Free Church. In the bloom of early manhood, six feet three in height, eager for battle as the war-horse in Job, but inspired only by the ambitions of the army of Christ, he had lately been discovered in a country parish and almost dragged to Edinburgh and fame. Less completely cased in the panoply of theological system than Cunningham, less brilliant and dazzlingly quick in his intellectual action than Candlish, and therefore less powerful than they in dealing with cultured and critical audiences, he could sway a common crowd more absolutely than either. If theirs was more close, formal, invulnerable logic, he had more of varying colour and of fascinating pleasantness. And as we look backward across the intervening years, we perceive that neither of those two rose subsequently so conspicuously above his Disruption renown as Guthrie, or had, at the time of his death, so unmistakably the whole English-speaking race for admirers and onlookers. Even Dr. Duff lived to see that Guthrie's fame had filled the world,— that no Scotchman's, and "assuredly no Free Churchman's, since the death of Dr. Chalmers, bulked so largely as his." The eloquence that had charmed the simple parishioners of Arbirlot proved potent to move great audiences in Manchester and London. Florid as a "careless ordered garden," or a picturesque forest avenue, festooned with tendrils and loosely hung with draperies of eglantine and the mountain rose,—exhaustless in anecdote, rich in broad innocent fun, and with pathos welling up straight from the heart,—the oratory of Guthrie was separated by a hair's-breadth from turgid and tawdry bombast, but yet was so absolutely sincere, so racy, so much in keeping with the aspect and enunciation of the man, that it was always and magnificently successful.

It would be wrong to infer that the perfect sincerity of the orator implied in every case that his anecdotes and illustrations were literal transcripts of fact. Or rather, we may say that, except in cases of arithmetical statement, his imaginative genius, perhaps without his knowing it, cast a light, a colour, an indefinable addition upon the naked fact. The eye sees what it brings with it the faculty to see, and the imaginative artist always obeys Turner's rule of painting his impressions. He gives the truth, but he has a way of putting it which is his own. The glance of Guthrie's eye made a thing more piquant than it found it. An illustration of our meaning, trivial in itself, occurs in one of his own illustrations, derived from his recollections of a stroll through London. We have all seen those collections of naturally hostile animals, forced to live in one cage, and suspend their natural instincts, whose listless and torpid repose belies too sadly their description as a "happy family." Guthrie saw one such family, and this is his account of it: "I saw the mavis asleep under the wing of a hawk; and an old, grave, reverend owl looking down most complacently on a little mouse; and, with the restless activity of his species, I saw the monkey sitting on a perch, scratching his head for an idea, I presume, and then reach down his long arm to seize a big rat by the tail, and, lifting it to his breast, dandle it like a baby!" The hawk, the mavis, the owl, the mouse, the monkey, the rat, were doubtless all there. Guthrie stated with veracity the impression they made upon him. But it is scarcely conceivable that their attitudes and avocations should have been so hyper-idyllic as he depicts them. Thus, however, it was that the flash of his genius, so full of humour and quaint feeling, lit up with a comicality, a pathos, a graphic vividness, circumstances which, to a common observer, might have been merely commonplace.

At other times, however, we are reminded, by a self-evidencing literalness of detail, that no rule can be laid down for the operations of descriptive genius. An indubitable literalness pertains to Guthrie's description of the proceedings of his large Scotch dog, Bob, which had been sent fifteen miles away in disgrace for worrying cats, and had come back of his own accord. "On going to the manse," says Guthrie, "I found Bob outside the gate, as flat, prostrate, and motionless as if he had been stone dead. It was plain he knew as well as I did that he had been banished, and had returned without leave, and was liable to be hanged, drowned, shot, or otherwise punished at will. I went up to him, and stood over him for a while in ominous silence. No wagging of his tail, or movement in any limb; but there he lay as if he had been killed and flattened by a heavy roller, only that, with his large, beautiful eyes half-shut, he kept winking and looking up in my face with a most pitiful and penitent and pleading expression in his own. There was no resisting the dumb but eloquent appeal. I gave way, and exclaimed in cheerful tones, 'Is this you, Bob?' In an instant, knowing that he was forgiven and restored, he rose at one mighty bound into the air, circling round and round me, and ever and anon, in the power and fulness of his joy, nearly leaping over my head." That is a photograph.

A word of apology may be due to the reader for beguiling him even momentarily into the trivialities of literary criticism, when our main subject is identified with the dearest and most sacred interests of nations: but Guthrie made conscience even of his methods of literary composition; and if we would know the man, and get close up to him,—to hear, so to speak, the beating of his heart,—we shall do well to realise how vividly awake he was to everything of which his observational faculty could take account, from dogs and monkeys up to street boys and State Churches. Interested in all things, he made all things interesting. "I have a distinct recollection," said one who knew him in his country charge, "of admiring the *vivaciousness* which he imparted to the sacred narrative;" and another, speaking also of what he had seen at Arbirlot, tells us how "the dull eye of the cow-boy and of the servant girl, who had been toiling all the week among the horses and cows, immediately brightened up" when Guthrie addressed them.

He got much from nature, little from books. No man could have been more characteristically Scotch, and no one can understand him and do him justice without understanding and doing justice to what there is of sterling worth and sound capacity in the noble type of Scotchmen. The blood of the Covenanting Guthries ran in his veins though he could not produce documentary proof of the fact, and his consciousness of this was among the influences that had strengthened and elevated him, and prepared him "to contend, and suffer if need be, for the rights of Christ's crown and the liberties of His Church."

His grandmother was notably Scotch. Fasting and praying one whole day every week, she showed that those who derived their faith from the Covenanters might practise the religious exercise of fasting as well as Anglo-Catholics. But she could "set to the mark," as his country neighbours said of Oliver Cromwell,—she could discern the essential thing and do it,—in other matters besides fasting and prayer. One of her sons, for example, was pining for a farmer's daughter whom he was too bashful to ask in marriage. What could be done? She "orders her sheepish lad to saddle a horse." He in the saddle, she on a pillion behind him, "she directs him to ride straight to the house of his sweetheart; and on arriving there, before he, the lout, has got the horse well stabled, she has done the work of a plenipotentiary, and got the affair all settled with the lass and her parents." Guthrie's habit of striking to the heart of things, and not going about them and about them in irrelevant gyrations, was quite in the style of this prevailing parent.

In his father's house he witnessed perfect honour in all transactions, and an unaffectedly sincere and not ungenial although constant and somewhat rigorous exercise of religion. It does not appear that he passed through any of those mental struggles and agonies which have frequently preceded the life-long devotion of themselves, by great preachers and missionaries, to the service of Christ; but on this point we cannot be quite sure, for though Guthrie was, generally speaking, as emotional and communicative as a child, the typical Scot is prone to silence as to the personal dealings of his soul with God. He said of himself with expressive truthfulness, that he had a "healthy constitution," and, so far as is known, this gradually developed, amid the kindly influences of a Christian household and a Christian country, into a healthy Christian manhood. As a boy he was frank, brave, adventurous, passionately fond of fighting, but with as chivalrous an absence of hatred or spite in his combats as ever a Bayard or a Cœur de Lion. Neither at school nor at college did he read much, and his education consisted mainly in drinking in from the atmosphere, during eight or ten years of life in Brechin and Edinburgh, the ideas of his time.

One might have expected him to be smitten in those years with the metaphysical enthusiasm that haunted Scotland's metropolitan University; but, boy and man, his grip was always on the concrete, and for abstractions he had no interest or care. So far as he was a student at all, it was science that charmed him; and he was so fond of medical subjects and medical treatises, that he would have made no bad shift as *locum tenens* for a general practitioner. If not bookish, he was constantly educating himself by the exercise of his observational and receptive faculties, and by judging among the questions of his day. A massive sense of what was right and true and simple, as contrasted with wire-drawn refinements and fantasticalities and affectations and posturings,—a mind decisively of the gravitative, not of the magnetic order,—rendered him marvellously trustworthy as an adviser in practical emergencies. Extremely valuable, therefore, to all who wish to ascertain the very truth in the matter, are his utterances and decisions in connection with the Church conflict.

As was natural for a pious and noble-hearted Scottish boy, he aspired to shine in the pulpit and beckon his fellow-men on the way to heaven. He had a profound enthusiasm for his profession. "As an ambassador for Christ," he said, "I regard a preacher of the gospel as filling the most responsible office any mortal can occupy. His pulpit is, in my eyes, loftier than a throne; and of all professions, learned or unlearned, his, though usually in point of wealth the poorest, I esteem the most honourable. That office is one angels might covet."

He was early enlisted in the anti-Moderate party, and in a manner creditable to him and little creditable to Moderatism. The son of an influential local politician, he found himself, before he had been half a year in the ministry, in a position to decline or accept presentation to one of the best livings in Scotland. If he would declare his adherence to the Moderate party, the living was his. Dr. Nicoll, of St. Andrews, was at the head of the party, and the faintest of assentient whispers in Dr. Nicoll's ear would secure the preferment. Dr. Nicoll "would ask no questions," said Guthrie's advisers, " nor attempt to bind" him by express paction. "But," says Guthrie, " regarding the waiting on him as, though a silent, a distinct pledge that he and the Moderate party would have my vote in the Church Courts, I refused to go." A sure proof of constitutional soundness of character! The case was evidently one in which a young man with any super-sublety in him, any lurking selfishness, any sneakish trick of self-deception, might have sophisticated himself into accepting the benefice.

He was from the first an Evangelical, but always more or less of a free-lance. Thus, while supporting Chalmers in his enterprise of Church Extension, and always ready for the *gaudia certaminis* in a platform tournament with Dr. Ritchie and the Voluntaries, he was prepared to share the benefits of Establishment with Dissenters to an extent which his brethren of the State Church hardly approved. " The Dissenters," he says in his Autobiography, " had preserved religion, and made up for her (the Church's) lack of service for many years in many parts of the country; and I would have had these services practically acknowledged by our asking the Government, when we sought the endowments for the purpose of extending the Church, to endow any and every party who, though seceders from the Church of Scotland, adhered to her standards." A most generous idea! He agreed, however, cordially with Chalmers, that the kindling of eloquent pulpit torches at intervals in great towns, to attract butterfly congregations from all points of the compass, is a matter of small importance as compared with the preaching of the gospel to the poor within limited parochial areas, where they can be visited, one by one, in their own dwellings. Many years afterwards, he avowed his conviction that the excitement of the Voluntary controversy had led the antagonists on each side to go further in the vehement assertion of their respective principles than truth required. In furious renunciation of State-Churchism, the Dissenting extremists would have "landed the country in practical Atheism," while "we" of the Establishment "perhaps erred as far and as much, in representing the Church of Christ as dependent almost for its very existence, certainly for its efficiency, on State countenance and support."

In few men have the nobly combative and the nobly social or aggregative instincts been so illustriously combined as in Guthrie. John Bright was equally combative, but his inability to work in harness made him a conspicuous failure as a Cabinet Minister. Of Guthrie's combative propensities the annals of the Voluntary Controversy and the Disruption Conflict are a succession of illustrative pictures; but before the Disruption he would have magnanimously offered the advantages of Establishment to any Presbyterian willing to accept them, and, after the Disruption, none welcomed more ardently than he the signs of union, none yearned more intensely than he for the day when the Reformed Church of Scotland, with its three main branches, should be again visibly one tree.

In point of fact, he governed himself by broad principles of sagacity and shrewdness, discerning when union was a hindrance and a folly, and when it was strength and beauty. On one occasion he illustrated, from his own experience, the occasional advantage, or indeed the necessity, of division. On his glebe he had a field of corn, and he hired a company of reapers, or "shearers," to cut it for him. They were Scotch rustics, theological and argumentative beyond their class in any land under the sun. They began to discuss the Voluntary Controversy, reaping-hook against reaping-hook, not only making it plain that his corn would never be reaped, but that they were in danger of actually plunging their weapons into each other's breasts. So he insisted upon it that the advocates of Establishment should go to one end of the field and the Voluntaries to the other. He once told this incident on a public platform with such humour, that an old man actually rose and implored him to stop lest he should die of laughter.

Loyal to Chalmers, and doing yeoman's service to his Church and party in Strathbogie and elsewhere, Guthrie nevertheless thought that a wiser course might have been adopted than that of passing the Veto Act. He believed that the desire of Chalmers and Lord Moncreiff to preserve patronage led them to take, fatally, the wrong turn in seeking to neutralise the evils of patronage by the Veto, and to retain what they considered its usefulness as a buffer to popular election of ministers. He would have had them apply to Parliament for its abolition. Liberal in his political sentiments, trusting more than

Chalmers in Democracy, even without the epithet "Christian" prefixed to it, he gloried in the parliamentary Reform Bill, and thought that, if he and his brethren had first made Scotland "from Cape Wrath to the Border" ring with agitation against patronage, and had then gone to the Legislature to have it "utterly abolished," they would have been successful. Who can tell?

Chalmers, at all events, took what seemed at the time to be the safer as well as the wiser and more moderate course; and with him agreed, not only Lord Moncreiff, but the law officers of the Crown. And Guthrie having seen the Church put her hand to the plough, would not have had her look back. That she held from Christ the right to reform herself, and to vindicate the spiritual liberties of her people, whether Parliament sanctioned her or not, he had not a shadow of doubt. He never, therefore, advocated the repeal of the Veto law. Nor could he fail to appreciate the beneficence of the Veto in its practical working. It was indeed most nicely fitted, thus attesting the statesmanlike genius of Chalmers, to exemplify the distinctive Presbyterian merit of securing and wedding together diverse advantages. Its method was neither popular election nor Church election, and yet it was both. Very important also is it to observe that the Veto was practically a success. In an overwhelming majority of instances, it satisfied not only the Church and the parishioners, but the patron. Sensible men, desirous to promote religion in the exercise of their Church patronage, did not consider that their rights were confiscated although one presentee was vetoed by the people, since they were themselves empowered to present another. It was, no doubt, natural for presentees to cling to what, for them, was real property, if they believed that they had a legal title to it; but they could have entered on their incumbencies only as intruded by sheer force on the congregations; and they might be expected to know that, from the earliest times of the Reformed Church in Scotland, intrusion had been against her genius and traditions.

While voting, therefore, with Cunningham against patronage, Guthrie went step for step with Chalmers and the general Evangelical phalanx, as Cunningham also did, in maintaining the Veto. Like Dr. Buchanan, he believed that the tap-root of the Church's trouble lay in the professional jealousy or perversity of lawyers. He was convinced that, as a general fact, "lawyers have always shown a strong bias to curtail the liberties of the Church of Christ, and, with legal bonds, to bind her neck and heel to the State." Like Dr. Buchanan, he signalised Dean of Faculty Hope as the man who, more than any other, by his machinations and manipulations in Edinburgh,—where the trimming, compromising "middleman," Dr. Muir, played clay to the Dean's potter,—and by his earwiggings of Premiers and Cabinet Ministers in London, brought about the catastrophe. The high powers "sitting away in London knew little or nothing of Presbyterianism; ignorant almost to an incredible degree, as Episcopalians in England are, of the characters and constitutions of other Churches than their own. In a quarrel between the Civil Courts, which were their creatures, and the Church of Christ, that claimed independence for herself,—owning no other authority but that of Christ, and no statute-book but the word of God,—naturally, the Houses of Parliament decided against us, and in favour of the Civil Courts: the contest being one whose merits they did not comprehend, and, familiar as they were with the slavish subjection of the Church of England to the State, did not seem able to comprehend."

Thus did Guthrie, great in common sense, advocate the cause of the Church without bitterness but without compromise,—without shilly-shallying, saccharine complaisance, or maudlin mixing up of essentials and nonessentials. Baptised into the science of the nineteenth century, he held no principle superstitiously, and was not fanatical in his State Churchism. He saw that, in subjection to the Court of Session, the Church of Scotland would have been reduced to a far more pitiful officialism even than that of the parliamentary Church of England. In Hooker himself he might have found recognition of the right of the Church to live and to grow, and this forms an adequate logical basis for the contention of the Church of Scotland. "All things natural," says Hooker, "have in them naturally more or less the power of providing for their own safety; and as each particular man hath this power, so every politic society of men must needs have the same, that thereby the whole may provide for the good of all parts therein. For other benefit we have not by sorting ourselves into politic societies, saving only that by this mean each part hath that relief which the virtue of the whole is able to yield it. The Church, therefore, being a politic society or body, cannot possibly want the power of providing for itself; and the chiefest part of that power consisteth in the authority of making laws."[1]

The Church of Hooker has from first to last been the Church of aristocrats. One of the express grounds on which he pleads her claims is that she makes religion acceptable to the rulers of this world, the mighty men of wealth and title. Yet he asserts her authority to make laws. The Church of Scotland, as Guthrie saw her in the past, had been a Church of the people; the Veto law was made by her for the restoration and safeguarding of the sacred rights of the people; and he would rather have gone to prison or to death than beheld the Veto rescinded, the call reduced avowedly to a mockery, and Christ's crown and covenant confessed to be no more than theatrical properties, or mere rhetorical phrases, with which turbulent, ignorant, and vulgar preachers had set off their ecclesiastical histrionism.

[1] Hooker, Book vii. chap. xiv.

CHAPTER XXVII.

Candlish in Shoals and Quicksands.

WE have been viewing the conflict mainly in the Assembly; but all Scotland was now a battlefield between the parties. And the man who was signalled out by the popular instinct as the Achilles of the fray was Candlish. Cunningham was more learned, Guthrie more pictorial and emotional, but no one seemed to appreciate with such piercing lucency as Candlish the interlacing of the people's cause with the Church's cause, the specialty of an Established Church guarding with the spiritual sword of Christ's Kingship the liberties of rustic parishioners.

Much of the enthusiasm with which he was regarded arose, we cannot doubt, from the fact of his glance being on the future. At a great public meeting, held in one of the largest churches in Edinburgh, in the August of 1841, when the Erastian schism of Strathbogie had fairly begun, he boldly contemplated, while earnestly deprecating, Disestablishment. He still hoped that the rulers of the nation would not commit "the great sin of which they would be guilty if they thrust out of the Establishment those who had committed no crime, unless it be a crime to sustain the honour of the great King and Head of the Church." But, if the worst came to the worst, if the inexorable alternative were an Erastian Establishment or none, he would relinquish Establishment and face Disruption. "I am not a worshipper of the principle of an Establishment." He repels the base idea that Establishment alone can lend cohesiveness to the Church, or prevent it from splitting up into sects. "As if that which united us together were our stipends, our manses, and our glebes!" He will not so "dishonour the Church of Christ, which in the beginning had no countenance from the State, and which needs none, and which can go on against the State." Valuing the principle of Establishment when, as in the history and constitution of the Church of Scotland, the freedom of the Church was deemed to be inviolable, he positively disapproved of, and was prepared to denounce, a Church enslaved by the State. "I hold an Erastian Establishment to be worse than none at all." "It is our bounden duty to bear this testimony, that the Church ought to be established on the principles which we are contending for, or that there should be no Establishment in the land at all."

A memorable saying. Perhaps if Candlish were still on earth, and surveyed the history of the Established Church and of the Free Church of Scotland in the light of fifty years, he might recall it, and express satisfaction at his *not* having addressed himself, as he certainly did not, in the years of his activity as a Free

Church minister, to the subversion of the Establishment. The vision that rose before him, when he spoke those words, was that of a Church of Scotland completely Erastianised,—reduced to an official machinery for enabling the Court of Session to thrust pastors upon unwilling parishes. It was not possible that he should realise that one part of the effect of the heroic exertions of himself and his associates was to be the sweeping away of all restrictions on the will of the people in choosing their own ministers in the Scottish Establishment, and that this was to be accompanied by ostentatious obsequiousness towards the Church by the conciliated Court of Session. We may, however, be quite sure that, with whatever comment on his original saying Candlish might have contemplated the result, he would not have regretted the stand he made for the principle of Christ's Headship over the Church, or his impassioned ardour in affirming that this principle is bound up with the rights of the Christian people. Equally confident may we be in affirming that he would not have been conscientiously content with spiritual independence by mere sufferance of the Court of Session, out of regard, not for the Church, but the Establishment.

As a platform speaker, Candlish probably never was surpassed for the precision and lucidity with which he distinguished between things constantly mixed up by confused and stupid persons. To the vague charge of refusing to let the Court of Session draw the line between things civil and things spiritual, he replies, "Do we ask them to take *our* definition of what is civil? Do we say, as the Church of Rome says, We pronounce a case of murder by an ecclesiastical person to be a spiritual matter, and we prohibit you from meddling with it? Do we exempt our persons or properties from their jurisdiction? No, we allow them the same liberty which we claim for ourselves. We do not presume to prescribe to them what is the law, or to describe what is civil; neither do we allow them to prescribe to us, and decide what is ecclesiastical." If the Civil Court gave force to its sentences in temporal effects, in assigning stipends, glebes, and church buildings, and if the Church were allowed to give force to her sentences in spiritual effects, deciding who should minister in the word and the sacraments, who should ordain and be ordained, there would be no collision. If, on the other hand, the Court of Session, directly or indirectly, commanded Presbyteries to ordain ministers, although the Church had commanded them not to do so, then the Court of Session was taking the place of the Church, and the Presbyteries obeying it and defying the Church were rebellious. If the Legislature sanctioned the Court of Session, then an Erastian schism would obviously proceed within the Church, and, in order to preserve her Divine life and liberty, she would be compelled to relinquish Establishment. Candlish's speeches wrote these distinctions in lightning for the pious intelligence of Scotland.

The spectacle of conflict in the headquarters of Presbyterianism attracted attention throughout the whole Christian world, and was viewed with keenest interest by the Presbyterian community in Great Britain and America. Among the champions of the Church, Candlish was recognised as the most conspicuous. Princeton College, New Jersey, unanimously conferred upon him the title of Doctor in Divinity. Intimation of the honour was made to him in a letter couched in terms of warmest admiration. The Church of Scotland is in it named with enthusiasm as "*our* mother Church," and glowing sympathy is professed with her in her contending. "Our whole Church," says the writer, "is awake to the importance of your conflict; nor do I know of a minister, elder, or layman in the length and breadth of this land who does not entirely sympathise with you and the beloved brethren who are so ready to hazard all, that the Lord Jesus Christ may rule as King in His own Church." "With one voice your Moderate Erastian party, led on by Dr. Cook, are condemned as the betrayers of Samson, and as delivering him over to the Philistines. If the unanimous approval of our whole Church can cheer you to continue the conflict, let whatever consequences ensue, be assured that you and your brethren have it." "Your name is as familiar to us as if you resided among us, and were a pastor of one of our churches."

Such sympathy was much required by Dr. Candlish at that point of time, for he was involved in what were for him the most painful and trying experiences of the entire conflict. Spread over many months, fatiguing for the student who now seeks to master them, and inexpressibly tantalising and irritating for those who were then tossed hither and thither in their distracting whirl of hopes and fears, an interminable interchange of negotiations took place. The very least that the Church could conscientiously accept from the State was nonintrusion in parishes, and unchallenged liberty to exercise her own spiritual jurisdiction. Statesmen, in the outset at least of the discussion, may be credited with a wish to preserve the Church as an Establishment, and with a sincere purpose to deprive her of no power or authority which she had previously enjoyed. As Chalmers and the eminent lawyers who acted with him in the Church, and the Law Officers of the Crown whom these consulted, had at first believed the Veto Act to be within the legal competence of the Church; so it had, as we know, been loyally accepted by the British Government, and given effect to, year after year, in the settlement of ministers. When the difficulty occurred, well-meaning politicians concluded that the dissension arose out of a mere misunderstanding, and the Earl of Aberdeen, Sir George Sinclair, and other more or less competent persons, came forward to solve the problem.

With Candlish it was "the very stuff of the conscience" that there should be no settlement of a minister without the consent of the people; and consent, he maintained, was a matter simply of will. To this Lord Aberdeen seems really to have believed himself prepared to yield a substantial agreement. But he insisted that the parishioners should be required to make a statement of their reasons for exercising their veto; and it proved to be impossible for him to define in a satisfactory manner the way in which they were to state those reasons. Since Cromwell's Parliament spent three months in the vain attempt to define an incumbrance, it has been familiarly known how difficult it is for men to agree in the chiselling of phrases, and in the distribution of lights and shades of meaning. For a long time Dr. Candlish applied all the powers of his keenly analytical mind to the production of such a measure as might, without the express abolition of patronage, exclude the possibility of intrusion. Chafing and fretting, he still resolutely endeavoured to make his way through the " shoals and quicksands of doubtful negotiations, depending on doubtful constructions and interpretations of doubtful clauses." But he bitterly felt the worry and the precariousness of such work. Never had he been so painfully exercised. What was mere matter of expediency with statesmen, was the life of his soul for him. " If we should consent to, or act under, such a measure," he cried, " which should come short by a hair's-breadth of a full non-intrusion measure, we should tempt Providence—we should offend God."

Impatient in proportion to the clearness and quickness of his intellectual glance, and of fiery temper though his heart was a well of tenderness, Candlish did at one moment almost, or altogether, lose his self-command in connection with the Lord Aberdeen " negotiations." It was at that crisis when, one impracticable solution after another having been tried, he had schooled himself to fronting all danger rather than recommence the windy war. Just at that moment he was startled by a new movement, initiated by a small but smooth-tongued and busy section in the Church, for beginning once more the dreary round of disputation. He gave way, and uttered his mind. " I have no doubt," he said, " that it will all turn out to be, if not a trick, at least an entire misunderstanding; a new edition of the old game at cross purposes. . . . But I must keep my temper. . . ." When a man comes to this point, he has evidently no longer his temper to keep.

CHAPTER XXVIII.

Lord Melbourne again.

AND if the prospect was thus clouded in the matter of non-intrusion, was it not still darker in respect of the spiritual jurisdiction of the Church? Was it not too clear that the principle of the Headship of Christ, for which he was prepared to shed his blood, was in the eyes of statesmen little more than a jest? We saw how little deference to this sacred principle was displayed by Lord Melbourne at an earlier stage in the conflict. On a later occasion, his Lordship was, by his own express appointment, waited upon on the subject by a deputation from Edinburgh. His demeanour was so rudely frivolous, that we can explain it only by supposing him to have been annoyed by the conduct of an Evangelical leader at a recent Perthshire election, and to have resolved to indemnify himself by making fun of the deputation.

"Who are you?" he began, "and whence do you come?" Reminded that they had been honoured by his own offer of an interview, he consented to hear a few words about the object of their visit. "The law is against you," was his prompt reply.

They ventured to recall to him that the Court of Queen's Bench was actually in collision as to a point of law with the House of Commons at the time.

"Yes, I see," said his Lordship, "the cases are similar,—questions of jurisdiction."

"It would really appear," he went on, "as if all religious bodies now-a-days were determined to be above the law. Why, there is Dr. M'Hale in Ireland. We made a law, saying, 'You shan't call yourself Archbishop of Tuam.' 'But I shall, though,' he replies; 'you had no right to make such a law.' And there is the Bishop of Exeter. We brought in a Church Discipline Bill into the House of Lords,—and immediately the Bishop starts up and tells us, 'You are interfering with the Divine rights of the episcopal office,— you are presuming to legislate on matters above the reach of Parliament, and if you do I won't obey your law.' And now here comes your Church of Scotland. You stand upon your spiritual jurisdiction, and wont allow civil authority to touch it. Eh! isn't that it—Eh?"

And Dr. Buchanan, who was present, tells us that his Lordship laughed heartily at his own joke.

It was indeed a joke to Lord Melbourne. Spiritual jurisdiction is either a jest, or a Popish assumption, or an enigma, for a multitude of persons. But in the sense of Church government by Christ's officers and Christ's law, it is the natural, obvious, and scriptural principle of unity for the Church Universal. It has been the glory of the Church of Scotland to unfold this banner of Christian unity. It is broad enough, when its folds are spread wide by the winds of God, to embrace all

National Churches, all forms of ecclesiastical administration, in so far as these are subservient to the enforcement and dissemination of Christ's principles. *Ubi homines sunt modi sunt;* wherever men congregate, there will be varieties of religious methods and institutions; and each and all of these, in so far as they can be breathed into by the Spirit of Christ, in so far as they guard and develop the life of the Christian organism, admit of being comprehended in the true catholicity of the Christ-governed kingdom of God. Between the scoffing, laughing Melbourne and the fervent Candlish, there could on this subject be no true harmony, no secure arrangement. And though Sir Robert Peel might be grave where Lord Melbourne was gay, they were in substantials at one on the matter.

Never, perhaps, has the office of the Civil Magistrate been more intelligently magnified, than was done by Candlish in a speech delivered in the heat of this conflict. "In a well-ordered Church Establishment," he said, "we hold the independence of the Civil Magistrate as strongly as we hold the independence of the Church; and the independence of the Civil Magistrate in all he is entitled to do *circa sacra*, as well as the independence of the Church in all she is entitled to do *in sacris*. It is of the utmost importance to understand this. The Church is not entitled to control or to resist him in the exercise of his duty. He is equally independent in all he does *circa sacra*, as the Church is independent in all she does *in sacris*. We hold that the Civil Magistrate is not only entitled generally to control all temporal matters, but that he has certain duties to discharge in reference to things spiritual; and we hold him to be entirely independent of the Church, both in his general control of civil matters and in all questions he has to determine and settle *circa sacra*. For example, we are not entitled to compel the Magistrate to establish a Church according to our views; it rests with the Magistrate to say whether he will establish the Church or not, and on what terms he will establish and endow it. In all he does to protect and favour the Church, he acts independently and on his own responsibility. In all his dealings with the Church he is not bound to take the will of the Church as his guide; he is bound to take the word of God in his hand and to act on his own responsibility to God alone. But then he is not entitled to assume the power of the keys; he is not entitled to set himself up in the Church as its governor. The Magistrate may only dispose of the temporalities which the Church enjoys, and do what he thinks fit in regard to all that he has himself given to the Church; that is an exercise of jurisdiction competent to him, which we may not resist."

Could the clearest-headed jurist that ever wrote upon the principles of universal law have treated the subject more temperately or more wisely?

From the officious busybodies who hurried uselessly forward with their nostrums,—their exquisitely poised phrases, by which non-intrusion of pastors was to be combined with non-exclusion of patrons, and harness provided wherein the Court of Session and the Courts of the Church could pull together,—Dr. Candlish pointedly excepted the father and son of the House of Argyll.

The Church, he acknowledged, lay under a debt of obligation to the Duke of Argyll, and not to the Duke alone, but to " a scion of that House, who, yet scarcely at the years of maturity, has put forth one of the best vindications of the Church in our day." This last allusion is to a nobleman who, in the serene and golden evening of an illustrious career, still survives, an object of proud and affectionate trust to all parties among his countrymen, to lend his counsel and guidance to the three branches of the Church of Scotland. His illustrious father aimed at inducing the House of Lords to accept, in substance, the unimprovable Veto Act. This was the best of all the suggested plans; but even this was hopeless.

CHAPTER XXIX.

The Claim of Rights.

WHEN the time came for the Assembly of 1842, the majority felt that the issue of the struggle could not now be long deferred. The Moderates, under the cautious and skilful guidance of Dr. Cook and the hooded Dean, were in a state of schismatic revolt within the pale of the Establishment. The simplicity of the Veto Law, and its unassailable righteousness in safeguarding the spiritual interests, and those only, of parishioners, had not availed the Church. The attempts to improve upon the Veto by the ingenuity of fussy phrase-makers had proved futile, and the Court of Session continued, like a great boa-constrictor, to throw fold after fold of its strangling apparatus over the body of the Church. Under these circumstances the view was more and more passionately held by Cunningham, that peace could never be permanently secured until patronage, by means of which the Court of Session might always contrive to entangle the Church, was abolished. Candlish and Guthrie concurred with him, and Chalmers at length threw the whole force of his influence into the movement of

Cunningham. In the Assembly of 1841, Cunningham was, we saw, defeated by three votes; in the Assembly of 1842 he carried his point by a majority of sixty-nine.

At first glance this course might seem to evince new and fierce aggressiveness on the part of the Reformers. But this was far from being the intention of Chalmers, Candlish, or Cunningham. The refusal of the State to repeal the Patronage Act, on being directly petitioned to do so, would let the Church know how she stood. Patronage, if irremovable, might be checked and qualified, as it had once before been in the history of the Church, without sacrificing the rights of the people or compromising the spiritual jurisdiction, which the Court of Session was now trampling into the dust. It seemed right and proper, under these circumstances, that the Government should be made aware, by a distinct expression of the conviction of the majority of the Assembly, that no effectual, permanent, and harmonious arrangement could, in their opinion, be made without repeal of that fount and origin of the Church's woes, the Patronage Act.

But the petition against patronage was a thing separate and apart from the general scheme or proposal for a settlement, which, under the title of Claim of Rights, the Church, at this Assembly, decided to present to the Government. This celebrated document, the most authoritative of all in respect to the origin of the Free Church, had been drawn up by Mr. Alexander Murray Dunlop. He has already been named in this narrative, and in the roll of Disruption worthies none holds a more tenderly cherished, a more affectionately honoured place than his. Macaulay says of Chatham, that "he loved England as an Athenian loved the City of the Violet Crown, as a Roman loved the City of the Seven Hills;" and with like fervour did Dunlop love the Church of his fathers. "The eldership of the Church in Edinburgh and its immediate neighbourhood," says Guthrie, "who supported the Evangelical or Non-intrusion party, was not less remarkable at that time than the Evangelical party among the clergy. At their head, *facile princeps*, was Alexander Dunlop. He was my most intimate friend. I loved him as a brother, and esteemed him almost above all men. He was so disinterested, so unselfish, so tender-hearted; a man of such delicate honour, so incapable by nature as well as grace of anything low or mean, and withal a devout, humble Christian! He had a grand head and a large heart, and wanted but a voice to have swayed popular assemblies at his will. He sacrificed his interests at the Bar, his prospects of a seat on the Bench, and many things else, to his attachment to the rights and liberties of the Church of Scotland."

Dunlop had been in the conflict from its beginnings, and all its particulars were imprinted in luminous order upon his memory. Never in the history of human character has there been record of a mind in which the innocent guilelessness, the simple transparency, of a child has been so signally combined with the acuteness and the discernment of a consummate lawyer. In stating the grievances of the Church,—in pointing out how her spiritual activities had been impeded, her power to delimit her own membership overborne, her profoundest principles put aside as histrionic phrases or egregious usurpations,—he uttered nothing but what was simply true and entirely unanswerable.

Dr. Buchanan, who prints the Claim of Rights in his Appendix, thus justly describes it: "Its style grave and perspicuous,—its tone calm and solemn,—its facts well chosen, accurately stated, and lucidly arranged,—its argument direct and powerful,—its conclusion clear and resolute,—it must ever be regarded, by all intelligent and candid readers, as every way worthy of the great occasion on which it was to be employed, and of the remarkable event with which it is destined to be inseparably associated in the ecclesiastical history of Scotland."

It opens with a declaration that the Lords of Session, who ought to have protected the Church in the enjoyment of her constitutional liberties, had become her assailants, and proceeds to prove in detail that they have invaded her jurisdiction, subverted her government, coerced her Courts in the exercise of their purely spiritual functions, ordination to the office of the ministry, Church censures, the preaching of the word, and the administration of the sacraments. It concludes with a solemn appeal to "the Christian people of this kingdom, and all the Churches of the Reformation throughout the world who hold the great doctrine of the sole Headship of the Lord Jesus over His Church, to witness that it is for their adherence to that doctrine, as set forth in the Confession of Faith and ratified by the laws of the kingdom, and for the maintenance by them of the jurisdiction of the office-bearers, and the freedom and privileges of the members, of the

Church, from that doctrine flowing, that this Church is subjected to hardship, and that the rights so sacredly pledged and secured to her are put in peril."

Mr. Dunlop, it has been said, was the author of the Claim of Rights. But, in drawing it up, he had been in close correspondence with Chalmers, who at this crisis towered into a pre-eminence worthy of himself. Never had he been raised, by the united force of genius, religion, and patriotism, to a serener or more intense exaltation of spirit. Dr. Gordon, glowing with sympathetic ardour as he thought of him, wrote: "Let us follow the course so plainly and powerfully laid out for us by our venerable and beloved father. I trust that his setting sun will exhibit him to Christendom in a brighter blaze than in all his other works,—leading his brethren in one of the noblest testimonies that have ever been borne to the glorious Headship of our adorable Redeemer."

It was through the influence of Chalmers, or mainly so, that the subject of patronage was kept apart from, and in fact all but directly and by implication out of, the Claim of Rights. He shared, no doubt, in the dislike to patronage. He voted with Cunningham for the petition against it. But he held that, as compared with the sacred principle of Christ's immediate rule in His Church, anti-patronage was a Scottish peculiarity. The central truth of the Headship was common to "the whole of Reformed Christendom," being an assertion of "the great generic and comprehensive privilege which is inherent with every true Church of deciding this" (the formation of the pastoral tie) "and all other purely ecclesiastical questions for themselves." Mr. Dunlop agreed with him as to the propriety of putting the question of jurisdiction " in the forefront of the battle, —or, indeed, making it the battle ; " but he more than doubted whether Chalmers was right in supposing that statesmen would have less objection to that than to Non-intrusion. " So far," said Dunlop, "as I have been able to judge of the sentiments and feelings of statesmen, I think their hostility to the Church's independence is far more intense and inveterate than their hostility to the people having a voice." Sir Robert Peel, he remarks, had said, " we *might* get more power to the *people*, but we would never again get so much to the *Church*."

In moving, therefore, the adoption of the Claim of Rights, Chalmers laid stress upon the encroachments of the Court of Session, and solemnly avowed that it was not possible for the Church to submit to them. Reluctantly but resolutely, " at the expense of every suffering and of every trial," he and his brethren would stand or fall with the " inherent " and not less the " constitutional " liberties of the Church of Scotland. They now sought a clear and final response from the ruling powers. " If the Government be satisfied with the conduct of their own servants, let them consummate the deed which themselves approve of, and let the act of our deprivation appear in its true character, not as the spontaneous doing of so many simpletons among ourselves, but as a great national act of injustice, a flagrant breach of all national honour and good faith."

It was a pathetic sight to behold this old champion of

Church Establishments calling upon his fellows to see the Establishment which he loved so well dismantled rather than degraded. As has often been characteristic of men of genius, there was a vein in his nature of childlike satisfaction in civic pomp, and the form and circumstance befitting great occasions and august institutions. He had been impressed with the ceremonial inauguration of the present Assembly by the Lord High Commissioner. An unusually brilliant circle had attended the representative of the Queen, and glittering carriages, lines of cavalry, martial music, had graced the procession from Holyrood. The contrast between all this and the humiliation of the Church, in being defied by her own ministers and contemptuously trampled on by the Court of Session, had struck him keenly. "It would truly," he had said, "be an egregious travesty, it would make a farce of the proceedings of our General Assembly, a complete laughing-stock of our Church, were there left her no authority to enforce obedience from her own sons. It would present a strange contrast between the impotence of our doings and the pageantry of our forms,—between the absolute nothingness of the Assembly and the mighty notes of preparation,—the imposing cavalcade which accompanied us,—the pealing of the clarionets with which we were conducted into the House on the present occasion. I must say, there is not a heart that beats with more gratification, or feels more elevation, than my own, at the countenance given to our venerable Church at present by the high and honourable of the land; but ours will be the fault, if, untrue to ourselves, if, untrue to our privileges, we shall allow our Church to become a sounding brass and a tinkling cymbal, a hissing and an astonishment to all passers-by."

The motion for the adoption of the Claim of Rights was seconded by Dr. Gordon. It is a name that has not for the first time come up in this history. Gordon was now in his wane, and he had never been of the meteoric kind, or much of a leader in Church Courts; but no man had shone with steadier, mellower, saintlier light in the pulpit or in private life than he. Intrepid and true-hearted, he had placed himself side by side with his country brethren when the Lords of Session had called them from their quiet manses to be scowled upon and reprimanded for having obeyed Christ. He had always been dearly loved and deeply honoured, and had stood on many a platform with Andrew Thomson. "Beautiful," writes one who spoke of what his eyes had seen, "was the repose of his (Gordon's) lofty brow, dark eye, and aspect of soft and melancholy meaning. It was a face from which every evil and earthly passion seemed purged. A deep gravity lay upon his countenance, which had the solemnity, without the sternness, of one of our old Reformers. You could almost fancy a halo completing its apostolic character."

Dr. Gordon now spoke without passion, but no voice could have expressed with deeper earnestness the determination of himself and his brethren, in the event of their claim being disallowed by the Estates of the Realm, to go forward in the path of duty. "We are bound as honest men and as Christian ministers, with all calmness and with all respect, but with all firmness and determination, to tell them that we cannot carry on the affairs of

Christ's house under the coercion of the Civil Courts; and, however deeply we may deplore the loss of those advantages which we derive from our connection with the State, if ultimately the Legislature determine that they will not listen to our claim, then those advantages we must relinquish, because we could not hold them with a good conscience."

The Court of Session party in the Church, with Dr. Cook as their wary Palinurus, and Mr. Robertson, of Ellon, as their most solidly able man and guiding mind, maintained their self-possession on this testing occasion. By way of explicitly declaring that they were on the Court of Session's side, they hung out from their mast-head the flag of surrender on the Veto question. The Veto Act, they submitted, had been referred to as an aggression upon civil rights, and until this aggression ceased the Court of Session proclaimed it to be its duty, in defending the property of patrons and enforcing the Patronage Act, to paralyse the whole jurisdiction of the Church. The Moderates, therefore, in formulating their policy, proposed, first, that the Veto Act should be rescinded. They proposed, secondly, that the principle of the Headship of Christ over the Church should be recognised as so abstract and theological that " conscientious diversity of opinion " might be allowed in its interpretation. " Much," said Dr. Cook, " as we have of late heard of spiritual independence, and much as has been spoken and written about it, it is still of moment to define it, or to endeavour to form clear notions of what is really included under it.

Meekly and with bated breath as the Moderates talked of the Court of Session, they were not prepared to endorse all the proceedings of the Court in its practical enslavement of the Church. Mr. Robertson, for example, admitted that one of the interdicts issued in the Strathbogie case could not be colourably alleged to restrict itself to the civil province. In this very Assembly an interdict of the Court of Session had been pleaded by a clergyman who had been deposed by his Presbytery for theft, and Dr. Cook and Mr. Robertson made no sign of remonstrance against the unanimous decision of the Church to disregard the interdict and ratify the sentence of the Presbytery.

But all the confusion, the seeming inconsistency, the civil and ecclesiastical chaos, which might be shown to exist in Scotland, arose, the Moderates averred, from the abnormal situation in which the Court of Session found itself placed. Let the Church repent, submit, surrender, and all would be well. And Mr. Robertson, of Ellon, laid great stress on what he maintained to be the unwarrantable severity of the discipline exercised by the Church upon those ministers who had appealed to the Court of Session and obeyed its commands. Dr. Cook and Mr. Robertson were now perfectly aware that, if the Claim of Rights were conceded without reservation, there would be a sombre outlook, not for the Strathbogie ministers alone, but for all except the undistinguished rank and file, if even for them, of the Moderate party. The day was past when hope could be entertained of a bloodless victory for the Church, with general amnesty, and obliteration of the old party distinctions.

Mr. Dunlop, whose name is immortalised and reputation imperishably established by the Claim of Rights, spoke very nobly on this the crowning day of his life. " Our forefathers," he said, signalising the illustrious part played by the Church of Scotland in history, " secured, in this corner of Christendom, the recognition, by the State, of the spiritual independence of the Church, showing how the Church, acknowledging the implicit obedience due to the temporal power in matters temporal, may yet, while supported and aided by the State, conduct her own government and advance the cause of religion in spiritual freedom and independence, with mutual harmony and peace. They thus obtained for the Church of Scotland a position among the governments of the nations which she has ever since retained." But a change had taken place. The powers of the world had endeavoured to enslave the Church. " From the very walls erected for our security they have assailed us, and the guards set to protect us have used the weapons entrusted to them for our defence to conquer and enslave us." The Court of Session had encroached, the land had rung with conflict. " But the din of the contest has recalled the multitudes, who had almost forgotten our existence, to a sense of the importance of the post which we occupy." The people of Scotland have seen that their Church is alive once more, and throughout the world a vivid interest is manifested by Christians in the task wherein they are engaged. " The sympathies of Christians in every part of the world are turning toward us; in this Assembly, from England, from Ireland, from America, from Switzerland, from Prussia, we have encouragement by letter, or by personal presence of ministers of the gospel, all deeply sympathising with us in our struggle for the rights of the Church of God in connection with the kingdoms of the earth. Defending the citadel which, as a Protestant Establishment, we possess, we afford a rallying point to the Christian world, and through it the Churches of Christ may yet establish themselves in the fortress of the world's power, and obtain universally a national recognition of the free and rightful dominion of our great Head and King."

The motion of Dr. Chalmers was adopted, and that of Dr. Cook rejected, by a majority of 241 to 110.

Apart from all question either as to the Christian tenderness or the worldly discretion of the majority in their dealings with the minority, the position taken up by the Church in the Claim of Rights was impregnably strong. As Dunlop simply and calmly said, the Church of Scotland had always claimed to be constitutionally established and yet free. If any man disputes this, he cannot be admitted into the arena of conference or debate upon the subject. She had based her claim to Establishment on her being a true, *i.e.* a free and spiritually independent, Church, always putting Establishment in the second place, not the first. Her distinctive doctrine had from time immemorial been the Headship of Christ over His Church, implying her right to exercise, in Christ's name, all the powers necessary to her life, growth, efficiency, prosperity. On this all authorities, from Oliver Cromwell and Walter Scott to Principal Hill, Dr. M'Crie, Andrew Thomson, Thomas Chalmers, and William Cunningham, are at one.

When had the Church of Scotland relinquished her right and power to make laws for herself, in accordance with the law of Christ, as contained in Scripture, and with the principles and traditions of the Church? When had she scrupled to declare herself a free Church, enjoying, in connection with the State, all the immunities and advantages of freedom? Had she not, from a hundred platforms, hurled back to Voluntaries who questioned her liberty the reply, "I am as free as you"? Could it be alleged of any non-established Presbyterian Church in Scotland or elsewhere that she was impotent to forbid Presbyteries to force ministers upon reclaiming congregations? Could it be alleged of the smallest community of non-established Christians in England or America,— Congregationalists, Baptists Wesleyans,—that they were not free to declare their ministers equal to each other in power and honour? If it really was no lie, but the simple, unadorned truth that the Church of Scotland had not bartered her freedom for Establishment, how could it be pretended that she had overstepped her powers in passing the Veto Act and the Chapel Ministers Act? Be it remembered, that in neither of these did the Church ask a shilling of property. Could she have hauled down the Veto Act and the Chapels Act at the bidding of the Civil Power, without acknowledging before God and man that she had blotted out the traditions in which she gloried, and that, from bearing aloft the banner of Catholic and Christian unity in the van of the Reformed Churches, she had slunk into the rear, and come to heel to the Court of Session, the most crouching and craven of them all?

CHAPTER XXX.

Forecastings of the Convocation.

ECCLESIASTICAL chaos reigned in Scotland. The Court of Session, confident of support from the Government, and tacitly but resolutely guided by the Dean of Faculty, shrank from no extreme in the assertion of its power to coerce the Evangelical majority. The country was convulsed by the dissension between those who put the State first and the Church second, and those who put the Church first and the State second.

We saw how, while the wintry wind moaned over a waste of snow, the parishioners of Marnoch had left their beloved church rather than see a pastor sacrilegiously forced on them by the tools of the Court of Session. At Culsalmond the parishioners had reclaimed almost as strongly as at Marnoch, and when the attempt was made by the Court of Session's ministers to thrust in a minister against their will, they had themselves abstained from violence as had the men of Marnoch; but the general democratic feeling of the country had been roused, and a noisy crowd from the adjacent districts, rushing into the church, interrupted the proceedings, shouted, mocked, and, in fact, compelled the enslavers of the people to beat a retreat to the manse and accomplish their purpose in secret. Lamentable this was, no doubt, but the surgings of sympathetic mobs have been among the accompaniments and indirect effects of many noble revolutions, and Scotchmen who are not ashamed of the doings of Jenny Geddes and her friends in the seventeenth century will not be oppressed with shame for the riotous interruption, in the nineteenth, of the forced settlement of Culsalmond.

In the August following the Assembly of 1842 the House of Lords pronounced judgment in what is known as the second Auchterarder case. The patron and presentee obtained a verdict in their favour, requiring the Presbytery to proceed to the ordination of the presentee, and awarding damages, which the pursuers estimated at £10,000. The actual amount levied might be altered by assessment before a jury, but it was now plain that Presbyters could be heavily fined for declining to obey the Court of Session, and for persisting in obeying the Church, in the settlement of ministers. Imprisonment had been threatened. Fines were imposed. The atmosphere of Scotland, becoming electric, vibrated with an excitement stronger than any she had known since the Union with England.

The dual system of the Church of Scotland, vaunted to be an example to the universe, had broken down. What was to be done? "Is one violent settlement after another," asks Dr. Candlish, "to be perpetrated in spite of the authority of the Church? Are men to rebel and set the Church at defiance? Is this to go on year after year?" With that penetrating keenness of intellectual glance which the simple have called prophecy and second sight, he has now discerned that the claims of the Church will not be conceded. We saw with what luminous precision he defined the power of the Civil Magistrate, not only in temporal things, but, *circa sacra*, in the external and mechanical matters connected with things spiritual. He was ready to yield anything that did not touch the life. He declared himself, however, no idolater of Establishment. Even in the mind of Chalmers there seemed to be at moments something like a superstitious horror as to what was called the Voluntary system. The vague notion appears to have been that this was some dogmatic and determinate scheme, tyrannically requiring Christians to pronounce it sinful in the Church to receive any aid from the State, and in the State to receive any aid from the Church. Candlish dismissed these spectral fancies. A Voluntary Church he saw to be merely a Church conducted, in relation to the maintenance of pastors, on the principles prevalent in the apostolic age, and indisputably sanctioned by Paul in his first letter to the Corinthians. It might or it might not be that, when circumstances altered, those who preached the gospel should "live of the gospel," as they did in Corinth and Galatia in Paul's time; but Presbyterians of all people, with their habit of insistence on the letter of biblical prescription, ought to have been the last to be shocked at the survival or revival of Paul's Church economics.

So early, also, as the autumn of 1841, Dr. Candlish

had anticipated Chalmers in the practical announcement of a Sustentation Fund. Referring to the "apostolic rule that all things in this matter should be in common," he expressed his conviction that, in the event of a catastrophe, the Church would adopt it. "There are some of us favourably situated," he said, "in the larger towns of the country, and in possession of youth and vigorous health, who might find little difficulty in retaining congregations who would devote their means wholly to the maintaining of the minister among them. But would this be reasonable to our fathers who have spent their days in lonely valleys of our land, to our brethren who have borne the heat and burden of the day, and that in districts where, willing as the people might be to support their beloved pastors, they are straitened from the want of means? There can be no doubt, I should think, that if God gave the ministers of this Church grace to be so faithful to our principles as to consent to the loss of their benefices rather than surrender this principle for which she is contending,—I cannot doubt, I say, that He will give us the further wisdom to provide in some such way as this that the ministry throughout the land should share in common from the freewill offerings of the whole people." This was spoken by the greatest preacher that had appeared in Scotland since the rise of Chalmers, the darling pastor of the richest congregation in the Church. To read it is like bathing in a well filled with the very dews of God.

The Marquis of Bute had transmitted the Claim of Rights and the petition against patronage to Sir James Graham to be submitted to the Queen. On the 20th of June 1842, Sir James Graham addressed a letter to Lord Bute, who passed it to the Moderator of the Assembly. If presentation of the document to Her Majesty "implied in the least degree the adoption of their contents," Sir James would not, he said, have presented these; but as their tone was respectful, and they purported to be "a statement of grievances from the supreme ecclesiastical authority in Scotland," he promised to do so. In this there was no glimpse of hope nor did the Government stretch out its little finger to stay the chariot in which the Court of Session was riding rough-shod over the liberties of the Church. Well was it for Scotland in those circumstances that her clergy, disseminated through the length and breadth of the country, were no mere *disjecta membra* of a vague, semi-organic whole, like the Church of England, but were pervaded with a sense of national and ecclesiastical unity, accustomed to act together, and possessed of leaders capable of confronting and dealing with the most difficult emergency.

It appears to have been with Hanna, the clear-minded, quietly eloquent, finely gifted biographer of Chalmers, that the idea of calling together a Convocation of the faithful among the clergy originated. Chalmers mentions the suggestion in a letter of 19th September 1842, and in his energetic hands it soon took practical effect. In a circular, initiated by him and signed by thirty-two clergymen, eminent and of reverend age, the Evangelical ministers of the Establishment were invited to assemble in Edinburgh, with a view to arriving at a perfect mutual understanding, demonstrating to the

Government and the nation that they were not a flock scattered on the mountains to be hunted down apart, but a host inspired with the inflexible determination of maintaining the spiritual independence of the Church or casting off the fetters of Establishment.

Candlish eagerly hailed the proposal. Of all forms of anguish for his impetuous spirit, that of teasing suspense and wordy disputation was the most painful. But both for him and for Cunningham, respecting whom, in Moderate circles in Scotland and in the ears of Conservative ministers in London, there were whispers of cunning detraction as to the mischief-making wizards who had brought Chalmers himself under their spell, it was wise to keep rather in the background. There was a breath of jealousy even among the country Evangelicals respecting the excessive influence of Edinburgh; and the Edinburgh influence centred in the great "twin brethren," Cunningham and Candlish. Perfectly agreed in their opinions, heroically pure and elevated in their motives, knit together in the tender brotherhood of Christian friendship, these were content to do their work without putting themselves forward.

Guthrie sketched beforehand with consummate accuracy the alternative courses of action which would be discussed at the Convocation, and which respective sections among the ministers were expected to favour. He was himself heart and soul with Candlish and Cunningham, resolute to go forward in the straight path. "Some of us," he wrote in a letter of the deepest confidence to his friend MacCosh, "entertain very decided opinions about the unlawfulness of the Church continuing in connection with a State which insists on Erastian conditions, and draws the sword of persecution against the reclaiming Church. Our idea of the Church's duty is this :—That on many accounts she should not rashly proceed to dissolve the connection, but should go to the Government of the land, explain how the terms on which she was united to the State have been altered to all practical purposes by the late decisions, how the compact had been therein violated, and how she cannot continue to administer the affairs of the Establishment unless she is to be freed from invasion and protected against persecution; that therefore unless the Government and Legislature shall, within a given and specified time, redress the wrongs we complain of, we shall dissolve the union, and leave all the sins and consequences at the door of an Erastian and oppressive State."

But there were others, prominent among them Mr. Begg, who took a different line. "Their idea," proceeds Guthrie, "is to remain in the Establishment till driven out, doing all the duties that belong to them. Well, our manifest duty, under the idea of remaining, is to purify the Church of Erastianism, and preserve it from it. So they agree that at this Convocation the ministers should resolve to admit no Erastian into the Church, to license no Erastian student, to translate no Erastian, and to thrust out of the Church without any mercy every man and mother's son that avails himself of these Erastian decisions, acknowledges them as binding the Church, or would in any way apply them in the face of our own laws." Guthrie admits that his section would have no conscientious objection to thus standing on the defensive and the offensive, and sketches, in a few masterly strokes, the circumstances that would arise under the proposed course and the probable issue. "We must cast out of the Church all that preach for, or in any way by overt acts countenance, the deposed of Strathbogie. We must cast out of the Church the Moderate majority of the late Synod of Aberdeen, and in less than two years we have all the Moderates declared to be no longer ministers of the Church of Scotland. They constitute themselves into *law* Presbyteries, depose our clergy within their bounds, declare their parishes vacant, ordain ministers of their own on the presentation of patrons, and then claim the stipends, and they are given them; and so, without the glance of a bayonet or ring of a musket,—the appearance even of a law functionary,—we are quietly dispossessed and put down." The Church would thus be transformed in the wrong way, and man after man the ministers would seem to be "struggling for a stipend," and no intelligible testimony would be borne to truth and principle. On the other hand, if, on calmly demanding their rights, and on being denied them, they in a body dissolved connection with the State, their deed "would fill the brightest page in Church history."

CHAPTER XXXI.

The Convocation.

IN response to Chalmers's invitation, the clergy flocked together from all parts of Scotland. One of the members of the Convocation noted that, on his way up to Edinburgh, he had met the minister of Maidenkirk, and that, having arrived, he found himself in the same lodgings with a minister from John o' Groats. There were four hundred and sixty of them by tale, and their quality was still more remarkable than their numbers. "This band," said Lord Cockburn, "contains the whole chivalry of the Church."

The Convocation opened in St. George's Church, Edinburgh, on the 17th of November 1842. Chalmers preached, choosing for his text the Scripture words, "Unto the upright there ariseth light in the darkness." More solemnly beautiful watchword for men contemplating an enterprise of great pith and moment could not be furnished by the literature of the world. A glance of courage, hope, and exultation flashed from eye to eye when the words were uttered. "The great lesson of this text," said Chalmers, "is the connection which obtains between integrity of purpose and clearness of discernment, insomuch that a duteous conformity to what is right is generally followed up by a ready and luminous discernment of what is true." "My venerable fathers and brethren of the Established Church of Scotland, I will not speak of it as a certainty that, if you persevere in the high walk of uprightness on which you have entered, the secularities of that Establishment will be wrested from your hands. It would not be venturing far, however, to speak of it as a probability and a hazard, and surely, at the very least, not to speak of it as a possibility were downright affectation. I rejoice to believe that, whatever be the shades or diversities of sentiment upon lesser questions, the tie of that great and common principle which hitherto has bound us together remains unbroken, —that I speak in the hearing of men firmly resolved as ever to lose all and to suffer all rather than surrender the birthright of those prerogatives which we inherit from our fathers, or compromise the sacred liberty wherewith Christ has made us free,—of men whose paramount question is, What is duty? that best stepping-stone to the solution of the other question, What is wisdom?"

The sermon was characterised by one who heard it as " solemn, tender, scriptural, faithful, full of tact and of power, much fitted to confirm the weak and embolden the fearful, and to animate us in an upright way." The temper of the assemblage was that of high-wrought spiritual enthusiasm. The proceedings were constantly interrupted by reading of the Scriptures, prayer, and praise. "O send Thy light forth and Thy truth." Unless we enter into their pervading sentiment of heroic faith and fervour, — if we permit any breath of worldly cynicism to blind us to the spiritual elevation of these men,—we absolutely fail to realise the situation.

> "Dark-brow'd sophist, come not a-near,
> All the place is holy ground."

And the principle of intellectual action, as cleared rather than clouded in the serene elevation of moral purpose, did not belie itself in the practical operations of the Convocation. Candlish had developed a capacity for business, a fineness and firmness of touch in managing men, which worked in marvellous harmony with his genius as an orator. To the seeing eye it becomes plain, as we glance along the notes of the sessions of the Convocation, preserved to us by Dr. James Henderson and published in the biography of Candlish, that it was in his creative brain that the masterly arrangements for discncumbering the discussion of non-essentials, minimising talk, procuring complete expression of opinion, and conducting the whole to a definite, clear, wise, and right conclusion, took shape.

On the first day there was much speaking, evidently a good deal of noise, of self-assertion, with traces of distrust, jealousy, discord. "On the whole, I," Dr. Henderson, "feel uncomfortable and anxious for results." But a Committee to arrange the order of business was got appointed, and Candlish was in it. Next day, at the morning diet, it appeared that the Committee, with Candlish in it, had not lost time in superfluous slumber. "Candlish," the other Committee men would probably have said, "hath murdered sleep." At all events he was ready with the report. It was a model of brevity and sagacity in the laying down of rules, and a masterpiece of comprehensiveness, lucidity, accuracy, in stating the subjects of discussion. Throughout the assemblage there was not a whisper of dissent, not a suggestion of improvement.

Dr. Henderson begins to feel much less uncomfortable. "On this matter of business," he notes, "perfect unanimity,—a great blessing, and a token for good." It gradually becomes clear that there will be considerable difference of view on the subject of patronage as related to spiritual independence. Dr. Chalmers, we saw, had voted with Cunningham and Candlish in the Assembly in favour of a petition for the abolition of patronage; but neither he nor, indeed, Cunningham and Candlish had held that it was impossible to secure Non-intrusion without absolute destruction of patronage; and therefore he opposed an "extreme anti-patronage proposal" tabled by Begg. The point was a fine one. Candlish, who combined Puritan fervour with a faculty for distinguishing and analysing equal to that of Aquinas, made it clear, in a speech "very clever and very fine," that Begg himself did not consider abolition of patronage indispensable to Non-intrusion; and the effect of his exquisitely lucid reasoning was summed up in the practical observation: "Certainly our existence under it hitherto shows that we may exist still (as an Establishment) though it should remain." But he was convinced that, in order to reconcile patronage with Non-intrusion, *i.e.* with consent of the people, such an elaborate, complicated, and delicate tissue of phrases was necessary, that the result of an attempt to provide such must be misunderstanding and disaster.

Cunningham agreed with Candlish. Too much of a Presbyterian to confound between Non-intrusion and popular election, too much of a Church historian to forget that even the Church of Scotland had not uniformly made abolition of patronage a *sine quâ non* of connection with the State, he did not say that the Church's spiritual jurisdiction must be sacrificed if patronage were permitted, in any form or to any extent, to remain. But he remembered that the prowlers of the Court of Session, if attracted by patronage, were sure to come for prey into perilous proximity to the sheepfolds of the Church, and "cautioned us most adroitly," says Henderson, "against our extreme present danger,—a Non-intrusion measure which does not rid us of the invasion of the Civil Courts."

The essential thing was felt by all to be spiritual independence, involving Non-intrusion. But Candlish held that it was fair to Begg and his friends to put on record their strong view against patronage. Chalmers admitted that this was "only keeping faith with Mr. Begg," but strongly urged him and his friends to forego the privilege. Candlish carried his point. We are unanimous, therefore. All, without ripple of difference, hold that it is a matter of life and death to guard the spiritual freedom of the Church, and a large number think that the best way to do this is to abolish patronage.

But the real difficulty had still to be encountered. What attitude was the Church to take up? Were the fathers and brethren in any case to stay in and show fight, or were they, in the event of being denied redress, to quit the Establishment? Ay, there's the rub. Some begin to be conscious of a certain qualminess in the region of the heart. Here, for example, is Dr. Dewar, of Aberdeen, a gentle, well-meaning, dignified person, truly Evangelical, liberal of his sermons on charitable occasions, the very pink of clerical respectability. "Dr. Dewar rose with deep solemnity; came up with the impression that it was too soon to contemplate a removal, or take any resolution regarding it;—don't outrun Providence." Let us judge no man. Sometimes one may conscientiously show the white feather. Mr. Brodie, of Monimail, the same who stood by Mr. Clark, of Inverness, in counselling tenderness in the matter of the Strathbogie rebels, now speaks out bravely. "If I am in doubt as to the course of duty when danger comes, I will cast in my lot with the losing party." Dr. Dewar did *not* come out.

Chalmers throws in his royal word to define the action of the Church in the event of a Disruption. There was no question, he said, of going out of the Church; "not *we*, but the endowments, were going out." On another occasion he adverted to "the cry of *schism*." It was a cry, he said, by which corrupt Churches disguised their faithlessness to truth. According to the principles on which these condemn schism, "there never could have been separation from the Church of Rome." In the present instance, as abiding by the Church's principles, from which others are departing, "*we* are the Church *minus* the endowments." It admits not of a moment's dispute, that the men who, expressly disobeying the Church, put themselves into subjection to the Court of Session, did really separate from the Church and commit schism. If an Italian Presbytery of Strathbogie were to defy their ecclesiastical superiors, and place themselves under the tribunals of united Italy, all the world would acknowledge that they, and not the Roman Church, were in schism. When we consider that Chalmers had been for thirty years the most splendid ornament of an Established Church, and that he had by common consent been recognised and crowned as the greatest living defender of Established Churches, we must grant that it was in him a fine illustration of combined moral and mental power to discern so clearly wherein lay the life, and wherein lay only the meat and raiment, of Established Churches.

The old argument that the Church ought to repeal the Veto Act came up, but the conclusive answer to it was ready on the lip of Candlish. The Church, he reminded his brethren, had always proclaimed herself willing to shelve the Veto, if only the principle of Non-intrusion, the sacred right of the people embodied in the ancient call, were conceded. But of this no promise or pledge had been given.

What is to be done? The highest mounted minds in the Convocation—happy Convocation, to have such a cluster of minds to lead it!—were unanimous. Looking into the "sacred morning" of the future, solemnly, not without awe, but yet calmly trusting in God, they saw that it was the duty of the Church to go forward. Chalmers, Candlish, Cunningham, Guthrie, Gordon, Robert Buchanan, saw, as with one flash of intuition, that if the Legislature gave no redress, it would be the part of the Church not to engage in an ignominious wrestle with the Court of Session, but to leave the Establishment. A great body of superior men, less distinguished than these, and a large proportion of the rank and file, were prepared to follow them.

But it soon appeared that there was a minority, not insignificant in numbers, and formidable from the ability of its chiefs, which was strongly bent on protracting the conflict, and staving off, for an indefinite period, separation from the State. By far the most remarkable man in this party was Mr. Begg. Still in the very prime of manhood, firm of fibre in body and in soul, there were few Non-intrusionists in Scotland better known, or better deserving to be known, than Begg of Liberton. He had won his spurs, as we saw, by audaciously facing an eminent Moderate orator in debate, and since that day he had never fallen into the background. He had defended the Church against the Voluntaries, on the ground that, though established, she was free. No one saw more clearly than he that if the Court of Session triumphed, this argument must vanish. "If," he had said in the Assembly of 1840, "they allowed the Court of Session to interpret the limit of their power, they gave to Voluntaries a weapon with which they would beat down any Establishment upon earth."

In that Assembly, two years before things had reached the present extremity of disorder and oppression, when the Church was being invited to accept the Aberdeen compromise, none had spoken out more clearly than Begg, or with more of the clarion note in his voice. "He saw nothing," he said, "for the Church but either a glorious dissolution from the State, retaining all her principles entire, or the abandonment of her principles,— the prostration of herself at the feet of the State, and her utter extinction piece-meal, from the desertion of the best of her people. It appeared to him that, although the Church of Scotland was a poor Church (and her poverty was principally owing to the faithful contending for her present principles), yet, being free, she was a noble Church. When they looked to all the Churches of the Reformation fettered and prostrated before the Civil Power, and thought of their own Church, free and independent though supported by the Civil Power, he felt that she was a noble specimen of the Church of Christ."

His next words might have been spoken, and most appropriately spoken, in his place as a member of the Convocation. "The question was now tried with regard to her, whether it was possible to have a Church Establishment and at the same time maintain her ecclesiastical freedom as a Church of Christ, and the rights and privileges of a Christian people. If by their vote they give the slightest countenance to any individual in determining that question so as to peril the existence of our spiritual independence,—so as to peril or endanger the rights of the people,—he saw nothing for it but dissolution to the Church. But if they stood true and united within, he had no fear of their enemies from without. Truth was great,—it had prevailed in times past over far mightier difficulties,—and he trusted that by the aid of the great Head of the Church, whose prerogatives they were endeavouring to defend, the Church would again be rescued from danger and perplexity; they would not fear, God Himself would defend and protect her, and that right early."

There are some who may be tempted to exclaim, that it had been well for Begg and for Scotland if he had died after uttering these noble words. Then would the garland of his fame have shone for ever on his brow, with the dews of dawn upon it. The difference, the disputation, that now emerged in the Convocation was the prognostic of a divisive influence, destined to tell with pathetic effect in the future history of the Church. That galaxy of glorious leaders,—that choir of morning stars that sang together at the birth of the Free Church,— how well had it been if they had remained, or if their inspiration had sufficiently remained, to keep the Church on the lines they indicated!

But we have perhaps no right to anticipate, and it must be clearly remembered that, while the galaxy of great ones continued to shine, nay even after Chalmers had set, and so long as Candlish, Cunningham, Guthrie, and Buchanan remained above the horizon, Begg did ever, as on the present occasion, with what mixture there might be of idiosyncrasy and self-assertion, yield finally to the celestial voices. His intense instincts of disputation and destruction were quelled by the mightier instincts of construction, of order, of expansion, of union.

Chalmers was now in his most exalted mood. "If free, the Church of Scotland might," he said, "be the rallying point for evangelical truths throughout the world." And as for the trouble, the danger, the apparent loss, involved in freedom, he feared them not. He launched into a description of the Divine enthusiasm, the spiritual passion, the sweet communion and fellowship, enjoyed by Christian brethren in times of persecution and excitement. "He was himself," says our reporter, "the most striking impersonation of the passion which he so eloquently and vividly depicted. I cannot recall it—it burst like electricity upon us—not less brilliant and effective than the most brilliant and striking of all the productions of his mind. The effect was astonishing." Truly a notable fact. It reminds one of the pathetically earnest and beautiful declaration by Jeffrey, that a quite peculiar influence, of a sacredly elevating nature, had been exerted upon him by this man. The visible glow of moral elevation in Chalmers—the Mosaic brightness of the face of one that had been on the Mount—has, when weighed in the severest scales of science, a real value, as casting light upon some difficult and mysterious but quite practical problems connected with genius and inspiration. Tennyson meant more than to say a merely pretty thing when he spoke of seeing, at moments of special elevation, "the God within him light the face" of his friend Arthur Hallam. And if the glow on one God-revealing face has been strong enough to light with spiritual radiance a vista of two thousand years, shall we hesitate to say that, whatever there may have been of myth or of miracle, there was, to begin with, an indestructible kernel of historical *fact* in the *transfiguration* of Jesus Christ?

Once more, however, we have to observe that Chalmers, though the most spiritually exalted man in that assemblage, was perhaps also the most practical. It was not strange, considering his fame as a political economist, that he should cheer the hearts of the brethren with calculations as to the probable provision to be made by a thoroughly roused and grateful people for a Church that had, for the people's sake, parted from the State. One might have fancied, from his sanguine trust in the generosity of the devout rich, and in his still fonder trust in the power of the unnumbered littles of Christ's poor, that he had been a Voluntary platformist all his days. So warmly did he paint the lifeboat, that some one cried out that he made it look better than the ship,—a pathetic jest which evoked one of the few laughs of the Convocation.

To go forward, then, following the glow upon the face of Chalmers, was the prevailing sentiment of the Convocation; but we are bound to take some note, were it only for the sake of historical fidelity, of the resolute effort of Begg and his section to perpetuate the struggle indefinitely within the Establishment. Begg admitted that, if the Civil Power had formally imposed Erastianism on the Church, then the hour would have struck for departure. But he refused to take the law of the Court of Session, or even of the Government, as final. He would take it only from the Estates of the Realm. Nay, he seemed at moments to fall back still further, and maintain what was theoretically true, that the rights of the Church were bound up with the Treaty of Union and the Constitution of the United Kingdom, and that not even Parliament could alienate them.

He proposed to confront law with the fulminations of Church discipline. The whole Synod of Aberdeen, he was reminded, sympathised with the schismatic Presbyters:

would he depose a whole Synod? "Undoubtedly," said the dauntless Begg. "Our ancestors in 1638 deposed by one stroke all the bishops of Scotland, and the result of this bold measure was that their cause triumphed, and in a little time the storm was past and gone." A most admirable debating hit. But in 1638 the bishops were a handful of individuals, and the Church had behind her the force of Scotland, ecclesiastical and civil; for at that time Montrose was still among the Church leaders. In 1662, when the Church really had the alternative placed before her of surrendering her principles or turning out on the hillsides, she made no attempt to struggle on against the Government. She quitted the Establishment; she chose poverty and worldly degradation; she saw her saintly peasants shot at their cottage doors, and her holy virgins drowned on her tidal sands; but she had her reward: she raised such a testimony to her distinctive principle that all men understood it and honoured her; she won the love and trust of the Scottish people for ever; and she now, in this autumn of 1842, had such men to guide her as Chalmers, Cunningham, Candlish, Guthrie, and Begg. Clearly, though a clever allusion to history might tell for a moment, in debate, Begg was not likely to convince a Convocation containing Cunningham, that the Church ought to remain at all hazards within the Establishment.

The constitutional argument, potent to mystify, and seducingly sweet in its suggestion that separation from the dignity and emoluments of an Establishment could *never* be a duty, was effectually disposed of by Chalmers as "a discovery, fetched from the depths of a metaphysical jurisprudence," which " left us independent of all decisions of Civil Courts free, or bound to keep our places." Evangelicals of the Church of England, hear these words!

Begg was too solidly able, too firmly based on common honesty and common sense, to make much of the constitutional argument, but he found it hard to reconcile himself to a surrender of the practical advantages of Establishment. What would they not lose! " We are driven from universities, from parish schools; we leave many parishes without the gospel, where not a spot of ground can be got to build a church upon. Let all this come if there was necessity for it; but he could see no necessity." It was no mean craving for the emoluments of Establishment that animated Begg. What sent a pang to his heart was to see that vision of spiritual possibilities vanish like a fading sunset.

One of the points on which he dwelt was that, in their rude haste to sweep aside the jurisdiction of the Church, the Civil Courts had made her answerable for the indirect and practically inevitable effects of Church discipline. In so doing, the Courts really declared war against the liberties of all Nonconformist Churches. Why go out, if the law will track you and persecute you as before? The answer was — or rather might have been, for it was not, to our knowledge, expressly given at the Convocation — that, whatever may be said or done by wrong-headed lawyers, the non-established Churches are really more free than Erastian Establishments. The Church of Scotland, the moment she stepped beyond the State pale, would be under the expanse of toleration. The liberty enjoyed by all the free Churches of England and of Scotland would be hers. The self-supporting Churches are guarded by the nation's sense of justice. In England or in Scotland a stupid judge may give trouble by ignorantly misunderstanding or maliciously misapplying the privilege of self-government exercised by the free Churches, but Britons love fair play, and their liberty and self-government are beyond general or serious attack. Their purely spiritual jurisdiction, — their strictly Church discipline, — which alone is a matter between them and Christ, requires no backing from the secular arm; and none of them— Wesleyans, Congregationalists, Presbyterians, Papists— have in their monetary arrangements found the operation of the common law unsatisfactory.

On this matter it was not possible either for Begg or any of the consummately able men who led the Convocation to see beyond the immediate future. Again and again it was declared by Candlish that the reckless aggressions of the Court of Session might bring into jeopardy that spiritual freedom on which the Voluntaries had plumed themselves. They actually did so in the Cardross case. Chalmers saw persecution looming as a clear possibility at a very measurable distance. But persecution has never been an insuperable difficulty for "holy and humble men of heart," whose allegiance to Christ was an affair of conscience. And the first attempt of the Court of Session to enslave a tolerated, self-maintained Church proved to be futile and the last.

No shadow of difference arose between Begg and his brethren on the point of standing by their guns in the sense of standing by their principles. The difference was that Begg clung with all the desperate tenacity of his nature to the idea that the guns of Establishment might possibly be used, if not permanently, at least for some time longer, in defence of the principles.

Chalmers, Candlish, Cunningham, Guthrie, Gordon, and Buchanan saw that this could not be,—that the Church possessed no arm of flesh to oppose to encroaching Courts or Legislatures, — that her spiritual freedom was now being trampled down,—and that, therefore, if relief did not come, and come promptly, she must go forth.

Let us be just to Begg. He was no traitor, no trimmer. He secured that the whole compass of alternative courses should be boxed, that the kaleidoscope of possible opinion on the situation should come full circle round. And, above all, be it distinctly admitted and realised that he did not hold out against the general sentiment. His biographer says justly that he acquiesced in the resolutions. Nor will all readers agree with Dr. Thomas Smith that Dr. Henderson's inestimable notes of the Convocation convey "an impression that Dr. Begg was less zealous than his brethren, or more cautious as to committing himself." No. The notes produce the impression that he would stick to the Establishment like limpet to the rock, so long as he thought the spiritual independence of the Church could in that way be preserved. But he formally withdrew his objections to the view taken by the brethren in general, and, when this was done, no man spoke out more clearly than he. The storm he had conjured up in the Convocation passed over, and he had the magnanimity to be swayed by wiser and greater men than himself.

CHAPTER XXXII.

The Court of Session's last Triumphs.

THE Convocation ended in harmony among the brethren, and fortitude and clear determination with reference to the future. As autumn deepened into winter, the ministers carried into every corner of Scotland the quickening power of the inspiration they had received. Among the causes of satisfaction with which all who have regard for the honour of human nature may be expected to view the results of the meeting, this, surely, is greatest, that no evasion was attempted, no theological phrase of disputable significance devised, under cover of which the Church might secure the sweet emoluments, and sweeter dignities and peaceful routine and comfort, of Establishment, and yet make pretence of retaining her freedom. No betrayal of Christ with a kiss, in the form of some verbal, visionary, and abstract recognition of His Headship! We came to you a free Church, we can part with you a free Church; we must, in any case, stand fast in the liberty wherewith Christ hath made us free. Such, in effect, was the message of the Convocation to the State.

The Church declined to continue an ignominious and anarchical struggle with the law Lords and their vassal clergy in Scotland. In the Memorial drawn up by the Convocation to be presented to the Legislature, it was declared that such a contest could not fail to be attended with pernicious consequences, " affecting both the majesty of law and the highest interests of religion." The question now was, whether the State would or would not commit " the heinous national offence of not only breaking the national faith, but disowning the authority of Christ in His own House, and refusing to recognise His Church as a free spiritual society, instituted by Him, and governed by His laws alone."

Scotland rang with agitation, the whole atmosphere quivering with an excitement so characteristic of Scotland, so strange to other lands. In hall and in cottage, in mansion and farm, in street and at market, men spoke of the grand struggle going on. Guthrie's biographers tell us that seven hundred and eighty-two distinct pamphlets might be noted among the phenomena of the time. The wrestle between the Churchmen, who were also the people's men, and the Court of Session's tools, was raging wildly. In most places the feeling of the pastors and of the population was ardently expressed in favour of the Church, but throughout the Synod of Aberdeen the influence of Moderatism prevailed. The Court of Session, encouraged no doubt by the approbation and acquiescence of a party in the Church, carried matters with a high hand, and scrupled not to make fresh inroads upon the spiritual jurisdiction.

Occurring with pathetic seasonableness as an illustration of the completeness with which the Court of Session was divesting the Scottish Establishment of all legislative power in the spiritual province, there was delivered, on the 20th of January 1843, the judgment of the Court in the Stewarton case. Its salient point was that, as the Auchterarder judgments had cancelled the Church's legislation combining the action of patronage with the will and consent of the people in the settlement of ministers, so the Stewarton judgment nullified the legislation of the Church giving effect to her principle of parity among ministers. In their dealings with the parish of Auchterarder, the law Lords had struck down the Church's barrier against intrusion; they now, by their Stewarton decision, struck down the Church's Chapel Act. Thus had they scornfully smitten into ruins the whole edifice of Church reform as it had arisen under the impulse of Chalmers.

The Dean of Faculty, now Lord Justice-Clerk, had done his work. If the Legislature did not restore what the Court of Session had taken away, and if the Church of Scotland acquiesced, then did the Church possess no jurisdiction. The respondents for the Church in the Stewarton case distinctly informed the Lords of Session that they would *not* obey them. "Whatever judgment your Lordships may pronounce, the respondents freely and at once avow that in regard to the matters here in question, they will continue to give obedience to the injunctions of the ecclesiastical judicatories to which they are subordinate."

During those days Candlish's whole nature burned with the intensity of his spiritual passion. The vague hopes, the busy weaving of cobweb compromises and gossamer explanations, that deceived feebler men, were shrivelled into dust by the impetuous lightnings of his mind. He knew that separation was inevitable. He frankly avowed that, were he a Congregationalist, were he not one of a company of Presbyterian brethren, he would go out at once. The May month and the Assembly were drawing near, and he panted for the decisive moment. Moving about from place to place, now in London, now in Edinburgh, now in the West of Scotland, wherever statesmen were to be interrogated, wherever great meetings were to be addressed, there was he; and wherever he came, he brought illumination. Never, however, was that superb intellect shaken from its calmness of vision, from its poised and perfect apprehension of the position, or from lucid moderation of speech. The jurisdiction he claimed for the Church was neither Popish, including infallibility, nor revolutionary, overleaping bounds, but liberty " to regulate the concerns of Christ on the principles of a Church of Christ, not by the determination of civil rulers in ecclesiastical matters, but by the word of Christ alone, interpreted by the prayerful study of our minds and hearts."

No arrangement which refused the spiritual jurisdiction, and left patronage in the way,—no arrangement which disallowed the original claim of the Church of Scotland to negotiate with the State on the footing of a jurisdiction derived, not from the State, but from Christ,—no mere independence by sufferance,—could he consider adequate or safe. " Unquestionably Parliament might lay down a form of proceeding which would enable the

Church to give effect to the Non-intrusion principle, and might say that if the Church adheres to that form of proceeding, her sentences shall not be reviewed by the Civil Courts. But still the Civil Courts will be entitled to come forward and say, You, the Church Courts, have transgressed that form which it is for us to interpret, and therefore we will subject you to actions of damages, and compel you to act on our view of the law. Here is the essence of the question. The slave may have his chain lengthened, the captive may have the range of his walk enlarged; but if the chain be round him still, he is not the less a slave; if the walls still enclose him on every side, he is not the less a captive."

They must take their stand, therefore, on first principles, and recur to the watchword of their Covenanting forefathers: "The Crown rights of the Redeemer." It may be that persecution will follow them out of the Establishment, but all the same, "Oh," cries Candlish, "let us be resolved and determined that we shall maintain the rights of Christ the King, whether in or out of the Establishment, under persecution, if need be." And solemnly, as the hour approaches when he must go one way, and those of his brethren who have disobeyed the Church and bowed their necks to the Court of Session another, he touches on the question of schism. "Very extraordinary words have been employed, not in random speeches, but in documents of Church Courts, imputing to us the sin of introducing a schism into the Church of Scotland. I won't venture to say that the sin of schism has not been committed; but let it be ever borne in mind that, in deciding on whose side the guilt lies, it is essential to discuss the question on which we have separated. *They* may be the schismatics who have consented to remain behind. Let it be remembered that the guilt of the schism is not to be determined by the question which party began, or which party have been most active; but simply and solely by the question, Which is the party who, on the point at issue, have acted in accordance with the word of God,—which party, I say, not in the manner of maintaining it only, but which party in the thing maintained, have upheld the testimony of the Lord Jesus Christ?"

On the 4th of January 1843, a letter was received in Edinburgh from Sir James Graham, who had the management of the Scottish Church question in Sir Robert Peel's Government. It held out no prospect that the Claim of Rights and the petition against patronage would be favourably considered. On the 31st of January the Commission of Assembly met. Dr. Welsh, the Moderator, having explained the circumstances of its meeting in view of Sir James Graham's letter, Dr. Cook, the ever vigilant and adroit leader of the Court of Session clergy, rose and called attention to the Stewarton decision as bearing on the constitution of the Commission. It was in virtue of powers conferred by the Church, and now cancelled by the Court of Session, that certain of the brethren had been enrolled as members of the Commission. Dr. Cook declared himself bound to require that these should be excluded. Mr. Dunlop pointed out, in reply, that the time legally available for appeal against the Stewarton decision had not expired. But the shadow cast before by the Court of Session sufficed for Dr. Cook. He pressed his motion, and 23 out of the 138 members of the Commission gave him their votes. Having read a protest, affirming the Commission to be illegally constituted, he and the minority withdrew.

Ecclesiastically this was an explicit act of schism. Tactically, however, the manœuvre was fine. The leader of the Erastian section had for his object to blazon it throughout the Church that the Court of Session had virtually decreed that there should be two castes in the clergy. The decree of the Court would add greatly to the force of Dr. Cook's party as a voting power in Presbyteries, Synods, and the General Assembly. The chapel ministers, emancipated by the Evangelicals, were naturally their allies; and now Dr. Cook would, of course, be prepared to challenge the right of any chapel minister to sit in the General Assembly. His withdrawal from the Commission with his followers may be justly described as a formal act of schism. "We," he virtually said, "are the Church constituted by the State." "And we," the others virtually replied, "are the Church constituted by Christ."

All the more smoothly, on account of the secession of the Moderates, did the Commission mature arrangements for making the final appeal of the Church to the Estates of the Realm during the approaching session.

CHAPTER XXXIII.

The Debate in the Commons—An imaginary Speech by Guthrie.

ON the 7th of March 1843, the case of the Church was brought before the House of Commons by Mr. Fox Maule. It was a memorable, a solemn occasion,— unique, perhaps, in the history of Parliaments, and deserving mention in the annals of the Universal Church. At the Reformation the Church in Scotland had assumed, as inalienably hers from Christ, that spiritual jurisdiction which Henry VIII. had usurped in England. At the Revolution Settlement this spiritual jurisdiction had formed an essential condition of Establishment. It was explicitly embodied, as clearly stated in the Confession of Faith, in the Constitution of the United Kingdom. There was no other instance in Europe in which the arrangements between Church and State, at the end of the Reformation period, had attained to such a consummation. The question now was, whether the experiment of a free, living, growing Church, exercising spiritual jurisdiction in friendly connection with the State, had or had not broken down. The Courts of law in Scotland had come into collision with the Church. The state of things was admittedly intolerable. The Church had announced her intention, if it must continue, of relinquishing Establishment. Would the House of Commons do aught to avert the catastrophe?

Parliament evinced no particular interest in the matter. There was not half a House. But too much stress must not be laid upon this circumstance. The attendance was larger than could have been looked for on the night of an Indian budget or an important Colonial debate. From 270 to 300 members were present. The leading men in all sections put in an appearance.

Sir Robert Peel had evidently taken pains to acquaint himself with the subject, and had mastered some of its superficial aspects; but he fell short in that practical sagacity, he lacked that penetrating glance, by which the inner truth, however veiled it may be in speciosities and superficialities, is reached.

Lord John Russell—the well-meaning, unimpassioned, superior but never superlative little John, who was born to come always so near greatness as to make his miss of it conspicuous—expatiated in generalities, dwelt on the difficulties of the situation, was so sorry that the excellent Church of Scotland was in trouble, would have been happy to help her if he could, but couldn't. The diminutive Lord John, however, was a gentleman. He had no part in the vileness of those churls who called the Scotch Churchmen hypocrites or tricksters. "Of this I am convinced," he said, "that there are many of the ablest, best, and most pious ministers of the Church, who, if you should shut the door to reconcilement completely, would think it their conscientious duty to leave the Church. I have said many able and pious ministers. There are two of them whom I have heard in the pulpit, though I am neither a Scotchman nor a member of the Scotch Church,—I mean Dr. Chalmers and Dr. Candlish—men in their separate ways as well fitted to expound the word of God, to enforce the obligations of morality, and to lead the people in the ways of the gospel, as any men belonging to any Church in any part of the world." Is it not pathetic that he should not have dared to say at once that these men could not be animated by any nefarious purpose in seeking to render their Church spiritually efficient?

Gladstone and Palmerston were present, but took no part in the debate. Charles Villiers and Cobden —*clarum et venerabile nomen!*—voted in favour of the Church. So did Macaulay, but his vote was silently given. He did not tell the House, as he might have done, that his friend Hallam, in his standard work on the Constitution, had declared the spiritual jurisdiction of the Church of Scotland to have been embodied in the Treaty of Union between England and Scotland. Nor did he anticipate his own denunciation of the Patronage Act, uttered in the House a couple of years later, as a "breach of the Treaty of Union." Charles Buller voted as became a friend of Carlyle. Sir George Grey spoke at some length on behalf of the Church. The debate occupied two nights, and fills thirty or forty of the doubled-columned pages of Hansard.

The speakers against the Church's claim, while using

courteous words, seemed one and all to be oppressed by a sense of some enormous absurdity, some extravagance of tyrannical usurpation, which the Scottish clergy were bent on perpetrating. Sir William Follett, an English lawyer of the highest reputation, professed himself unable to believe that the law of Scotland could possibly embrace the theory of concurrent and co-ordinate jurisdictions, each supreme in its own province, as put forward by the advocates of the Church. On such a theory he pronounced it absolutely incredible that the Civil Courts and the Ecclesiastical Courts could act harmoniously. He was willing to acknowledge the supremacy of the Church in spiritual things, but he started as at an adder in his way when the Church insisted upon drawing for herself the line of demarcation between spiritual and civil. What Sir William Follett said was so lucid and looked so reasonable, that his speech was eminently fitted to deepen, in the minds of simple, straightforward Englishmen, the suspicion that these Scotch parsons were either very bad or very mad, and that the House ought to make short work of their nonsense.

Sir Robert Peel's speech, elaborately plausible, its sophisms lying, for the most part, well hid under its generalities, would have passed off finely as an oration by some leading Moderate in the General Assembly. He praised the Church with honest cordiality. He had enjoyed, he said, "an opportunity of observing the worth of the ministers of that Church." He had marked in them a combination of solid learning and theological acquirement, of sterling worth and great energy in the work of their parishes, which made a deep impression on him. That impression, he said, "had not been effaced by what had since occurred." Coming to closer quarters, "There is no disposition," he made bold to affirm, "on the part of the House of Commons to deprive it (the Church) of any privilege which is essentially necessary to its efficiency as an Establishment." He did not scruple to admit the spiritual independence of the Church. "We all admit that to the Church belongs the exclusive jurisdiction in ecclesiastical matters." Is it not astounding to come upon a declaration like this by the Prime Minister of Great Britain, made a couple of months before the Disruption? On the Veto Law he pronounced slight censure or none. Practically he might be said to have sanctioned its working. The Government patronage had, as we know, been exercised in Scotland for years after its enactment in harmonious accordance with its provisions. But by persisting in it after its legal character had been denied by the highest authority, the Church, he held, had put herself in the wrong. The law had been declared; and need it be said that, to Sir Robert Peel, the law was a spectre at whose approach all resistance ought to give way?

It was when he took up the question of the discipline practised by the Church that Sir Robert's tone sharpened into severity, and he used terms of angry condemnation. He referred to the "violent and tyrannical act by which the Church deposed those ministers who, having taken the oath of allegiance, considered it to be their duty to obey the laws of their country." Again and again he repeated his denunciation of this infliction of the severest punishment upon clergymen for yielding "obedience to the law of the land." He maintained that they were "deprived of their civil rights." He would not hear of severing spiritual things in parishes from things temporal. The obvious meaning and purport of the Patronage Act was, he insisted, that the minister of the parish should both perform the parochial duties and enjoy the living. "What becomes of the stipend?" Was one man to receive it from the patron, while the Church declared that he was no minister at all? And was another man, ordained pastor of the parish by the Church, to receive none of the money? It could never have been rationally contemplated that two men should thus struggle against each other in one parish. Such a state of things would be anarchy.

But, apart from all question as to the stipend, there were other effects of deposition, said Sir Robert, to be considered. The stipend, in fact, is "not the most important." There were things dearer to a man than stipend. "It is the degradation of character to which these men are subjected that most affects me." In short, Sir Robert Peel distinctly and indignantly included within the civil jurisdiction those indirect effects of spiritual sentences which the Church always admitted to be inevitable. Warming as he spoke, he accused the Church of outdoing Rome herself in domineering pretensions. "I do maintain that, even in times that preceded the Reformation, the Church of Rome never laid claim to a greater power than that involved in the claims now set up."

The idea of some monstrous solecism and incredibility having been blundered into by the clergy manifestly haunted him as it did Sir William Follett. As the clearheaded English lawyer refused to regard the existence of two independent jurisdictions in Scotland as credible, so Sir Robert refused to believe it possible that the House of Lords had sanctioned any real encroachment by the Court of Session on the spiritual jurisdiction of the Church. "I will venture to say, if the civil tribunals attempted to control the Church in a matter purely spiritual, there would at once be an intervention on the part of Parliament to control the tribunals."

Towards the end of the speech he came upon delicate ground. "Take," he said, "the case of the Roman Catholics, or any of the Protestant Dissenters in this country, who are not connected with the State by way of Establishments. Their right, so far as voluntary jurisdiction is concerned, is quite supreme, and we do not attempt to interfere with it." But these were not established; and that made all the difference. He evaded, or overlooked, the question, in this instance, of indirect effects.

The presentation of the Church's case was creditable to the speakers, but not original, not masterly, not adequate to the requirements of an unprecedented and most difficult occasion. Fox Maule, afterwards Earl of Dalhousie, a nobly patriotic, devout, and capable man, beautiful in person and character, intrepidly loyal to his native land and his ancestral Church, deserved the immortality of fame which his speech and his conduct of the debate secured him. He shirked no labour, spoke for hours, but did not convince his audience. Rutherfurd was a lawyer of recognised ability, a lucid and effective pleader, not a commanding, statesmanlike mind, to lift the debate out of commonplace ruts and suggest an original solution of an original and perplexing problem. Speech after speech was spirited, argument after argument was telling and seemed conclusive, and yet the gloom and oppressiveness, as of some dark mystery, continued to pervade the atmosphere of the House. In vain did the advocates of the Church quote Scotch statutes from the time of John Knox downward. In vain was the historical and notorious claim of the Church of Scotland to an independent spiritual jurisdiction again and again appealed to. You could not say that the speakers were at any point wrong, and yet the clouds would not lift, the general nebulous haze continued to float around, the vessel was drifting full upon the rocks.

Consider the situation. It is perfectly certain that, if the leaders of the Church had been certified that the spiritual jurisdiction was safe, and that unedifying ministers would not be forced upon congregations, they would have joyfully remained in the Establishment. It is perfectly certain also, that in this debate the Prime Minister and the first Law Officer of the Crown expressly declared that they recognised the spiritual jurisdiction of the Church. Sir Robert assuredly did not wish to break up the Establishment in order to force unedifying presentees on parishes. Since Job cried in his anguish for a daysman to come between God and him and enable them to understand each other, there had never been an instance in which a mediator was so much wanted to remove the misunderstandings, the suspicions, the hallucinations which lay like a malignant spell upon both parties.

A Scotchman thinks of Sir Walter's words, when
Scotland's chance at Flodden was flung away,—

> "Oh for one hour of Wallace wight,
> Or well-skilled Bruce to rule the fight!"

There were in the Convocation nearly half a dozen men
who could have handled the Church's business with the
House more effectually than any of the speakers.
Imagination pictures the impression that might have
been made by a few words from royal Chalmers. What,
he might have asked, had they taken him for? Had he
ever, in all those years when he had defended the Church
of Scotland as the paragon of ecclesiastical Establishments,
omitted to say that it was as a living, a spiritually independent Church that he praised her? Had he been an
impudent impostor, or a wily trickster, or a theatrical
histrio, or a mere rhapsodising fool, when, in the presence
of nine English bishops and a Prince of the Blood, he
declared, four years before, in London, that the King could
not put his foot across the threshold of the Church of
Scotland? The Church now claimed, as essential to
Establishment,—for she did *not* now demand the total
abolition of patronage,—only what she had always in
essentials claimed; and she had never asked an iota
more than that she should be allowed to serve Christ
as strenuously in connection with the State as she could
serve Him if she were not in connection with the State.
In the whole course of her history she had never been
more efficient in teaching the poor, never more efficient
in preaching the gospel to all classes, than during the
last ten years; and for this she was to be disestablished.

Candlish, whose unparalleled skill, both strategical and

tactical, in the management of large bodies of men, had been illustrated in the Convocation, was probably the likeliest man (for Candlish at his best could work miracles) to have presented the claim of the Church to the House of Commons so convincingly, and at the same time to have indicated a method of restoring tranquillity so practicable, that the Disruption might, even at this the eleventh hour, have been averted. Not only could Candlish, with his Aquinas-like power of drawing accurate distinctions and stating them with exquisite precision, have cleared up misunderstandings and solved enigmas, but he might, with his marvellous faculty for framing schemes of action and his unexampled velocity in outlining them in resolutions, have suggested to Government a plan of campaign.

This, in the pass things had now reached, was a matter of paramount importance. Peel's references to the deposed ministers touched the crux of the difficulty. Scotland was the battlefield of two sets of clergymen. One set obeyed the Church, the other set obeyed the Civil law. The Government might regret having to choose between the two, but the continuance of their battle was clearly out of the question. Of the two, the Government, if forced to make a choice, would be shut up to stand by the party that obeyed the Civil law. All that the Strathbogie mutineers and those who sympathised with them had suffered was on account of their having, as the first of all necessities, obeyed the State. Sir Robert Peel might pardonably decide that it was better to let the Evangelicals leave the Church, than to see the whole Moderate party, or even a large proportion of that party, not only thrust out of the Church, but thrust out in a state of professional degradation and disqualification.

Candlish, however, was the man who could have shown the Government how to solve the problem presented by the divided Church. He had publicly said that he did not wish to see the Moderates excluded. Had he obtained a patient hearing from the House, and had he stated the case of the Church, and made his practical suggestions, in that Demosthenic language of his which needed no other ornamentation than the running glance of its electric fire along the keen unerring lines of its logical distinctions, a change might have passed over the situation.

One is tempted, since the audacity of even in imagination trying to put words into the mouth of Candlish is out of the question, to fall back upon Guthrie as the dramatically extemporised spokesman of the Church before the House of Commons. Not Guthrie the florid pulpit orator, but Guthrie the sound strong head that always instinctively, putting aside irrelevancies, trivialities, and obscurations, went to the core of a matter; Guthrie of Arbirlot, Guthrie the sympathetic friend and familiar of all sorts and conditions of men, Guthrie whose enchanting simplicity and cordial humour disarmed suspicion, inspired confidence, and never on one of a thousand platforms failed to appreciate and win his audience.

Guthrie is supposed to Speak.

It is naturally gratifying to me to have heard the high-flown praises bestowed by successive speakers upon the Church of Scotland. Quite a garland of flowery compliments has been vouchsafed her; but I cannot help remembering that in ancient times, creatures richly adorned with garlands have been led to sacrifice; and I must say that, when the eloquent gentlemen passed from general eulogies on the Church to a particular consideration of her claim, they changed their tone. Incredibility, absurdity, tyranny beyond that of the Papacy before the Reformation, are, in their view, the proper terms in which to describe the position she takes up. Now I have no doubt that the gentlemen of this House cherish no wish to inflict wrong either upon the Church or the people of Scotland; I have the firmest persuasion that the Church makes no demand which is not both just and simple; and I regard it therefore as indubitable that, in some way or other, a fog, a haze of misunderstanding, is the source of all the mischief. Pardon an illustration from the annals of the sea. Two noble vessels have made many a voyage prosperously and pleasantly together. Many ports have "exulted at the gleam of their masts," and at the wholesome merchandise they brought. But a fog crept over the deep. The treacherous dusk, worse than night's honest blackness, distorted the appearance they presented to each other, caused them to mistake each other for enemies, to misinterpret each other's signals, to run out their guns against each other. Gentlemen, we are in the fog. It is *light* that is wanted, in order that Church and State in Scotland may resume their harmonious and happy co-operation in the service of God and man.

The head of Her Majesty's Government, Sir James Graham, Sir William Follett, and every English gentleman in this House, must be held to know that the Confession of Faith is part of the constitutional law of the Church of Scotland. No man disputes that statement. The words of the Confession are these: "The Lord Jesus Christ, as King and Head of His Church, hath therein appointed a government in the hand of Church officers distinct from the Civil Magistrate." Are these words challenged by the House? If so, there is an end of the question. But if the British Parliament is unchallengeably bound to maintain the Confession of Faith, then we can understand each other. The Premier has told us that it is foreign to the intentions of Her Majesty's Government to cancel any essential condition of the hitherto existing alliance between Church and State in Scotland. Well, then, there are no words in the language that could more exactly define the essential condition of that alliance than those of the Confession of Faith. The alliance is based upon the recognition by the State of a Church government, which is characterised, first, as "therein" or within the Church; secondly, as "in the hand of Church officers;" and thirdly, as "distinct from the Civil Magistrate." I now ask, Is the Court of Session a Civil Court? It is. Can the Court of Session, then, be distinct from the Court of Session? If not, it cannot be the government of the Church of Scotland. I might ask also whether the Lords of Session are "Church officers." If not, they cannot be the persons to have the government of the Church in their hands. Once more,—to leave no hole of evasion unstopped,—I ask, would any straightforward man look upon the epithet "distinct," applied to the government in the hand of "Church officers," as satisfied and fulfilled by the stipulation that the Civil Court might, by enslaving the Church, thus convert the Church officers into Court of Session officers?

I submit that, by reasoning as simple, as clear, and as cogent as that of any proposition in Euclid, I have proved that the Court of Session can have no governing power over the Church of Scotland. And I will thank the House to observe particularly that the Confession of Faith is part of the law of the land for Scotland,— embodied in the Treaty of Union, and implied in the oath of allegiance.

I am anxious not to deviate from the straight road of a simple honest argument, but I take leave to interpose the remark that the enormity and solecism of our position, if we are indeed a parcel of cunning hypocrites, bent on establishing a spiritual despotism, are greatly enhanced by the pretensions we have always, as advocates of the Church of Scotland, made to be the all-round upholders of law. In our championship of Establishments, we have scouted the notion that there is any conflict between the moral, social, political law of nations and the spiritual law of the Church. Incredibility for incredibility, it is surely more incredible that hundreds of men should turn their life and character into a contradiction and a lie, than that two or three lawyers should have taken the wrong turn, and, having taken it, should refuse to go back. A crotchet, a prejudice, a wire-drawn metaphysical idea may ensconce itself in the brain, and step forth robed in all the infallibility of law. A small numerical majority gives the cue to the profession, and thus the world of politics and the press is influenced, "the whole ear of Denmark is abused," and the conclusion is lightly arrived at, that the clerical fellows are, as usual, in the wrong. It may be less credible that three lawyers have made a mistake than that some twice three hundred clergymen, one of them being such an one as Dr. Chalmers, have turned their whole existence into a falsehood.

Resuming the main course of my observations, I call the attention of the House to the circumstances under which the Court of Session took, as I say, the wrong turn. The patron, Lord Kinnoull, presented Mr. Young to the parish of Auchterarder. The congregation, by an all but unanimous majority, testified their unwillingness to receive him as their pastor. He was therefore rejected by the Presbytery. A suit was brought into the Court of Session with a view to putting the Patronage Act in force in Mr. Young's favour, and the Court of Session decided that he was legally entitled to be minister of the parish. Up to this point, having it as my object to discriminate and deal with none but essentials, I assume that the Court of Session was in the right. Property had been applied for; whatever else was craved, property was claimed; and the jurisdiction of the Court to hear all claims touching property is beyond dispute. But it appeared that, in order that Mr. Young might be put in possession of his property in the regular way, he required to be ordained pastor of the parish. And what I call the wrong turn was taken by the Court when it proceeded to command and coerce the Church to ordain Mr. Young.

Let us not fall back into mist. We are in no danger if we keep our eyes open. Every member of this House, every educated man, is aware that ordination to the office of the ministry is one of those things which in all ages and in all Churches has ranked as spiritual. The Premier knows perfectly that ordination is a spiritual matter, and that it must be included in that government which is defined in the Confession of Faith as "distinct from the Civil Magistrate." Reminding him, then, of his statement as to the desire of the Government to preserve all the essentials of the alliance between Church and State in Scotland, I call upon him to admit that the Lords of Session, when they reached this point, ought to have paused and said, "We cannot govern the Church, for we are not 'therein,' we are not 'Church officers,' and we are not 'distinct from the Civil Magistrate.'" Now the Court of Session, instead of having respect to a government "distinct" from its own, usurped the right to coerce or absorb that government, and to treat the "Church officers," who alone could exercise it, as if they were its own servants. By so doing it has violated the Union. Its conduct has resulted in a comprehensive interruption of the government of the Church.

The method of the Court of Session has been the most contemptuous that could have been adopted. Their Lordships have simply *ignored* the existence of a "distinct" ecclesiastical government, and proceeded on the tacit assumption that it was sheer affectation, or farce, or hypocrisy, on the part of the "Church officers," to object, on spiritual or conscientious grounds, to ordain, depose, or admit to full ministerial brotherhood, as the Court of Session pleased to command. Let no one delude himself for a moment by supposing that the Lords of Session debate with us as to the line of demarcation between spirituals and temporals. They do not say what *is* spiritual, if ordination and deposition are *not*. They simply ignore any government "distinct from the Civil Magistrate;" and if the officers of that government come between their decrees and temporals, and refuse to be coerced, they inflict severe punishment. That is all. If the House look into our Claim of Rights, they will find that, along the whole line of Church government, the authority of the Church is struck down. It is taken out of the hands of "Church officers" in the sense of officers obeying the Church, and put into the hand of officers disobeying the Church and obeying the Court of Session. The direction of the Confession of Faith is *reversed*.

Is this what the honourable Baronet calls preserving the essentials of the alliance between Church and State in Scotland? The statute of patronage is not alleged to have repealed the Confession of Faith. The Civil Court could not legally take the place of a government, or even instruct and correct a government, defined in a fundamental muniment of the constitution *verbatim et literatim* as "distinct" from its own. The most gifted man, and perhaps the shrewdest practical lawyer, among the law Lords told them that they were utterly without jurisdiction in ecclesiastical matters; and the fact was illustrated by their attempting to press Church officers into their service and punish them for refusing to be enslaved.

Vainly did the Church offer to let the Court dispose of the property. The Lords might fairly allege that the Patronage Act, interpreted by common sense, meant the stipend and the duties to be assigned to one and the same man. We do not deny that. By leaving the parish duties to be regulated by the Church and the people, and giving the money to the patron's man, division and dissension would be fostered in parishes. The Church never contemplated this as a feasible, permanent arrangement. But she would submit to such an arrangement rather than dissolve the alliance with the State. She would not go out, though stripped of her endowments. But since she scrupulously respected the Court of Session in its own sphere, it was conspicuously blameworthy in the Court of Session to vault completely out of its own sphere and begin a course of disdainful domineering in the spiritual province,—the sphere expressly marked off for the " Church officers." Repeating, then, that the essential, all-comprehending grievance complained of by the Church of Scotland is, that the Court of Session has transferred to itself the government declared by the Confession of Faith to be distinctive of the Church, I proceed to ask what is that wrong— surely a monstrous one—in redressing which the Court of Session thrusts itself into a sphere from which " the Civil Magistrate" is peremptorily excluded.

Church patronage, no one hearing me will dispute, possesses the nature of a trust. The property involved is held in trust for the spiritual benefit of parishioners. The Church of Scotland has always professed a supreme regard for the spiritual interests of parishioners, and,

nearly ten years ago, embodied, in the Veto Act, the
principle that no one should be ordained pastor of a
parish if a majority of the male heads of families, being
communicants, disapproved of him on spiritual grounds.
The Church thus associated the parishioners with herself
in the guardianship of their spiritual interests. She
secured that the men who ministered to them spiritually, who lived among them as soul-healers, friends,
counsellors, should not be ordained as their pastors *against*
their will. The will of the people had been anciently
expressed in the "call." This had been allowed to fall
too much into abeyance, and for a long period it had
been overborne, but it had never been abolished; and
that party in the Church which, after long struggling
as a minority, has in the present century become the
majority, always contended that the call was constitutionally Presbyterian, and that patronage was the
foreign and questionable element. By the Veto Act
the Church reinforced the call. To whatever extent
she may have fallen short in the past, she thus intimated
to all the world that it was with her a vital principle
to ordain no minister to a parish against the will and
consent of the parishioners. If the Premier considers
this determination incompatible with the essential conditions of the alliance between Church and State in
Scotland, then we must quit the Establishment. If the
call remains, as Lord Brougham said, as completely
a nonentity as the wagging of the champion's horse's
tail at a coronation, the Establishment must be broken
up. Through many a dark day the people of Scotland
have stood by the Church, and the Church will now

stand by the people. But let the House recollect that the Veto Act did not abolish patronage, that in the great majority of cases the patrons were satisfied with the Act, and that the Crown patronage was worked smoothly in connection with it. The Church went rather further than a majority of three Lords of Session held she was legally entitled to go in securing the spiritual interests of parishioners, and for this the Court of Session, regardless of the Confession of Faith, has unhinged her whole system of government. At this moment the Church cannot, except under severe penalties, depose ministers guilty of theft; proceed against ministers accused of fraud and swindling; send ministers into particular districts to preach.

I need scarcely remark that, if the paralysis to which the Church is at present condemned must continue, we could never, should we remain in the Establishment, look the Dissenters of Scotland again in the face. We always told them that, unless we could serve our Lord Christ as well in the Establishment as out of it, we should not be in it; and if the "distinct" government in the Church "in the hand of Church officers" is at an end, we must tell them that the State Church in Scotland has proved a failure. The right honourable Baronet has reflected in most vehement terms on the severity of discipline with which the Church has visited those of her clergy who, directly disobeying her, have made themselves the instruments and officers of the Court of Session. He carefully points out that he disallows the indirect effects of the discipline. "It is," he says, "the degradation of character to which these men are subjected that most affects me." He looks with friendlier trust upon non-established denominations. Of Roman Catholics, Wesleyans, Congregationalists, he says, "Their right, so far as voluntary jurisdiction is concerned, is quite supreme, and we do not attempt to interfere with it." But a Roman Catholic priest, when deposed, is affected by the "degradation of character" as inevitably as a Presbyterian clergyman. The honourable Baronet must think very meanly of us, and believe us to think very meanly of ourselves, if he expects us to ordain and depose at the bidding of the Court of Session, when the Voluntaries ordain and depose in the exercise of their own discipline.

No doubt the Premier may insist that the men we have put under discipline declare that they have obeyed the law of the land. But for every minister of the Church of Scotland, the Confession of Faith is indisputably the law of the land. By their ordination vows our ministers have expressly accepted and sworn to that ordinance by which the government of the Church of Scotland is declared in the Confession of Faith to be "distinct" from the Civil Magistrate. Is it not really an insult to the human understanding that men who had vowed to obey a government in the Church, "distinct" from that of the Civil Magistrate, should excuse themselves by simply reiterating that they *had* obeyed the Civil Magistrate,—that is to say, by confessing and reconfessing their fault.

But the Premier need not be haunted by a spectral apprehension of being compelled, in case of reconciliation with the Church, to witness the expulsion from her borders of the Strathbogie ministers and all who have sympathised with them. The actually deposed ministers are but a handful. If they express contrition,—if they manifest a sincere desire to return to the arms of the Church,—then it is, to say the least, highly probable that they will be restored. Dr. Candlish, expressing the general sentiment, has publicly declared that he has no wish to see the party opposed to us—the Moderates—driven out of the Church. It is, moreover, a fact that the Moderates have never repudiated the spiritual jurisdiction. They profess merely to be in a difficulty as to its application. And it has at all times been a principle and rule of our Presbyterian discipline to judge overt acts and uttered words, not to pry into motives, or to pretend to see what is visible to the eye of God alone.

I suggest that a provisional arrangement should be formed on the basis of resolutions of the House to the following effect:—1. That there is not any intention to invade the independent spiritual jurisdiction of the Church of Scotland as defined in the Confession of Faith. 2. That immediate legislation is contemplated with a view to obviate any detriment or disadvantage in temporals, to clergymen of the Church, on account of their recognising, submitting to, and giving full effect to, the spiritual jurisdiction. 3. That legislation will be undertaken with a view to securing, in the settlement of pastors, that the property placed in trust of patrons in Scotland for the spiritual benefit of the people, shall be assigned to no minister against the will, expressed for purposes of edification, of the parishioners. Grant this, and separation will be averted.

And now, to close all, I shall make two short appeals. In the first place, I entreat honourable gentlemen not to allow themselves to be influenced by the earwig whispers, the stabs in the dark, of those who say that only a handful of head-strong, hare-brained men—interested demagogues wanting to pose as martyrs—will in any case leave the Establishment. It were better to make a noble mistake—to trust too generously, too bravely, too magnanimously—than to estimate human nature so vilely. To approach a member of your honourable House with these insinuations and suspicions is to insult him.

In the second place, addressing myself specially to the English members of the House, I ask them not to treat this question with impatient indifference as a mere alien and Scotch affair. It is their duty—they will not in terms deny it—to extend to Scotland, which at the Union became one with England, the same care and consideration which are due to England. Scotland maintained her national independence against England for ages. She entered the Union, on the faith of England, as a free and independent nation. The hostile feeling of the earlier time has given place to a sentiment of the warmest loyalty to our common realm. There was a day when the voice of Scotchmen attracted the notice of Europe, by proclaiming that, while a hundred Scotchmen remained alive, and there was a Scottish hill on which to plant their feet, they would not be reigned over by a King of England. It is now nearer the truth to say that, while a hundred Scotchmen remain alive, the imperial flag will not be rent asunder or the head of England brought low. Never, then, let it be alleged that, on this most intensely Scottish of all Scotch questions, in which petitions presented to your House prove hundreds of thousands of the worthiest people in Scotland to be supremely interested, the English members of Parliament, overruling the judgment of the Scottish members, and refusing to pause and consider, precipitated the break-up of the Scottish Establishment.

Alas! there was no Guthrie present in the House of Commons,—no Chalmers, no Candlish, no Cunningham, no Buchanan, no Hugh Miller,—to plead the cause of Scotland and her Church. In the dusk of suspicion, misunderstanding, vague apprehension, a great wrong was done. Out of 287 members, only 75 voted with Mr. Fox Maule. In the minority voted 25 Scotchmen, in the majority 12,—two to one true to Church and country. Never did the arrogant and icy indifference, so narrow, so ungenial, so unjust, so insular, that shows Englishmen at their very worst, more signally display itself. In the records of the British Parliament it might be difficult to find a more discreditable exhibition.

CHAPTER XXXIV

Thank God! they come, they come!

THE Claim of Rights had been presented, the House of Commons had been appealed to, the Government had been as inexorable as a marble Jove. And yet the Church made no sign. Over the face of society, like the moan of a malarious wind, crept the vile hope, the mean suspicion, that the Presbyterian party would play false. " They are not out yet! Good, sympathetic people, who had floods of tears ready to shed on the occasion, may bottle them up, not forgetting to cork them well, for they must stand long before they be needed."—Thus wrote one who ought to have known his countrymen better. Sooth to say, cause had been given, though never by the Church of Scotland, for questioning the fibre of the clerical conscience. The ghastliest of all the spectacles of the French Revolution was that of troop after troop of clergymen appearing before the Convention to announce that their profession of religion had been a sham. The uneasy sceptic, the man who knows in his heart that *he* is not at peace with God, is comforted beyond expression by what strengthens his conviction that *all* conscience is a lie, a nonentity, an echo from no Divine Voice, a thing not to be taken account of among the realities of the world. And so, during the weeks preceding the meeting of the General Assembly,—on the 18th of May 1843,—the whole Satanic school of treasonous theology, and atheistic philosophy, and mere cynical worldliness, continued to mock and moan.

But the great heart of Scotland knew better. Scott's romantic town, Wordsworth's peerless Edinburgh throned on crags, knew that a day to be remembered was about to rise upon her guardian hills and clustered dwellings. The excitement was intense, and from earliest morning there was a stir in the streets. Never had the gathering at Holyrood to meet the Queen's Commissioner, who again was the Marquis of Bute, been larger or more distinguished. It was remarked, as a pathetically felicitous coincidence, that the portrait of William of Orange, which had hung in the reception room, and opposite to which Lord Bute took up his position, fell from the wall. It was in no small measure due to the common sense and honest firmness of William that no attempt had been made, at the time of his accession, to foist some ecclesiastical compromise, or at least to impose some shadow of Anglican Erastianism, upon the people of Scotland, instead of giving them their own genuine Church. It was appropriately, therefore, that a voice cried out, "There goes the Revolution Settlement."

With extraordinary pomp, through crowded streets, the procession moved to St. Giles's Church. There, for the last time, the lineal descendants of those who rose in the rear of Jenny Geddes's stool to begin a revolution that changed the course of Britain's history, met around Dr. Welsh, the retiring Moderator, one of their own most resolute leaders, to hear him preach. He told them that the eyes of Christendom were upon them, but that this was a small matter compared with that of getting their feet upon the adamant of conscience, and feeling themselves in the presence of their Divine Head.

It was between two and three in the afternoon when Dr. Welsh took the chair as Moderator of Assembly in St. Andrew's Church. A few minutes later, Her Majesty's Commissioner entered. The great church was filled from floor to ceiling. Never perhaps in its history had the heart of Edinburgh been more deeply touched, its brain more keenly stirred. The cause had always been in some peculiar sense the cause of Edinburgh, a town whose fine intellectuality, nurtured on learning, law, literature, science, and theology, elicited the keen admiration of Charles Dickens. The intellectuality of Edinburgh was now raised to highest temper by glow of religious emotion; and the vast audience, in the church and in the street, knowing that, in logic as well as religion, the ministers of Christ had on this occasion the advantage of the lawyers, vexed with no faithless fear lest the Scottish clergy might fail in moral heroism, expected breathlessly but exultantly the decisive moment.

Having opened the meeting with prayer, the Moderator, whose manner we may realise as an impressive combination of solemnity and intrepidity, made the announcement that, in consequence of an infringement on the liberties of the Church, they could not constitute the General

Assembly, and he would read a protest embodying reasons for declining further proceedings. The document in question was signed by 203 ministers and elders, members of the House. It consisted of a brief but substantial summary of the Claim of Rights, with the all-important addition that the Legislature, by refusing to concede the Claim, or even to take it into full and fair consideration, had "recognised and fixed" conditions of Establishment which were subversive of the spiritual jurisdiction of the Church. Having made good, by a sufficient number of irrefragable facts, this position, the protesters declare it to be their duty to separate, in a way of peace and order, from the Establishment, which in its constitutional verity they love and prize, carrying with them the Standards of the Church, ceasing in no whit to be the Church, but "enforced" to rupture of the State connection by "interference with conscience, the dishonour done to Christ's crown, and the rejection of His sole and supreme authority as King in His Church."

The reading ended, Dr. Welsh laid the protest on the table of the Assembly, turned to Her Majesty's Commissioner, "who rose in evident and deep emotion," and bowed. It was a courteous but resolute farewell. The Church of Scotland, in the person of her Moderator, handed back to the State that property which she could no longer retain with due regard to her duties to those Scottish parishioners for whose spiritual benefit it had been confided to her, and without surrendering that spiritual jurisdiction which, as part of the Holy Catholic Church, she possessed from Christ her Head. He moved calmly towards the door.

Chalmers had been standing immediately on Welsh's left. A thousand eyes had been on him as the protest was being read, and it was observed that there was about him a look of dreaminess and abstraction. Was he, in that supreme hour, thinking of the picturesque manses and manse-gardens of Scotland, or of the nine prelates and the Prince of the Blood that had welcomed him in London, so lately, as a defender of Church Establishments? Suddenly, when Welsh began to move, he awoke to the present, and followed him with the air of one impatient to be gone. Dr. Gordon, Dr. Macdonald, of Ferintosh, rose and went after Chalmers. Another, and another, and gradually whole benches, moved away. Intense interest pervaded the vast audience. Many, both men and women, were weeping; but the tears were of pride, of exultation, of inexpressible joy. When the head of the column reached the open air, when the crowd recognised the familiar but loved and honoured figures of Chalmers, Gordon, Cunningham, Guthrie, Candlish,—these and so many others,—then a shout, "They come, they come! Thank God, they come!" rang through the air.

Dividing spontaneously to receive the column of Presbyters as they advanced, the great multitude escorted them down the long slope of the hill, looking across the Firth of Forth to Fife and the Highlands, toward Tanfield Hall, Canonmills, which had been prepared for their reception. About four hundred clergymen had withdrawn from St. Andrew's Church, and in the course of the next day the number of those who relinquished the dignities and endowment of Establishment had risen to nearly five hundred. "We did not," said Guthrie, "come out a small and scattered band; but, on the day of the Disruption, burst out of St. Andrew's Church as a river bursts from a glacier,—a river at its birth. In numbers, in position, in wealth, as well as in piety, our Church, I may say, was full grown on the day it was born. Above all, and next to the prayers that sanctified our cause, we were followed by a host of countrymen, whose enthusiasm had been kindled at the ashes of martyrs, and who saw in our movement but another phase of the grand old days that won Scotland her fame, and made her a name and a praise in the whole earth."

So the mockers and the moaners, the cynics, the sceptics, and the whole Satanic school of critics,—those true sinners against the Holy Ghost, who blaspheme the Divine gleam of moral heroism when it appears among men,—were in the wrong. It is roughly estimated that in annual income the ministers of the Free Church surrendered £100,000. But it will be readily admitted that, even when the large addition that falls to be made to this on account of glebes and manses has been reckoned, the most difficult part of the sacrifice, as involving the rupture of dear and tender associations, and the forfeiture of cherished dignity, will remain to be counted. The act has been recognised by all generous and candid observers as a piece of honest adherence to principle, the simple heroism of truth and worth, the matching of profession with performance. On this ground it was looked upon with proud sympathy by Jeffrey, whose true-hearted patriotism led him both to do justice to his native Church at every stage in the conflict, and to affirm, as he witnessed the Disruption, that such a spectacle could have been seen only in his native land. Carlyle, in those melancholy years when his visionary optimism was darkening into despair, may have let some sneers escape him about the Free Church, but within ten years of the Disruption he signalised it as the best bit of moral performance that had been transacted in his time. Mr. Justin MacCarthy has generously honoured it in his eloquent and admirable history of the Victorian Epoch.

And Macaulay, no prejudiced, and surely a well-informed witness, pronounced in these words his judgment as to which of the Assemblies, the departing or the remaining, represented the true Church of Scotland. "Suppose that we could call up Carstairs; that we could call up Boston, the author of the *Fourfold State;* that we could relate to them the history of the ecclesiastical revolutions which have, since their time, taken place in Scotland; and that we could then ask them, 'Is the Established Church, or is the Free Church, identical with the Church which existed at the time of the Union?' Is it not quite certain what their answer would be? They would say, 'Our Church, the Church which you promised to maintain unalterable, was not the Church which you (the legislators of Great Britain) protect, but the Church which you oppress. Our Church was the Church of Chalmers and Brewster, not the Church of Bryce and Muir.'"

It is related that when the movement to follow Welsh and Chalmers began in St. Andrew's Church, Robertson, of Ellon, the ablest and at the same time the most respected and earnest among the Moderates, rose from his place, took his station near the door, and watched with anxious face what was taking place. When he saw that the great body of those men who had been the light of the Church were actually departing, the blood, it is said, left his face and he became pale with sorrow. It was a nobler demeanour than if he had looked with cynical pride or harsh resentment upon his retreating antagonists. It was a tacit but eloquent acknowledgment that the men who were going had been no ignoble opponents, and that their departure was a deep loss to the Establishment. Let the figure of Robertson, as he at that hour appeared, stand for a symbol of the willingness of all that is best in the Established Church of Scotland to greet the day when the flimsy partitions that still stand between the sections of the whole Presbyterian Church of the land shall be removed. If not in theory, then in practice, all that the fathers and founders of the Free Church asked on behalf of the Establishment has, through their contendings, through sacrifices that were, for them, the very cracking of the heartstrings, been granted. They want no thanks from their successors. They seek no compliments, no detailed endorsement of their proceedings; but, even as they stand with their King around the throne of God, they ask to see, as the result and reward of their sacred passion, all branches of the Church of Scotland ranged under one banner, and that banner inscribed with the Crown Rights of the Redeemer.

CHAPTER XXXV.

The Queen's Letter.

BEFORE following Chalmers and his column into the hall at Canonmills, we may cast one glance on the truly miserable attempt, or pretext at an attempt, made by Sir James Graham and the Government, when the eleventh hour had struck, to avert the separation.

The Queen's letter to the Assembly was found, on being opened, to contain the following sentences: "The Church of Scotland, occupying its true position in friendly alliance with the State, is justly entitled to expect the aid of Parliament in removing any doubts which may have arisen with respect to the right construction of the statutes relating to the admission of ministers. You may safely confide in the wisdom of Parliament; and we shall readily give our assent to any measure which the Legislature may pass for the purpose of securing to the people the full privilege of objection, and to the Church judicatories the exclusive right of judgment."

Had this declaration and this promise been made in good time and in good faith, and with a candid desire to respect the spiritual independence of the Church, some good result might have ensued. But it seems impossible for any one who has sufficiently followed the conflict to know its catchwords, its pitfalls, its openings for that interminable hair-splitting which almost drove Candlish frantic, to read these words—the mature fruits of Sir James Graham's genius—without feeling that, brought forward at this time, they were cruelly frivolous. There was not an ordinarily clever and patriotic schoolboy in Edinburgh—the statement is made with the utmost deliberation—who, upon coming to the word "objection," might not have cried, "Objection,—privilege of objection, —why, that brings back the old question, Is the objection reasonable or unreasonable? and you may split hairs about that for ever."

More subtle is the comment, and yet not trivial or captious, that the last words of our quotation, which constitute, in fact, the offer of a bribe to the clergy, in form of power over the people, if only they will accept them, as parochial serfs, from the State, are pitiful. Not possessing the gift of prophecy, the ministers could not tell but their successors might tyrannise over the people, as their predecessors, the Moderates, had tyrannised. They would not accept unlimited right of judgment, while the people could only formulate objections. They demanded that the spiritual will of the people should be sacred from enforcement, either by Church officers or by State officers.

If anything could lend a tragic dignity to this letter, it would have been its formal association with the sovereign. That kind, good lady, whose heart and the heart of Scotland found each other out so soon, and have remained faithful to each other so long, knows and values all the branches of the Church in Scotland. Her Majesty, with her revered Consort, sent to Scotland, at the time of the Disruption, the distinguished and able Sydow, who drew up a luminous, nobly-toned, and conclusive vindication of the Free Church. Had it been constitutionally Queen Victoria's part to deal *proprio motu* with the Church business, it would never have been so ignorantly and negligently mismanaged.

CHAPTER XXXVI.

The Free Church.

WHEN the column had entered the hall, and the ministers had taken their place in the centre, all other parts of the immense building being densely crowded, the first breath of the new-born Church went up, from the lips of its retiring Moderator, in a prayer of such "thrilling pathos" and "overpowering solemnity," as befitted this appeal from earth to heaven.

The first business was to appoint a new Moderator. So soon as Dr. Welsh uttered the name of Chalmers, a burst of acclamation ascended from the audience, and they rose to their feet as one man. In a few well-chosen words Dr. Welsh alluded to his fame, his genius, his crowning glory in being among those who, "having turned many to righteousness, shall shine as the stars for ever and ever." Chalmers rose, briefly acknowledged the honour, and gave out the forty-third Psalm,—

"O send Thy light forth and Thy truth,
Let them be guides to me,
And lead me to Thy holy hill,
Even where Thy dwellings be."

The voice of the vast audience rose with such a volume of sound, that it seemed, said Dr. James Hamilton, who was present, "as if the swell of vehement melody would lift the roof from off the walls." Just at that moment the sun, which a heavy thunderstorm had thrown into almost complete eclipse, pierced the clouds and brilliantly lighted the place.

The address of Chalmers was in all respects worthy of himself and of this great historical occasion. He began by stating simply and calmly that the Legislature had declined to concede the claim of the Church, and had thus made subjection to the Civil Power in spiritual things a condition of Establishment. With as serene a sense of consistency, therefore, as he had ever felt in defending State Establishments of religion, he now announced that he and his brethren had dissolved their alliance with the State. "We are compelled,"—these were his words,—"though with great reluctance and deep sorrow of heart, to quit the advantages of the British Establishment, because she has fallen from her original principles, in the hope that we shall be suffered to prosecute our labours in peace on the ground of toleration."

Clear, comprehensive, conclusive! If any fact admits of historical verification, it is historically true that, in the period preceding 1843, the Court of Session had assumed complete jurisdiction over the Church of Scotland. The sole and supreme Headship of Christ, as explicitly affirmed in the Confession of Faith to involve a government "in the hands of Church officers DISTINCT from the Civil Magistrate," had been superseded.

Constitutionally and in Christian peacefulness the Church sought refuge in toleration. A thousand times have feeble or half-honest rhetoricians woven webs of sophistication to confuse persons weaker than themselves, under the notion that toleration offers no sounder guarantee of spiritual independence than the weighed and measured specifications of Erastian Establishment. But whatever allowance must be made for the occasional perversity or extravagance of lawyers, it remains certain that, under the blue vault of toleration, the free Churches of Great Britain enjoy every essential of spiritual freedom. Could Queen or Parliament command Dr. Dale, of Birmingham, to ordain a man pastor to a reclaiming congregation? If the person in question told the Court of Queen's Bench that ten thousand pounds of property depended for him upon Dr. Dale's being commanded to ordain him, would the Court fine, or reprimand, or threaten to imprison Dr. Dale for declining to do so? The justice of a strong, free, and noble nation is a mighty guarantee, and so long as British freedom endures, and Congregationalists, Romanists, and Presbyterians pay their own way and break no civil law, they will enjoy spiritual freedom and self-government under the open sky of toleration.

Chalmers then alluded in seemly and modest terms to the sacrifices made by the brethren. "It is well that you should have been strengthened by your Master in heaven to make the surrender you have done of everything that is dear to nature, casting aside all your earthly dependence rather than offend conscience, incur the guilt of sinful compliance by thwarting your own sense of duty, and run counter to the Bible, our great Church Directory and statute-book." And from this he passed on to expatiate on one of his favourite ideas. "We read," he said, "in the Scriptures, and I believe it will be found true in the history and experience of God's people, that there is a certain light and joyfulness and elevation of spirit consequent upon a moral achievement such as this. Apart from Christianity altogether, there has been realised a joyfulness of heart, a proud swelling of conscious integrity, when a conquest has been effected by the higher over the inferior powers of our nature; and so among Christians there is a legitimate glorying, as when the disciples of old gloried in the midst of their tribulations when the spirit of glory and of God rested on them, when they were made partakers of the Divine nature, and escaped the corruption that is in the world; or as when the Apostle Paul rejoiced in the testimony of his conscience. But let us not forget in the midst of this rejoicing the deep humility that pervaded their songs of exultation."

Thus was inaugurated the Free Church of Scotland. The State Church experiment, conducted under circumstances of peculiar advantage, had broken down. Dr. George Hill, the glory of the Moderates, had told his students, of whom the most illustrious headed this exodus, that "as the Church did exist before it was united with the State, it may exist without any such union;" and Chalmers now obeyed his teacher, and led the Church into freedom. What did we hear Hill saying at the outset? "If the Church, instead of deriving any benefit from the State, were opposed and persecuted by the Civil Magistrate, it would be not only proper, but necessary, to put forth of herself those powers which, in more favourable circumstances, she chooses only to exercise in conjunction with the State." When we read the unanswered and unanswerable Claim of Right, and realise how completely, how contemptuously, the Court of Session had in those years scoffed aside as a mere nonentity — a fantastic invisibility interposed between property and the Civil Power — the spiritual jurisdiction of the Church, we may indeed wonder how Dr. Cook and his associates could believe themselves true, in act as well as in word, to the noblest traditions even of the Moderate party. The State Churches that arose in the wake of the Reformation deserve that respect which pertains to all institutions that have been used by Providence, and have done good in their time. The best and bravest of them now broke first into freedom, — appropriately so, as the strongest bud is first in bloom, and the strongest eaglet is the first to leave the sheltering eyrie on the crag.

CHAPTER XXXVII.

The Testimony.

IT will be in place to devote a few sentences to knitting up historically the event just witnessed, and estimating its bearing upon the testimony of the Church of Scotland to the grand principle of Christian catholicity, the Headship of our Lord.

It was under favouring providential conditions that the Church entered, in the sixteenth century, on the particular path of witness-bearing that lay before her. Knox and her reformers in general were thoroughly cosmopolitan, having been at home in England, in Frankfort, in Geneva, wherever the foremost ideas of the time were most visibly in front. A weak monarch in Scotland presented opportunities which the hard, able, and tyrannical Tudors denied to the Reforming party in England. In her early history the Church laid her hold upon the affections of the people, and possessed in her Assembly, to use the words of Professor Charteris, "a free and popular Parliament when the Crown was despotic and when the nobles were in anarchy." It was hardly perhaps so much in the way of expressly formulating a dogma, though this was by implication effected, as by practical exercise of the natural rights of life and of growth, that the Church came to realise her sole spiritual allegiance to her Head. The spirit in which she recognised herself, not as the Church of Christ in any exclusive sense, but as one section of the Church of many nations, was in strictest harmony with this view.

In the seventeenth century, though it is difficult to repel the idea that the Church of Scotland was in some respects decadent, for there was a narrowing Catharism in the seventeenth century alien to the larger spirit of the sixteenth, she did not forget her catholicity, and she inscribed for ever in the annals of the world her devotion to the Headship of Christ. The Solemn League and Covenant, as she intended it, was to be a token of amity and Catholic union throughout Reformed Christendom. She placed upon the portals of the Shorter Catechism, as the beginning and end of education for every Christian child, the glorious words, closely akin in sound and sense to some of the sublimest ever uttered by Plato, "Man's chief end is to glorify God and to enjoy Him for ever." And it may be claimed as due to her influence, that her great principle of the Headship of Christ was lucidly, exactly, indelibly inscribed on those Westminster Standards which have been accepted by the Reformed Church throughout the English-speaking race.

But distinguished as her seventeenth century record had been, it was shadowed by serious drawbacks. If it could not be said that the Church did ever, as such, avail herself of material weapons, it could not be denied that, in the plenitude of her power, she was perilously free in making the Civil Magistrate indirectly her minister, and even the sword indirectly her weapon. And beyond question she had not, in the seventeenth century, attained to the grace of tolerance. This great attainment had been facilitated for all Churches, long before the Disruption, by the century of suspended enthusiasm and vivacious reason, of waxing science and waning superstition, the much maligned but not unprofitable eighteenth century. The last vestige of a disposition to encroach upon temporals, the last trace of intolerance and superstition, had departed from the Church of Scotland before 1843; and the Church of Chalmers, Welsh, and Gordon, of Candlish, Cunningham, and Guthrie, bore, it may be candidly maintained, the most precisely correct and the most impressively eloquent testimony to the sole and supreme Kingship of Christ over the Church that has been uttered since the Reformation.

A few points bearing directly on the edification and the efficiency of the Church, in relation to this doctrine, deserve to be briefly noted.

It fixes the gaze of the Christian army upon its King, the Divine Personality, Christ Jesus, whom all wise men discern to be the epitome of the revelation of God.

It reminds Christians of their privilege and duty to carry with them, as emanating from Christ, a certain kingliness of spiritual authority, a call to speak in the accent of conscience, the tone of the moral imperative, commanding morally sick men in His name to be well, and morally dead men to arise, and all men to repent.

It broadens out into the blue expanse of catholicity the little tent of sectarian peculiarity, and tempers with a loving spirit the arid intellectualism and negativism that beset Protestants. Thus is smitten down and refuted, in the way which is at once most conclusive and most conspicuous, the cruel and wicked lie against the Reformers that they were founders of sects, preachers of dogmatic specialties, instead of restorers of the truth and unveilers of the Church. No words ever came from the heart of Luther of more impassioned earnestness than those in which he expressed the wish that every syllable he had ever written should perish rather than that his comments should be put in the place of Holy Writ. Such was the spirit of all the great Reformers, who with one voice virtually adjured Christians, as Paul did, in tones of piercing, poignant entreaty, not to put them in the place of Christ.

It throws upon the proper shoulders, to wit her own, a sense of responsibility for the order of the Church and the defence of the truth, not permitting Christians to trust for the purity of their doctrines to civil lawyers; or to political assemblies, in which atheism and infidelity may prevail, for their worship, discipline, or the settlement of their ministers.

It pours a consecrating ray, direct from heaven, upon all those operations, missionary, philanthropic, educational, in which Christians work together for the promotion and extension of Christ's cause. When we observe the clumsy, haphazard, anarchical machinery of societies, unions, associations, talking-clubs, extemporised conferences, congresses, committees, by which Christian undertakings and Church work are generally carried on in England, are we not tempted to ask whether some men imagine that Christ has positively forbidden His Church to manage her concerns in His name, on the principles laid down in His law, on methods found to be expedient, and in the spirit of His disciples? Let the sacred right and duty of spiritual self-government be but duly apprehended by the Christian communities of Europe and America, and the chaos of denominationalism will beam gradually into a world of order, light, and beauty.

The Headship of Christ is the principle of catholicity; and the day it is made light of, the day it is put aside as obsolete, will be a day of perishing for the Church. Better were it for her that she should once more betake herself to the hill and the moor, that her membership should dwindle to two Christians and Christ on Scottish ground, than that her life-principle should be compromised and the Headship foresworn. But while the living Christ is her Head, there can be no risk of narrowness, no mistake about catholicity. The Vine with the surface of the world for its vineyard,—the Good Seed with the area of the world for its field,—the Leaven with the atmosphere of the world for its medium,—these are our Master's own symbols of the catholicity of His Church.

CHAPTER XXXVIII.

The Sustentation Fund.

CONVOCATION had been the spiritual birth-hour of the Free Church. All who felt themselves embraced within the fellowship of its brotherhood, and linked together in the inspiration of its sacred purpose, were henceforth free; and it was as a Free Churchman that M'Cheyne, who did not live to join the procession to Canonmills, rose, on the wings of his long-remembered Convocation prayer, to heaven. Assembled in their hall, under those same leaders who had helped them to realise Christ's presence in the Convocation, the brethren and their adherents felt that a great step had been taken, that it was well with them, that there was a sound of timbrels and of dances in the air, and that the Red Sea and the land of bondage lay behind.

Need it be said that the foremost leader shone in the practical part of the enterprise? The name of Chalmers is not more closely connected with the Church's spiritual independence, and the proclamation of the monarchy of Christ upon earth, than with those principles and methods of Church finance which are suggested by the mention of the Sustentation Fund. The point to be realised is, that those principles and methods, while intensely practical, partake of the ideal character of the Christian Church. As a political economist, Chalmers had the healthiest sympathy with commerce; but he would not have admitted that Christian pastors were competitive tradesmen, or even had a right to look upon their calling, as lawyers and physicians are allowed to do, with an eye to social and pecuniary success. They were bound to merge the personal motive in the sympathetic glow of pastoral brotherhood, the sacred *esprit de corps* of ministers of Christ, and to teach their flocks to rise above congregational selfishness into regard for the interests of the Church. Not competition but Christian communism was the principle adopted, and no door was left open for that fortune-making which has so grievously tarnished the spiritual glory of the Christian pulpit in London and New York.

The principle of a Sustentation Fund, equality of distribution, and this alone, can obviate the extremes of luxurious affluence on the one hand, and of strangling poverty on the other. Not that rigid rules can be laid down. It is out of the question that absolute uniformity of income should be prescribed, or that the attempt should be made to prevent congregations from making any special additions to the amounts received by their pastors from the common fund. But the benefits of the system, in securing a fair average, have been abundantly proved, and are incalculable.

Chalmers had been strenuously engaged for many weeks before the Disruption in making his financial preparations. Six hundred and eighty-seven associations had been organised, and two hundred and thirty-nine of these were in actual operation. Had all the pastors who adhered to the Free Church been thrown for maintenance upon the members of their own congregations who came out with them, then, in upwards of two hundred instances, the charges must have been abandoned. In any other country except Scotland,—and not even for Scotland can the exception be pleaded save in this instance,—it would have been thought sufficiently generous on the part of wealthy congregations and their pastors, *after* providing for their own requirements, to start a society in aid of those crippled congregations,— a society that should institute inquiries, make condescending suggestions, and at the end of that humiliating process, with which poor pastors in England are agonisingly familiar, hand out doles. The Free Church received all those brethren and their congregations into her arms, providing endowment for almost the whole of the Highlands. This involved a self-denying ordinance on the part both of the popular Free Church ministers and the well-to-do Free Church congregations, as deeply imbued with celestial fire, as instinct with moral nobleness, as anything in the entire transaction.

Candlish, of whom Dr. Gordon said that he was "essentially an unselfish man," and whom we saw anticipating the principle of the Sustentation Fund in 1841, was at the time of the Disruption loved beyond measure by one of the richest congregations in Edinburgh. In the first year of freedom, that congregation subscribed about £10,000 to the purposes of the Church. By

merely being silent, by simply letting his friends enjoy
what would have been for them the luxurious delight of
showering gold upon him, Candlish might have been far
richer than before. What he did receive from his congregation was £200, having refused to accept of more.
And of this £200 he returned £50, besides declining to
take his share from the Sustentation Fund. There is a
chord in every human heart that vibrates to Christianity
like this!

It was part of Chalmers's idea that the duty and
privilege of supporting the service of the Master should
be shared in by all members of the Church, artisans
and day-labourers and domestic servants, as well as
by marchionesses and millionaires. It is beautiful to
observe how giving became, under these Christian circumstances, more blessed than receiving. It was not
on the thousands handed in by the rich that Chalmers
dwelt with fondest satisfaction, but on the pence of the
poor. "The liberalities," he said, "which have been
poured forth on our great enterprise, even by the
humblest of our artisans and labourers, and the grateful
responses which these have called back again,—the words
of kindness and encouragement which have been sent
from all places of the land, to bear us up on the field
of conflict, and our thankful sense of the friendship which
prompted them,—the amalgamating power of a common
object and a common feeling, to cement and knit together
the hearts of men,—the very emulation to love and to
good works, which has given birth to so many associations, each striving to outrun the other in their generous
contributions for the support of what is deemed by all

to be a noble cause,—even the working of these associations, in which the rich and the poor are often made to change places, the former visiting the houses of the latter, and receiving the offerings of Christian benevolence at their hands,—the multiplied occasions of intercourse thus opened up between those parties in the commonwealth which before stood at the greatest distance, and were wont to look with the indifference, if not the coldness, of aliens to each other,—these are so many sweetening and exalting influences which serve to foster the sympathy of a felt brotherhood among thousands and tens of thousands of our countrymen, and will mightily tend, we are persuaded, to elevate and humanise the society of Scotland."

It is beautiful to see how the experiences of Free Church finance charm the ingenuous soul of Chalmers, who seems never to have once bethought him of the hard things he used to think, if not to say, of the Voluntary system. It must, however, be confessed that Voluntaryism never appeared in so fine a form as that it assumed under the auspices of this champion of Establishment. Nor ought it to be disguised that, unexampled as was the success of Voluntaryism in the Church of Chalmers, it nevertheless failed to reach the height of his ideal. Never did he see congregational selfishness so completely smitten down as he could have wished,—never did he see the cause of the poor, relatively to that of the rich, in country or in town, so well cared for as he demanded,—never did the liberality of Christians, splendid as Free Church liberality was, appear to him liberal enough.

But in truth Free Church finance was, and has continued to be during these fifty years, a notable success, a cause of thankful, honourable pride to Scotland and to Christendom. Though in the first year there were cases not a few of painful privation, of suffering to the death, —though the tremendous effort in the outset to build churches, procure dwellings, and provide incomes, told with great severity both upon pastors and people,—yet the position of the Free Church clergy has, in economical respects, been one of many advantages. Relations of warm friendliness have subsisted between them and their flocks; and if their money income has not been large, it has been the delight of their people to make them partakers in all the bounties of the season—fruit, fish, game —as they came round. Owing to the beneficent mechanism of the Sustentation Fund, they have been spared the perils and the pains of dependence upon one, two, half a dozen opulent or well-to-do persons in their congregations, and have been under no necessity to wait the convenience of heritors or factors. " For the twenty years consecutively," said Mr. Sage, of Resolis, " in which I was a minister of the Established Church, I did not receive a farthing of my stipend without a *grudge*, or even without the *curse* of my heritors along with it." Their delays, their litigious disputes, their desperate niggardliness, vexed and impoverished him. " How different," he exclaims, " was all this from, and how contrary to, the treatment which I have uniformly received since I joined our beloved and truly nobleminded Free Church of Scotland! Its managers, instead of opposing me or adding to my expenses, more than half-way meet my wants, and even anticipate them. After shaking myself free of the Establishment and its annoying, unhallowed appendages, in joining the Free Church I may truly say that I exchanged debt and poverty for peace of mind and a competency, enabling me to supply my everyday wants and to pay all debts."

CHAPTER XXXIX.

The Missionaries.

THOSE were not days of cablegrams, when responses from India, Australia, Canada, Chicago could have reached Canonmills in an hour. It was only in faith and hope that the Free Churchmen could in any measure realise the extent to which they commanded the sympathies of Christendom.

At the very first, indeed, the leal and gallant Presbyterians of Ulster held out to them the right hand of fellowship, and the Presbyterians of England greeted them with acclamation. In due course the envoy sent to report upon them by Queen Victoria and Prince Albert pronounced their argument invulnerable; and Hase, in his masterly epitome of Church history, ranked their exodus among the sacred episodes of Christian progress. A large proportion of the probationers of the Church—the ministers who had not yet obtained charges—cast in their lot with them, and almost in a body the students of theology joined them. Dr. Rabbi Duncan, and all who, with him, were inspired with ardent zeal for the conversion of the Jews, saw in the Free Church the most accurate realisation achieved, since the days of Paul, of the Christian Israel. As weeks and months went by, Dr. Chalmers received about a score of congratulatory letters or addresses from the same number of distinct Christian communities, representing the vast and various ramification of the great tree of Reformed Christianity.

So soon as it was possible to hear from India and other outlying portions of the Mission Field, it became known that, without a single exception, the whole of the missionaries, with Dr. Duff at their head, adhered to the Free Church. No testimony in her favour can be conceived more weighty and impressive than this. The missionaries felt themselves spiritually in touch with the Free Church; nor can it be doubted that the larger part of their material support had reached them from men who were now Free Churchmen. And we cannot wonder at this, for it is first and foremost of the Church of all Christian missionaries that Christ is King and Head. It is of a Church in motion rather than of a Church at rest that we have a description in the New Testament. It is marching orders, rather than directions for the pitching of tents or for the employment of time in camp, that the Master has left us. And it is in connection with the mission enterprises of the last half century that the Church in all its sections has most conspicuously blessed the world, and that blessing has most manifestly been reflected back upon the home congregations. The missionary has approved himself the most efficient minister of civilisation, the man who enables the untutored child of nature to realise that civilisation has a heart and a conscience, and is not necessarily an invasion of fraud and cruelty.

In India, in Africa, in the islands of the Pacific, the missionaries of the Free Church have done noble work, and have been honoured by the Universal Church. When they have gone out into the great wilderness of pagan humanity, the difference between a social atmosphere impregnated with Christian elements and one where the name of Christ is unknown, has been felt by them and all missionaries to be so great, that the things on which Christians disagree have seemed to dwindle, and the things on which they agree to rise into supreme importance. It is seen that there are but two religions in the world,—the religions which, having served their providential ends, are dying of decrepitude, perishing in the dawn; and the religion whose God cannot be eclipsed by civilisation until civilisation reveals something purer than Light and better than Love. Duff, Moffat, Livingstone are household words, not in the Free Church alone, but in all Christian circles. "The lights begin to twinkle from the rocks." There are points of Christian illumination gleaming out here and there in the dusk, which seem to announce a vast extension of Christian influence in the councils of the world. On international peace, on commercial righteousness, on all philanthropic questions, on the mercy and tenderness due from man to the animal tribes, the voice of the Church's Head, speaking through the many voices, in great part missionary voices, of His Church, is making itself heard.

Remembering that liberty to obey Christ, though infinitely different from anarchy, is the most expansive

form of freedom ever bestowed upon men, do we not find
it pleasant to realise that, in sending forth ever new
waves of missionary zeal, the Free Church may quicken
in the future, as she has done in the past, the energies of
her own home life, and realise with fresh vividness her
sympathy with other branches of the Church? Such
mission journeys as those of Dr. Norman Macleod and
Dr. A. N. Somerville have been rich in benefit both at
home and in the outlying field. Why should they not
be taken boldly into precedent, and a circulating system
be established, the blood pulsing out warm towards the
extremities and returning in healthful current to the
heart? Why should not mission-pilgrimages visit India,
making the simple native Christians by Ganges feel that
they are brothers and sisters of the Christ and the
Christians of Britain? And if India is visited, may
not even China be reached, where one of the smallest
but not the least loving of the sister Churches of the
Free Church, the Presbyterian Church in England, has
long had a flourishing mission?

Nor can a word of reference be omitted to that
missionary enterprise which arose under the influence
of that remarkable man who was referred to as Rabbi
Duncan. Mr. Taylor Innes, an enthusiastic admirer of
the Rabbi, tells us that, in his youth, he had been so far
off the Evangelical lines, that the strong hand of Dr.
Mearns was required to bring him back from atheism.
In his wild days, *teste* one of his college friends, he
fell, like Burns and many another gifted Scot, into
intemperance; but in his most eccentric moments
the fire of public spirit never died within him; and

one night, when his boon companions were bearing him homewards on a shutter, and there arose an alarm of fire, he shouted lustily from his elevation, "Water for the fire, citizens,—water for the fire!" John Duncan did nothing by halves. He was a highly successful student. A period of struggle and of crisis in his spiritual life issued in what he definitely named his conversion; and no sooner was he converted than he became an importunate preacher of his new faith to his companions. Addressing himself with his usual ardour to the study of Hebrew, he became one of the first Hebraists in Europe, and, as head of the Christian mission of Buda Pesth, opened up a sympathetic connection between the best type of devout minds among the Jews and such as, being brothers of Christ, claim to be children of Abraham. Through his means the Saphir family, distinguished for talent and fine moral qualities, passed from Judaism to Christ.

Acquaintance with the best Hebrew scholarship—Gesenius, Hengstenberg, Ewald, and the like—tended doubtless to temper and expand the somewhat rigid dogmatism of Dr. Duncan's first earnest belief; and innate intrepidity and honesty kept his ear open to the moral voices of his time, so that, as Professor Knight has taught us, he could take a hint from Carlyle, and detect the true accent of Christian song in the hymn of a Roman Cardinal. He gave the New College, Edinburgh, its reputation as a seat of Hebrew scholarship,—a reputation it has splendidly sustained under his favourite student and successor, Dr. A. B. Davidson. And now, when some one-eyed personages ask whether Christianity is not dying off the earth, we behold, under various forms, a development of that sympathy between the best Hebrews and the best Christians, which Rabbi Duncan initiated at Buda Pesth, and which may presage much in the evolution of spiritual civilisation. Are not men puzzled in the classification of a Montefiore,—is he Jew or is he Christian? Are not heavy-laden Jewish populations in the east of Europe beginning to ask wistfully whether Jesus was not *their* brother, and why the Gentiles have had all the joy of Him? Has not an Adler, leader of the Hebrew community in London, told his brethren to take note that the deepest spiritual consciousness of mankind has been embodied in the sayings of Christ?

CHAPTER XI.

Royal Chalmers.

HIS part in the founding of the Free Church was the last grand public enterprise in the life of Chalmers. Never did a film of doubt cross his mind as to the rightness of what he had done; and in 1847, in giving evidence before a Committee of the House of Commons, he distinctly avowed his belief that the schismatic conduct of the clergy who forsook the Church to place themselves under the Court of Session, deserved an extreme exercise of discipline. But though the brief period of life that remained to him was beautiful in its serenity and spiritual elevation, there was a quietude in it, an absence of jubilancy, which might have been different if duty had not compelled him to part with so many friends of his youth, and if the end of all his hoping and promising, in relation to the Established Church of Scotland, had not been so different from what he had expected.

The peace of Christ, however, left him not for a moment. Perfectly sincere religion approved itself to be in his case, as in that of millions, a well of living water in the soul, and he needed no further mechanism than that of his pocket Bible to quicken its healing virtue. He delighted beyond expression in the society of those Christian friends, of whom even he could count but few, who really loved to engage with him in sympathetic interchange of thought upon the incorruptible riches and the immortal life. "We have a warrant in the Bible," he wrote to a lady friend, "for loving much :—'Love one another with a pure heart fervently.' It may be fervently, if it be *first* with a pure heart." He rejoices in the universality of the gospel offer. The Bible "does not bear your name and address, but it says, '*whosoever*' —that takes you in; it says '*all*'—that takes you in; it says, 'if *any*'—that takes you in. What can be surer than that?"

Having passed beyond the pale of ecclesiastical establishment, he soon began to perceive and to welcome the growth of a sentiment towards union among free Churches. Were there but cordial fealty to the Head, he set small store by forms of administration, and was careful that the liberty of any one body of Christians should not be made a restraint for any other. He too, although he did not live to see the express initiation of movements in that direction, may be enrolled among the Apostles of Union. "Co-operation now," he said, "and this with the view, as soon as may be, to incorporation afterwards." In May 1847, silently and painlessly, he passed away. "He sat there, half-erect, his head reclining gently on the pillow; the expression of his countenance that of fixed and majestic repose."

The Christian gentleman! So stainless, so lofty, in all his moods and habitudes of soul. "Chalmers," said

Robertson, of Ellon, "understands little of the ways of men." What a compliment! Meanness was incomprehensible to him,—he had no organ, no sense, by which it could be evinced to his perceptions, or rendered intelligible to his mind. This is the greatest man of the whole Evangelical movement. He preached philosophical virtue, and left his weighty testimony to its practical ineffectiveness, and to the practical effectiveness of another kind of preaching. "To preach Christ is the only effective way of preaching morality in all its branches." He drew out in theory, and exemplified in practice, exhausting both, the Christian method, which is also the sole right method, of dealing with the poor. If you meet with any true word on this subject, however new it may look, or any sound suggestion, however original it may appear, put forward by slum-worker or oracle of Toynbee Hall, be you quite certain that Chalmers has anticipated it. And as a piece of unanswerable reasoning, sound in theology, sound in science, sound in common sense, his *Astronomical Discourses*—an antidote to morbid humility on the one hand and to spiritual pride on the other—cannot be bettered. His ideal of Christ's kingdom on earth could not be realised in connection with the State; and great is the honour, but great also is the responsibility, of the Free Church, in having received from him that ideal, to be realised under God's blue sky.

CHAPTER XLL

Cunningham, Scholar and Controversialist.

CUNNINGHAM had not the brilliant ideality of Chalmers, nor the lightness and velocity of Candlish; there was beyond question an element of ponderousness about him, and there was little magic in his pen; but he conveyed to a vast multitude of minds the idea of being substantially an abler, stabler man than either. The prevailing sentiment among Free Church students and Free Church ministers has always been, that the authority of Cunningham on any theological or ecclesiastical subject was the highest that could be quoted.

He was a born controversialist in the best sense of the term,—endowed, that is to say, with a transcendent capacity for discerning and recollecting the essential points of difference between opposing systems of thought, weighing them against each other, and striking with exact precision the balance between them. His specialty was that, with this faculty in transcendent development, he was not intellectually a trimmer, but a man of decisive belief, and energetic, or even impetuous action. It was truth he sought. In rhetoric, he had no skill. Seeking truth, he ended in conviction; and to end in conviction was to reach the beginning of action. Conscientious in the quest for truth, conscientious in the examination of *all* the evidence, he could not without insufferable pain behold his conclusions overlaid by the cobwebs of clerical mediocrity, or obscured and misrepresented by the quibbles of professional law pleaders. His trains of reasoning, accordingly, were apt to terminate in the rise and thunderous roll of his moral indignation.

Cunningham was exactly the man to be at the head of a great institute for training candidates for the Christian ministry. Acquainted with all the great systems of thought, philosophical as well as theological, he combined with his dogmatic firmness a very large capacity of intellectual toleration. His students learned from him that the difficulties which come up in theology, have come up before in philosophy; that a man may, as a philosopher, intelligently enough hold any one of the great contrasted systems, idealist or materialist, and yet be a Christian; that for wise men all systems lead up, by various ways, to mystery and reverent silence; and that a sure mark of the sciolist and of the vulgar, voluble, flippant coxcomb, is readiness to solve insoluble problems. He knew infidelity too well to think it would conquer. "No school of infidelity," he said, "had exercised influence over more than a generation." The trepidation and the exultation raised by each new chameleonic variation of infidelity south of the Tweed, he accounted for in a way not highly complimentary to England, or to the theological colleges of

England: "There is so little *in* the English mind; there is a want of clear, definite, theological views, they are at the mercy of every wind of doctrine."

His Calvinism was for him what it was for Paul and Calvin, a taking of refuge from the agonies alike of philosophy, and of theology, and of nature, in the bosom of God. "Shall not the Judge of all the earth do right?" Faith in His sovereignty is surely more reasonable than make-believe in any optimistic trifling with the mystery of things. Cunningham liked to expatiate on the innumerable multitude of the redeemed. He looked upon the Articles of the Church of England as fulfilling all the requirements of Calvinistic orthodoxy. Under his auspices at the New College, speculative thought among the students was bold and free, but he never displayed the slightest jealousy on the subject.

He reflected with humility but gratitude on the circumstance that it was he who, in a motion made in the Presbytery of Edinburgh, initiated the movement that issued in the Disruption. The principles contended for had, he held, been "the peculiar deposit of the Church of Scotland in every age;" and he viewed it as a "marvellous token" of Divine kindness to the Church, that she had been again honoured to contend, "as before, for the sole Headship, and for the sole and exclusive right of Christ to reign in His own kingdom." In the first and by far the greatest period of the Reformation, the general system adopted in outline by all the Reformers, not through invention or excogitation, but by simple rediscovery in the newly-opened Bible, and specially in the New Testament, had, he held, been substantially that of Presbyterianism. So it was throughout the vast ramification of the Reformed Catholic Church, in the national Churches of Switzerland, Holland, France, England, and Scotland. It was in England, and there not so much through fault of the people of England, or even of the Church of England, as of the Erastian monarchs of England, that what Milton calls "a schism from all the Reformation, and a sore scandal to them," took place. Cunningham thought, however, that the Reformers had themselves been greatly to blame, having become involved in "contentions and divisions which, in the course of a single generation, arrested the whole course of the Reformation."

During the years of life that remained to him after the Disruption, he was the steadfast friend of union among Christians, wherever it was based on essentials, and recognised the Head. But although he was cheered by tidings of harmony and concord from Canada and from Australia, he found that proposals for home union were strangely, lamentably productive of wrangling. This vexed him deeply; and in his last illness, when his mind wandered in the near approach of death, he twice repeated Melanchthon's prayer, "From the rage of theologians, good Lord, deliver us." He died in perfect peace, saying he was going home.

It was December 1861. A year before, his great antagonist in the Church's battle, Robertson, of Ellon, had died. "It deepens our solemnity," Professor Charteris touchingly says, "to remember that, when a year had shed its showers and snows on the grave of James Robertson, bleak December, which had carried him away, bore from his brethren William Cunningham. They were set face to face in many a fight, and now they rest together. They cherished mutual respect throughout the hard encounters; and ere their labours on earth were closed, when one had retired from public life to study the theology of past ages, and the other had sacrificed learned leisure to the great cause of the evangelisation of Scotland, they spoke of each other as was to be expected of true men drinking at a purer source than the muddy waters of controversy. But now, when they see eye to eye, and dwell in the light of God's eternal love, how unworthy must seem to those saints every feeling that erewhile marred the fulness of their Christian brotherhood!" Yes, every feeling that did injustice to each other, but no feeling that was only the glow of impetuous ardour in the service of their Lord.

CHAPTER XLII.

Candlish and Union—James Hamilton.

FREED from the cerements of Establishment, Candlish realised, with his own peculiar lucency of apprehension, the position held by the Church in relation to sister Churches. "It was as maintaining great principles, and suffering for them, that the Church of Scotland became a rallying point of union to all the Churches of the Reformation; and God has brought us into this position again." He struck out a wider principle of unity in variety than had been discovered by Presbyterians in earlier ages, but one that is of vital and priceless importance to the Reformed Catholic Church in our time. "We have now got hold of a principle of which the Westminster Divines did not seem to be aware,—at least the practical application of it was not before their minds,—I mean that of Christian Churches coming ever nearer and nearer to one another in point of doctrine and discipline, yet still deeming it right to keep up their different forms of Church government," while sympathising in their efforts for God's glory and man's good, and, of course, owning the supreme Headship of their Lord.

There was a beautiful consistency, a precise and peremptory logic, in the historical account he gave, from the distance of 1856, of the Established and Free Churches. "The date of the existence of the present Established Church of Scotland is 1843; the date of our existence is 1560. We can trace our unbroken pedigree through many vicissitudes, trials, and persecutions, from that eventful year when first the General Assembly met in Scotland; by all the historical signs and marks which can possibly identify a national Church, we can certainly trace our descent, far more clearly than any bishop can trace back his to the apostles. That being our position, we are not, in the exercise of any false and spurious charity, to be found for a moment admitting that the Established Church, as it now exists, is a Church of older date than the last thirteen years."

Very soon after the Disruption, he asked the question whether, since the States and kingdoms of the world refused to establish Churches without extinguishing their spirituality and freedom, Churches were bound, or were permitted, to put off their union with each other from abstract considerations as to the duty of States and kingdoms in the matter of Establishment. "Is the division and schism of the Christian Church to be kept up by a question as to the duty of another party over whom we have no control?" His brain and conscience answered, No.

It may fearlessly be affirmed that each and all of the galaxy of Free Church leaders who secured unanimity in the Convocation were prepared to give the same answer to this question. Chalmers, Cunningham, Guthrie,

Buchanan, would have seen the reasonableness of leaving the State to answer for itself, and proceeding with the positive duty of gathering, so far as was practicable, under the Church's wing, those chickens which the Establishment had driven into the waste. Candlish, Buchanan, and Guthrie entered with high spiritual enthusiasm into this new movement, and round these the young men of forward-looking mind, with Dr. Rainy at their head, were prompt to range themselves. Union was, in the view of these men, and first of all union with the United Presbyterians, the normal, constitutional, catholic path for the Free Church to take. In heartfelt accordance with them, Dr. Cairns and the great body of United Presbyterian clergymen and laymen hailed the prospect of union. The great Union party in both Churches forged no new fetters for their brethren, added no iota to what it was already permitted them to believe or disbelieve, but merely asked that the belief entertained as to the duty of a third party should not be an insuperable bar to union among brethren. Again, again, and yet again did the remaining Titans of the Disruption, with *one* exception, and the foremost Free Churchmen of the newer generation, vote by overwhelming majorities that the gates of the Free Church should be thrown open, and the free Presbyterians of Scotland invited to enter.

Not a little was accomplished. The principle of mutual eligibility was adopted. Four hundred ministers and elders of the Free Church signed a most important manifesto, setting forth the beneficial results of the conferences, and inscribing Union, not as "a matter of discretion, to be ultroneously undertaken or abandoned at the Church's pleasure, but a duty of deep and abiding obligation," on the banner of the Free Church. But Dr. Begg, whom the heavenly influences at the Convocation, after his frank and honest speech, had constrained into still nobler silence of assent and acquiescence, headed an irreconcilable minority. Union could not have taken place without a rending of the Free Church. Strange to say,—and even if one does not quite agree with him, one cannot help loving him the better for it,—Guthrie, the genial, kindly Guthrie, who, as boy and man, so dearly loved an honest, stand-up fight, was so deeply imbued with the sacred passion for union, that "he would," says his biographers, " even at the risk of a partial secession from his own Church," have carried out the hallowed enterprise. " It clouds the evening of my days," he said, " to think that we cannot, while retaining our differences, agree to bury our quarrels in a grave where no mourner stands by,—a grave above which I can fancy angels pausing on the wing, and uniting in this blessed song, ' Behold how good and how pleasant it is for brethren to dwell together in unity.'" But Candlish, Buchanan, Moncreiff, Rainy, and with them Cairns and Ker and their brethren, felt that it was more in the spirit of Christ—more consistent with Christian magnanimity— to postpone formal union. And this, we may reverently believe, was most of all in harmony with the Master's will.

There was a perfect absence of affectation in all that Candlish said or did, and his boyish naturalness, combined with what may be called the fiery honesty that was his habitual mood of mind, caused him to convey to superficial observers some idea of harshness. As a disciplinarian he certainly was stern. But this arose exclusively from his sense of duty. At heart he was one of the tenderest of men, and no one could thoroughly know him who had not rowed with him in a boat, or seen him among his children.

His estrangement from Cunningham, which almost broke *two* of the noblest hearts, showed that both were forgiving men. Cunningham spoke bitterly of Candlish, his choler for the moment fairly getting the better of his reason. But the provocation was severe. Cunningham justly felt that his services to the Free Church had been great, and, knowing his unrivalled learning, and being Principal of the College, he could not but feel that much was due to his opinion on questions of theological education. He was convinced of the importance of erecting one great seminary of theological education in Edinburgh, to be a Pharos of spiritualised intellectual light for the whole Reformed Church. Candlish held that there ought to be Colleges in the neighbourhood of the Universities of Glasgow and Aberdeen. The Church took the view of Candlish. The Principal saw himself eclipsed. He felt it bitterly. All friendly relations were suspended between the men. Cunningham's health gave way, and it reached Candlish's ear that a journey abroad, with medical attendance too expensive for his means, was desirable. In careful secrecy, with studious delicacy, Candlish initiated a movement for procuring the necessary funds, and the suggestion was so energetically taken up that a testimonial of upwards of £7000 was presented to Cunningham. We need not inquire whether the latter ever knew where the movement originated, but the friendship of the men was renewed, and Candlish was relieved from what, while it lasted, had been one of the greatest sorrows of his life.

And how beautiful does he appear in his relations with Dr. James Hamilton! The men were of contrasted types, Candlish having a strong trace of the Dantesque austerity, the Miltonic Puritanism, "ever in the great Taskmaster's eye;" Hamilton being an incarnation of sympathy, gentle as a woman, melodious in all his moods of mind. You could not be long in a room with James Hamilton without believing in the real presence of Christ. He and Candlish found each other out. Candlish said of Hamilton after his death, that "under the spell of his benign and blessed temper, always giving thanks, converse was sure to cease from being mere earthly and idle talk, and to become serenely, happily, and even joyously, fellowship of a more heavenly sort." It had been, doubt it not, in the ardency of their love for their Master, that they became known to each other as brother friends. They used to exchange pulpits, and were perfectly at home in each other's houses. "I write home," says Candlish to Hamilton, in a note from London, "to say that they may expect the pleasure of your staying with them from Thursday till the beginning of the following week. Don't steal the hearts of my children as you did before! You may help James in his lessons, but don't captivate my namesake Bo." No one who had seen him pulling about Bo in romping games, enlivening the fun with jokes, quite on a level with Bo's understanding, about the Goose-dubs of Glasgow, would have had much apprehension as to the security of his hold upon Bo's affections.

And what beauty of tenderness could excel this, in a letter to his daughter, Mrs. Archibald Henderson, who had lost an infant son? "Your nice letter greatly pleased me. I thank the Lord from the bottom of my heart for the grace granted to you and Archie. I cannot say or write much to comfort you. But you are seldom long out of my thoughts, and I inwardly mourn and weep with you. I feel it is a knock-down blow to myself when I look back on the delight and joy of having you here, so bright and radiant, with so darling a boy. But, like you, I try to be grateful for these few weeks, and would not for worlds part with the dear recollection of them. It is good for you, and a blessed reflection, to have had a little one in your arms whom Jesus has now taken into His own."

And think of this,—the time now being very near his death: "That forenoon he saw little Mary and John, his eldest daughter's children. They were lifted up on his bed, and sang 'Rock of Ages.' He kissed them, and said, 'Love Jesus, and meet me in heaven.' After they left he was very much overcome, and said, 'How these monkeys get round one's heart. I would like to have seen them up a bit.'"

His last effort of consciousness was a warm pressure of the hand when his son-in-law, Mr. Henderson, repeated these words of Isaiah: "The mountains shall depart, and the little hills be removed; but my kindness shall not depart from thee, neither shall the covenant of my peace be removed, saith the Lord that hath mercy on thee."

Of Buchanan, the candid, eloquent, and convincing historian of the conflict, and of so many others, time now fails us to speak. A chapter, and a long one, might be devoted to the eminent men, Hugh Miller, Fleming, Sir David Brewster, who pledged the Free Church to a conscientiously bold and resolute acceptance of the truth of science as the truth of God. Much might be said also of the contributions of the Church to education, to temperance, and all good social causes. Illustrious among the labours of Free Churchmen, lay and clerical, have been the various literary efforts and issues by which the fountains of theology have been continuously replenished, and the devout learning and reverent speculation both of Christian antiquity, and of Christian Germany, France, Switzerland, and America, communicated to the religious world of Great Britain. Under the auspices largely of the Free Church, with the assistance of many eminent authors and publishers, the reproach of being unlearned has been effectually removed from the Reformed Catholic Church.

WORKS BY PROFESSORS AND MINISTERS

OF

The Free Church of Scotland

PUBLISHED BY

MESSRS. T. & T. CLARK, EDINBURGH.

'*The Free Church of Scotland, the most theological and literary Church in the world.*'
—METHODIST TIMES.

Adam.—EXPOSITION OF THE EPISTLE OF JAMES. By the late JOHN ADAM, D.D. 8vo, price 9s.

Bannerman.—THE CHURCH OF CHRIST: A Treatise on the Nature, Powers, Ordinances, Discipline, and Government of the Christian Church. By the late Prof. J. BANNERMAN, D.D. Two vols., demy 8vo, price 21s.

Bannerman.—THE SCRIPTURE DOCTRINE OF THE CHURCH HISTORICALLY AND EXEGETICALLY CONSIDERED. By D. DOUGLAS BANNERMAN, D.D. Perth. In demy 8vo, price 12s.

'A noble volume, and reflects credit on the author's industry, learning, and vigour both as a theologian and a writer.'—*Freeman.*

Binnie.—THE CHURCH. (*Handbook Series.*) By the late Prof. BINNIE, D.D. In crown 8vo, price 1s. 6d.

Blaikie.—THE PREACHERS OF SCOTLAND FROM THE SIXTH TO THE NINETEENTH CENTURY. By Prof. W. G. BLAIKIE, D.D., Edinburgh (*Moderator of the General Assembly*, 1892). In post 8vo, price 7s. 6d.

'Incomparably the best and most popularly written book on the subject that has appeared for many years.'—*Spectator.*

Blake.—HOW TO READ THE PROPHETS. Being the Prophecies arranged Chronologically in their Historical Setting. With Explanations, Maps, and Glossary. By Rev. BUCHANAN BLAKE, B.D., Clydebank. Four volumes, now ready, crown 8vo.

PART I.—THE PRE-EXILIAN MINOR PROPHETS (with JOEL). 2nd Ed. Price 4s.
PART II.—ISAIAH (Chapters i.–xxxix.). Second Edition. Price 2s. 6d.
PART III.—JEREMIAH. Price 4s.
PART IV.—EZEKIEL. Price 4s.

'Mr. Blake seems to have hit upon the right thing, and he has proved himself competent to do it rightly. While these books are the very best introductions to the study of the prophets, even the accomplished scholar will find them indispensable.'—*The Expository Times.*

Brown.—COMMENTARY ON I. and II. CORINTHIANS. By Principal BROWN, D.D., Aberdeen. (In Schaff's 'New Testament Commentary,' Vol. III.) Imperial 8vo, 12s. 6d.

'The Epistles to the Corinthians are commented on by Dr. Brown with his well-known solidity, shrewdness, and pointedness, and occasional piquancy.'—*Wesleyan Methodist Magazine.*

——— THE EPISTLE TO THE ROMANS. (*Handbook Series.*) Crown 8vo, price 2s.

'We do not know a better book to recommend to Bible-class teachers or scholars in their study of this Epistle.'—*Glasgow Herald.*

——— CHRIST'S SECOND COMING; WILL IT BE PRE-MILLENNIAL? Sixth Edition. In crown 8vo, price 7s. 6d.

EDINBURGH: T. & T. CLARK, 38 GEORGE STREET.

WORKS BY PROFESSORS AND MINISTERS OF

Bruce.—APOLOGETICS; OR, CHRISTIANITY DEFENSIVELY STATED. By Prof. A. B. BRUCE, D.D., Glasgow. (Vol. III. of *The International Theological Library*.) Second Edition. Post 8vo, price 10s. 6d.

'In this noble work of Dr. Bruce, the reader feels on every page that he is in contact with a mind and spirit in which all the conditions for a genuine apologetic are fulfilled. . . . At the end of Dr. Bruce's work the reader is uplifted with a great and steady confidence in the truth of the gospel; the evangel has been pleading its cause with him, and he has felt its power.'—*British Weekly.*

——— THE KINGDOM OF GOD; OR, CHRIST'S TEACHING ACCORDING TO THE SYNOPTICAL GOSPELS. New Edition, Revised. In post 8vo, price 7s. 6d.

'The astonishing vigour and the unfailing insight which characterise the book mark a new era in biblical theology. In fact, as in all Dr. Bruce's writings, so here we find ourselves in the company of one whose earnest faith in the matter of the Gospel narratives prevents him from treating the doctrine of Christ merely in a scholastic style, or as an interesting subject for theory and speculation.'—Prof. MARCUS DODS, D.D.

——— THE TRAINING OF THE TWELVE; OR, EXPOSITION OF PASSAGES IN THE GOSPELS EXHIBITING THE TWELVE DISCIPLES OF JESUS UNDER DISCIPLINE FOR THE APOSTLESHIP. Fourth Edition. In demy 8vo, price 10s. 6d.

'A volume which can never lose its charm either for the preacher or for the ordinary Christian reader.'—*London Quarterly Review.*

——— THE HUMILIATION OF CHRIST IN ITS PHYSICAL, ETHICAL, AND OFFICIAL ASPECTS. Third Edition. In demy 8vo, price 10s. 6d.

'The title of the book gives but a faint conception of the value and wealth of its contents. . . . Dr. Bruce's work is really one of exceptional value; and no one can read it without perceptible gain in theological knowledge.'—*English Churchman.*

Candlish.—THE KINGDOM OF GOD BIBLICALLY AND HISTORICALLY CONSIDERED. By Prof. J. S. CANDLISH, D.D., Glasgow. 8vo, price 10s. 6d.

'As to the ability of this volume there can be no question; it is of profound interest, is scholarly and able, and worthy of the reputation and position of its author.'—*Evangelical Magazine.*

——— THE CHRISTIAN SACRAMENTS. (*Handbook Series.*) In crown 8vo, price 1s. 6d.

'An admirable manual; sound, clear, suggestive, and interesting.'—*Free Church Monthly.*

——— THE WORK OF THE HOLY SPIRIT. (*Handbook Series.*) In crown 8vo, price 1s. 6d.

'A masterly, succinct, and suggestive résumé of the highest Christian thought on the personality and office of the Holy Spirit.'—*Baptist Magazine.*

——— THE BIBLICAL DOCTRINE OF SIN. (*Handbook Series.*) In crown 8vo, price 1s. 6d.

'What Prof. Candlish has given us here in such admirable clearness and welcome brevity is the fruit of the most accomplished modern study.'—*The Expository Times.*

Cunningham.—HISTORICAL THEOLOGY. A Review of the Principal Doctrinal Discussions in the Christian Church since the Apostolic Age. By the late Principal CUNNINGHAM, D.D., Edinburgh. 3rd Ed. Two vols., 8vo, 21s.

Davidson.—AN INTRODUCTORY HEBREW GRAMMAR. With Progressive Exercises in Reading and Writing. By Prof. A. B. DAVIDSON, D.D., Edinburgh. Eleventh Edition. In demy 8vo, price 7s. 6d.

——— THE EPISTLE TO THE HEBREWS. (*Handbook Series.*) In crown 8vo, price 2s. 6d.

'For its size and price one of the very best theological handbooks with which I am acquainted—a close grappling with the thought of the Epistle by a singularly strong and candid mind.'—Prof. SANDAY in *The Academy.*

Dods.—THE BOOK OF GENESIS. With Introduction and Notes. By Prof. MARCUS DODS, D.D., Edinburgh. (*Handbook Series.*) In crown 8vo, price 2s.

'Of the care with which the book has been done, and its thoroughness in every point, it is not possible to speak too highly.'—*Congregationalist.*

EDINBURGH: T. & T. CLARK, 38 GEORGE STREET.

Dods.—THE POST-EXILIAN PROPHETS: Haggai, Zechariah, and Malachi. (*Handbook Series*.) In crown 8vo, price 2s.
> 'When the Books of the Old Testament are treated in this way, there is some hope that the standard of popular teaching will be sensibly raised. . . . We can only congratulate the rising generation in having guides like these.'—*Literary World*.

—— COMMENTARY ON I. AND II. THESSALONIANS. (In Schaff's 'New Testament Commentary,' Vol. III.) Imperial 8vo, price 12s. 6d.
> 'A fine specimen of careful, finished work.'—*Methodist Recorder*.

—— THE SUPERNATURAL IN CHRISTIANITY. (In conjunction with Principal RAINY and Professor ORR.) Crown 8vo, price 2s.

Douglas.—THE BOOK OF JOSHUA. By Principal G. C. M. DOUGLAS, D.D., Glasgow. (*Handbook Series*.) In crown 8vo, price 1s. 6d.

—— THE BOOK OF JUDGES. (*Handbook Series*.) Cr. 8vo, 1s. 3d.

—— THE SIX INTERMEDIATE MINOR PROPHETS: Obadiah, Jonah, Micah, Nahum, Habakkuk, Zephaniah. (*Handbook Series*.) Cr. 8vo, price 1s. 6d.

Fairbairn.—PASTORAL THEOLOGY: A Treatise on the Office and Duties of the Christian Pastor. By the late Principal FAIRBAIRN, D.D., Glasgow. With a Biographical Sketch of the Author. In crown 8vo, price 6s.

—— PROPHECY VIEWED IN ITS DISTINCTIVE NATURE, ITS SPECIAL FUNCTIONS, AND PROPER INTERPRETATION. Second Edition. 8vo, price 10s. 6d.

—— THE REVELATION OF LAW IN SCRIPTURE, CONSIDERED WITH RESPECT BOTH TO ITS OWN NATURE AND TO ITS RELATIVE PLACE IN SUCCESSIVE DISPENSATIONS. (Third Series of 'Cunningham Lectures.') 8vo, price 10s. 6d.

Hastings.—THE EXPOSITORY TIMES, Edited by Rev. JAMES HASTINGS, M.A., Kinneff. Published Monthly, price 6d. Annual prepaid Subscription, post free, 6s. Bound volumes—Vol. II., 4s.; Vol. III., 7s. 6d.; Vol. IV., 7s. 6d.
> 'The third volume of "The Expository Times" is a perfect thesaurus of interesting and suggestive matter. Mr. Hastings has his eyes open to all the drifts which are telling around us, and it is not his fault if his readers are not in expository connections kept abreast of the age.'—*Free Church Monthly*.
> 'The leading magazine of its kind published.'—*Evangelical Magazine*.

Henderson.—PALESTINE: Its Historical Geography. With Topographical Index and Five Maps. By Rev. A. HENDERSON, D.D., Crieff. (*Handbook Series*.) Second Edition, Revised. In crown 8vo, price 2s. 6d.
> 'The only geography of Palestine within reasonable compass (or unreasonable either for that matter) worth taking into our hands at present.'—*The Expository Times*.
> 'The best, cheapest, and most trustworthy introduction to the geography of the Holy Land.'—*British Weekly*.

Hetherington.—APOLOGETICS OF THE CHRISTIAN FAITH. By the late Prof. W. M. HETHERINGTON, D.D.

Iverach.—THE LIFE OF MOSES. By Prof. J. IVERACH, D.D., Aberdeen. With Map. (*Primer Series*.) Paper covers, price 6d.; cloth, 8d.
> 'Accurately done, clear, mature, and scholarly.'—*Christian*.

Kilpatrick.—BISHOP BUTLER'S THREE SERMONS ON HUMAN NATURE. With Introduction and Notes. By Rev. T. B. KILPATRICK, B.D., Aberdeen. (*Handbook Series*.) In crown 8vo, price 1s. 6d.
> 'The best edition of the famous sermons that we have ever seen. . . . No student of Butler should fail to procure it.'—*Literary World*.

Lilley.—THE LORD'S SUPPER: Its Origin, Nature, and Use. By Rev. J. P. LILLEY, M.A., Arbroath. In crown 8vo, price 5s.
> 'A seasonable piece of work, well and thoroughly done . . . There is an underlying glow of genuine devotional feeling which adds to the attractiveness of the book.'—*Critical Review*.

Lindsay.—THE GOSPEL ACCORDING TO ST. MARK. With Introduction, Notes, and Maps. By Prof. T. M. LINDSAY, D.D., Glasgow. (*Handbook Series.*) Crown 8vo, price 2s. 6d.

—— THE GOSPEL ACCORDING TO ST. LUKE. With Introduction, Notes, and Maps. (*Handbook Series.*) Part I., price 2s.; Part II., 1s. 3d.

'Invaluable aids to Bible-class teaching.'—*Sword and Trowel.*

—— THE ACTS OF THE APOSTLES. With Introduction, Notes, and Maps. (*Handbook Series.*) Two Parts. Crown 8vo, price 1s. 6d. each.

—— THE REFORMATION. (*Handbook Series.*) Crown 8vo, price 2s.

'The best popular account we have yet seen of the causes, principles, and results of this momentous movement. As a handbook, the work is complete.'—*Baptist Magazine.*

Macdonald.—INTRODUCTION TO THE PENTATEUCH. By the late Rev. D. MACDONALD, Edinkillie. Two vols., 8vo, 21s.

Macgregor.—'SO GREAT SALVATION.' By the Rev. G. H. C. MACGREGOR, M.A., Aberdeen. With Introduction by Principal MOULE, Ridley Hall. Cloth, price 1s.

'A full gospel is presented not only clearly, but sympathetically; not only tenderly, but searchingly.'—*Principal MOULE.*

Macgregor.—THE APOLOGY OF THE CHRISTIAN RELIGION: Historically regarded with reference to Supernatural Revelation and Redemption. By Rev. JAMES MACGREGOR, D.D., Oamaru (late Professor of Systematic Theology, Edinburgh). 8vo, price 10s. 6d.

'Fresh and original, sustained and powerful, it is an apology of the noblest kind.'—*The Expository Times.*

—— THE REVELATION AND THE RECORD. 8vo, price 7s. 6d.

—— THE BOOK OF EXODUS. With Introduction, Commentary, Special Notes, Plans, etc. (*Handbook Series.*) 2 vols., cr. 8vo, price 2s. each.

—— THE EPISTLE TO THE GALATIANS. With Introduction and Notes. (*Handbook Series.*) Crown 8vo, price 1s. 6d.

Macpherson.—COMMENTARY ON ST. PAUL'S EPISTLE TO THE EPHESIANS. By Rev. JOHN MACPHERSON, M.A., Findhorn. 8vo, price 10s. 6d.

'Mr. Macpherson is a minister of the Free Church of Scotland—the most theological and literary Church in the world. . . . It is an advance, and a great one, on anything we yet possess. . . . The author goes to the root, and neglects nothing that usually comes under the eye of the careful student. . . . Besides all this, the book is a living book. One is conscious of the heart of a man in it as well as the brains.'—*Methodist Times.*

—— PRESBYTERIANISM. (*Handbook Series.*) Crown 8vo, 1s. 6d.

—— THE WESTMINSTER CONFESSION OF FAITH. With Introduction and Notes. (*Handbook Series.*) In crown 8vo, price 2s.

—— THE SUM OF SAVING KNOWLEDGE. With Introduction and Notes. (*Handbook Series.*) In crown 8vo, price 1s. 6d.

Nicoll.—THE INCARNATE SAVIOUR. A Life of Jesus Christ. By W. ROBERTSON NICOLL, LL.D. (formerly of Kelso Free Church). Cr. 8vo, 6s.

'It commands my warm sympathy and admiration. I rejoice in the circulation of such a book, which I trust will be the widest possible.'—*Canon LIDDON.*

Rainy.—DELIVERY AND DEVELOPMENT OF CHRISTIAN DOCTRINE. By Prof. R. RAINY, D.D., Principal of the New College, Edinburgh. 8vo, 10s. 6d.

'We gladly acknowledge the high excellence and the extensive learning which these lectures display. They are able to the last degree, and the author has, in an unusual measure, the power of acute and brilliant generalisation.'—*Literary Churchman.*

—— THE SUPERNATURAL IN CHRISTIANITY. (In conjunction with Professor DODS and Professor ORR.) Crown 8vo, price 2s.

Reith.—THE GOSPEL ACCORDING TO ST. JOHN. With Introduction and Notes. By Rev. GEORGE REITH, D.D., Glasgow. (*Handbook Series.*) In two vols., crown 8vo, price 2s. each.
'We have often commended Messrs. Clark's Bible-Class Handbooks, and this is one of the best of them.'—*Church Bells.*

Salmond.—THE CHRISTIAN DOCTRINE OF IMMORTALITY. By Prof. S. D. F. SALMOND, D.D., Aberdeen.   [*In the Press.*

——— THE CRITICAL REVIEW, Edited by Prof. S. D. F. SALMOND, D.D. Designed to furnish Quarterly a critical survey of current literature in Theology and Philosophy. Annual Subscription, post free, 6s.
The Academy says:—'The editor's name is a guarantee both for learning and for moderation.'

——— COMMENTARY ON I. AND II. PETER. (In Schaff's 'New Testament Commentary,' Vol. IV.) Imperial 8vo, price 12s. 6d.
'The exposition by Prof. Salmond leaves very little to be desired for popular, or indeed for critical, ends. The exegetical discussions and elucidations are full and conclusive; the style is clear, crisp, and chaste. The analysis of the ethical teachings so characteristic of these Epistles is masterly.'—*Presbyterian Review.*

——— THE LIFE OF CHRIST. (*Primer Series.*) Paper, 6d.; cloth, 8d.
'Nothing could possibly be better.'—*Free Church Monthly.*

——— THE LIFE OF PETER. (*Primer Series.*) Paper, 6d.; cloth, 8d.

——— THE SHORTER CATECHISM. (*Bible-Class Primer Series.*) Three Parts, price 6d. each; cloth, 8d. Three Parts bound in One, cloth, 1s. 6d.

——— THE PARABLES OF OUR LORD. (*Primer Series.*) Paper, 6d.; cloth, 8d.

——— THE SABBATH. (*Primer Series.*) Paper, 6d.; cloth, 8d.

Salmond.—OUR CHRISTIAN PASSOVER: A Guide for Young People in the Serious Study of the Lord's Supper. By Rev. CHARLES A. SALMOND, M.A., Edinburgh. (*Primer Series.*) Paper, 6d.; cloth, 8d.

Scott.—THE LIFE OF ABRAHAM. By Rev. C. A. SCOTT, M.A., London (formerly of Free St. John's, Edinburgh). With Map. (*Primer Series.*) Paper covers, price 6d.; cloth, 8d.
'In literary quality and scholarly accuracy, this little book leaves nothing to be desired.'—*British Weekly.*

Scott.—PRINCIPLES OF NEW TESTAMENT QUOTATION ESTABLISHED AND APPLIED TO BIBLICAL CRITICISM. By Rev. JAMES SCOTT, D.D., Aberlour. Second Edition. Crown 8vo, price 4s.

Scrymgeour.—LESSONS ON THE LIFE OF CHRIST. By Rev. WILLIAM SCRYMGEOUR, M.A., Glasgow. (*Handbook Series.*) Cr. 8vo, 2s. 6d.
'A thoroughly satisfactory help both to teacher and scholar.'—*British Messenger.*

Skinner.—THE HISTORICAL CONNECTION BETWEEN THE OLD AND NEW TESTAMENTS. By Prof. J. SKINNER, D.D., London (formerly of Kelso Free Church). (*Primer Series.*) Paper covers, price 6d.; cloth, 8d.
'As a skilful *résumé* of the period, this little work is beyond praise.'—*Sunday School Chronicle.*

Smeaton.—THE DOCTRINE OF THE HOLY SPIRIT. By the late Prof. GEORGE SMEATON, D.D., Edinburgh. Second Edition. 8vo, price 9s.
'One of the ablest works ever written on the Holy Spirit.'—*Presbyterian & Reformed Review.*

Smith.—MEDIÆVAL MISSIONS. By Prof. THOMAS SMITH, D.D., Edinburgh. In crown 8vo, price 4s. 6d.
'A work which will well repay careful study.'—*Watchman.*

WORKS BY MINISTERS OF THE FREE CHURCH.

Stalker.—THE LIFE OF JESUS CHRIST. By Rev. JAMES STALKER, D.D., Glasgow. Large Type Edition, handsomely bound, price 3s. 6d. Handbook Edition, price 1s. 6d.

'Even with all our modern works on the exhaustless theme, from Neander to Farrar and Geikie, there is none which occupies the ground of Mr. Stalker's. . . . We question whether any one popular work so impressively and adequately represents Jesus to the mind. . . . It may be despised because it is small, but its light must shine.'—*Christian.*

———— THE LIFE OF ST. PAUL. In crown 8vo, price 1s. 6d.; Fine Edition, large Type, price 3s. 6d.

'A gem of sacred biography. . . . Well does it deserve the new and handsome dress in which it now appears.'—*Christian Leader.*

Thomson.—MEMORIALS OF A MINISTRY: A Selection from the Discourses of the late EDWARD A. THOMSON, Free St. Stephen's Church, Edinburgh. With a Portrait, and a Biographical Sketch by Prof. LAIDLAW, D.D. Crown 8vo, price 5s.

Thomson.—LIFE OF DAVID. By the late Rev. P. THOMSON, M.A. (*Primer Series.*) Paper covers, price 6d; cloth, 8d.

'I think it is excellent indeed, and have seen nothing of the kind so good.'—Rev. STANLEY LEATHES, D.D.

Thomson.—THE CHRISTIAN MIRACLES AND THE CONCLUSIONS OF SCIENCE. By Rev. W. D. THOMSON, M.A., Lochend. (*Handbook Series.*) Crown 8vo, price 2s.

Troup.—WORDS TO YOUNG CHRISTIANS: Being Addresses to Young Communicants. By GEORGE ELMSLIE TROUP, M.A., Broughty-Ferry. On antique laid paper, and in neat binding, crown 8vo, price 4s. 6d.

Walker.—THE THEOLOGY AND THEOLOGIANS OF SCOTLAND, CHIEFLY OF THE SEVENTEENTH AND EIGHTEENTH CENTURIES. By the late JAMES WALKER, D.D., Carnwath. Second Edition, Revised. In crown 8vo, 3s. 6d.

'Eloquent, interesting, and informing. . . . We know of no volume so well calculated to set things in their right light.'—*Literary World.*

Walker.—SCOTTISH CHURCH HISTORY. By NORMAN L. WALKER, D.D., Editor of *The Free Church Monthly.* (*Handbook Series.*) Cr. 8vo, 1s. 6d.

'A very beautiful account of the history of Church matters in Scotland.'—*Presbyterian Churchman.*

———— THE CHURCH STANDING OF CHILDREN. Price 4d.

'No better contribution has been made in recent years to the discussion of the question of infant baptism. . . . The argument stands forth, as it seems to us, impregnable.'—*United Presbyterian Church Missionary Record.*

Welsh.—ELEMENTS OF CHURCH HISTORY. By the late Prof. DAVID WELSH, D.D., F.R.S.E. (*Moderator of the General Assembly,* 1842). 8vo, 7s. 6d.

White.—THE SYMBOLICAL NUMBERS OF SCRIPTURE. By Rev. M. WHITE, Blairgowrie. Crown 8vo, price 4s.

Whyte.—A COMMENTARY ON THE SHORTER CATECHISM. By ALEX. WHYTE, D.D., Free St. George's, Edinburgh. (*Handbook Series.*) Cr. 8vo, 2s. 6d.

'So clear, so true, so lively. . . . Theology of this stamp will do us all good. Scatter it; its leaves are for the healing of the nations.' C. H. SPURGEON.

Innes.—CHURCH AND STATE. An Historical Handbook. (*Handbook Series.*) By A. TAYLOR INNES, Advocate. 2nd Ed., Revised. Cr. 8vo, 3s.

'In the field of the historical relations of Church and State, we do not know its superior.'—*Guardian.*

Smith.—SHORT HISTORY OF CHRISTIAN MISSIONS: From Abraham and Paul, to Carey, Livingstone, and Duff. By Dr. GEORGE SMITH, F.R.G.S., C.I.E. (*Handbook Series.*) 3rd Ed., with additional matter. Cr. 8vo, 2s. 6d.

'As a handbook of missionary history, the work is invaluable.'—*Sunday School Chronicle.*

EDINBURGH: T. & T. CLARK, 38 GEORGE STREET.

www.ingramcontent.com/pod-product-compliance
Lightning Source LLC
Chambersburg PA
CBHW031425230426
43668CB00007B/432